Lecture Notes in Computer Science 13103

More information about this subseries at http://www.springer.com/series/7409

Wanlei Zhou · Yi Mu (Eds.)

Advances in Web-Based Learning – ICWL 2021

20th International Conference, ICWL 2021
Macau, China, November 13–14, 2021
Proceedings

Springer

Editors
Wanlei Zhou
University of Macau
Macau, China

Yi Mu
University of Macau
Macau, China

ISSN 0302-9743 ISSN 1611-3349 (electronic)
Lecture Notes in Computer Science
ISBN 978-3-030-90784-6 ISBN 978-3-030-90785-3 (eBook)
https://doi.org/10.1007/978-3-030-90785-3

LNCS Sublibrary: SL3 – Information Systems and Applications, incl. Internet/Web, and HCI

This Springer imprint is published by the registered company Springer Nature Switzerland AG
The registered company address is: Gewerbestrasse 11, 6330 Cham, Switzerland

Preface

The 20th International Conference on Web-based Learning (ICWL 2021) was held in Macau, China, during November 13–14, and it was organized and hosted by the City University of Macau.

ICWL is an annual International Conference on Web-based Learning, founded by the Hong Kong Web Society. The first ICWL was held in Hong Kong in 2002. Since then, ICWL has been held in Australia (2003), China (2004, 2008, 2010, 2015, 2020), Hong Kong (2005, 2011), Malaysia (2006), the UK (2007), Germany (2009, 2019), Romania (2012), Taiwan (2013), Estonia (2014), Italy (2016), South Africa (2017), and Thailand (2018), Germany (2019) and China (2020). ICWL 2021 featured a technical program of refereed papers selected by the international Program Committee, and keynote addresses offered by eminent scholars.

Due to the influence of the COVID-19 pandemic, this year the conference received 29 submissions. All the submissions were reviewed on the basis of their significance, novelty, technical quality, and practical impact. The Program Committee (PC) consisted of members with diverse backgrounds and broad research interests. After careful reviews by at least three experts in the relevant areas for each paper, and discussions by the PC members, 10 submissions were accepted as full papers (with an acceptance rate 34%) and seven submissions as short papers for presentation at the conference and inclusion in the conference proceedings. The accepted papers cover multiple topics, from algorithms to systems and applications.

ICWL 2021 was made possible by the joint efforts of many people and institutions. There is a long list of people who volunteered their time and energy to put together the conference and who deserve special thanks.

We would like to thank all the PC members for their great effort in reading, commenting, and finally selecting the papers. We also thank all the external reviewers for assisting the PC in their particular areas of expertise.

We sincerely thank the authors of all submitted papers and all the conference attendees. Thanks are also due to the staff at Springer for their help with producing the proceedings and to the developers and maintainers of the EasyChair software, which greatly helped simplify the submission and review process.

October 2021

Wanlei Zhou
Yi Mu
Kuai Peng Ip
Aniello Castiglione
Xiang Yang

Organization

General Chairs

Wanlei Zhou	City University of Macau, Macau, China
Weijia Jia	United International College, Beijing Normal University-Hong Kong Baptist University, China
Baltasar Fernandez Manjon (Balta)	Universidad Complutense de Madrid, Spain

Program Chairs

Yi Mu	City University of Macau, Macau, China
Kuai Peng Ip	City University of Macau, Macau, China
Aniello Castiglione	University of Naples, Italy
Xiang Yang	Swinburne University, Australia

Steering Committee Representative

Qing Li	Hong Kong Polytechnic University, Hong Kong, China

Publicity Chair

Shuying Sean Li	City University of Macau, Macau, China

Local Organization Co-chair

Wenjian Liu	City University of Macau, Macau, China

Web Chair

Andrew Jiang	Macau Expo Group, Macau, China, and Hong Kong Polytechnic University, Hong Kong, China

Program Committee

Alessio Bonti	Deakin University, Australia
Adriana Botha	University of Pretoria, South Africa
Maiga Chang	Athabasca University, Canada
Lu Chen	Aalborg University, Denmark
Wei Chen	Chinese Academy of Agricultural Sciences, China
Dickson K. W. Chiu	University of Hong Kong, China
Maria-Iuliana Dascalu	Politehnica University of Bucharest, Romania
Damiano Distante	University of Rome Unitelma Sapienza, Italy
Giovanni Fulantelli	National Research Council of Italy, Italy
Denis Gillet	Swiss Federal Institute of Technology in Lausanne (EPFL), Switzerland
Sabine Graf	Athabasca University, Canada
Tianyong Hao	South China Normal University, China
Andreas Harrer	University of Applied Sciences and Arts Dortmund, Germany
Michael A. Herzog	Magdeburg-Stendal University of Applied Sciences, Germany
Rafiqul Islam	Charles Sturt University, Australia
Mirjana Ivanovic	University of Novi Sad, Serbia
Ioannis Kazanidis	Eastern Macedonia and Thrace Institute of Technology, Greece
Michael Kickmeier-Rust	Graz University of Technology, Austria
Ralf Klamma	RWTH Aachen University, Germany
Tomaž Klobučar	Jozef Stefan Institute, Slovenia
Milos Kravcik	DFKI GmbH, Germany
Zuzana Kubincová	Comenius University, Bratislava
Amruth Kumar	Ramapo College of New Jersey, USA
Elicia Lanham	Deakin University, Australia
Luigi Laura	International Telematic University UNINETTUNO, Italy
Frederick Li	Durham University, UK
Carla Limongelli	Università Roma Tre, Italy
Qing Liu	Hong Kong Baptist University, China
An Liu	Soochow University, China
Matteo Lombardi	Griffith University, Australia
Ivana Marenzi	L3S Research Center, Germany
Alke Martens	University of Rostock, Germany
Harald Mayer	Joanneum Research, Austria
Xiaoye Miao	Zhejiang University, China
Yuan Miao	Victoria University, Australia
Tanja Mitrovic	University of Canterbury, New Zealand

Wolfgang Mueller	University of Education Weingarten, Germany
Umberto Nanni	Sapienza University of Rome, Italy
Wolfgang Nejdl	L3S and University of Hannover, Germany
Leanne Ngo	Deakin University, Australia
Kyparissia Papanikolaou	School of Pedagogical and Technological Education (ASPETE), Greece
Hans Põldoja	Tallinn University, Estonia
Elvira Popescu	University of Craiova, Romania
Francesca Pozzi	Istituto Tecnologie Didattiche - CNR, Italy
Julia Prior	University of Technology Sydney, Australia
Demetrios Sampson	University of Piraeus, Greece
Olga C. Santos	aDeNu Research Group (UNED), Spain
Flippo Sciarrone	Roma Tre University, Italy
Marcus Specht	Delft University of Technology, The Netherlands
Marco Temperini	Sapienza University of Rome, Italy
Lorna Uden	Staffordshire University, UK
Carlos Vaz de Carvalho	GILT - ISEP, Portugal
Pierpaolo Vittorini	University of L'Aquila, Italy
Riina Vuorikari	Institute for Prospective Technological Studies, Spain
Fu Lee Wang	The Open University of Hong Kong, China
Shiting Wen	Zhejiang University, China
Naomi Whiteside	RMIT University, Australia
Tak-Lam Wong	Douglas College, Canada
Charoenchai Wongwatkit	Mae Fah Luang University, Thailand
Jianqiu Xu	Nanjing University of Aeronautics and Astronautics, China
Keyu Yang	Zhejiang University, China
Yang Yang	University of Science and Technology of China, China
Zhenguo Yang	City University of Hong Kong, China
Sergej Zerr	L3S Research Center, Germany
Detian Zhang	Soochow University, China
Yunhui Zhuang	City University of Hong Kong, China

Contents

Online Learning Methodologies, Trust, and Analysis

Decentralized M-Learning Platform with Trusted Execution Environment

Wennan Wang[1], Linkai Zhu[1,2(✉)], Baoping Wang[1], Li Guang[1], Sheng Peng[1,3], and Zhiming Cai[1]

[1] Institute of Data Science, City University of Macau, Macau, China
linkai@iscas.ac.cn
[2] Institute of Software Chinese Academy of Sciences, Beijing, China
[3] Zhuhai Yingying Technology Co., Ltd., Zhuhai, China

Abstract. With the rapid growth in E-learning, Mobile learning (M-learning) is one of the most widely used ways in distance education compare to the traditional classroom environment. However, Mobile learning has accentuated the problem of data privacy disclosure and low performance. Blockchain is an important step in smart contracts with peer execution, immutability, and provenance may bring a new level of protection and confidence to M-learning. In combination with Trusted Execution Environment, we proposed a decentralized M-learning platform prototype within TrustZone technology for ARM devices where the learner identity key is encrypted and stored in Hyperledger Fabric with a peer-to-peer network. Our platform resolves the difficulties with privacy data in E-learning and reduced workload. An evaluation demonstrated that It is available to execute encryption algorithms in a trusted execution environment.

Keywords: M-learning · E-learning · Blockchain · TrustZone · Privacy

1 Introduction

With the impact of the new coronavirus epidemic on normal teaching activities in colleges and universities [1], school teaching methods have changed to online methods in most countries. Online education platforms provide new solutions to ensure online teaching during the epidemic prevention and control period. School students can be free from space and learn online anytime, anywhere through the Internet.

With the development of wireless Internet technology and the widespread popularity of mobile devices. The software and hardware platforms of mobile devices run faster and more abundant applications [2]. People are also paying more and more attention to the advantages of mobile learning, focusing on creating a high-performance Mobile learning (M-learning) platform to better serve the majority of learners [3]. The equipment of M-learning includes an Android phone, iPhone, tablet, iPad, and notebook.

Intelligent push platform can solve the problem of content value judgment, but this is based on the user's privacy data exposure. The root cause of the problems encountered

W. Wang and L. Zhu—These authors contributed equally to this work.

W. Zhou and Y. Mu (Eds.): ICWL 2021, LNCS 13103, pp. 3–13, 2021.
https://doi.org/10.1007/978-3-030-90785-3_1

in the education industry is the lack of trust relationships and opaque mechanisms under the central network [1]. These devices collect and transmit large amount of privacy data in educational area when students or learners' study off campus using their smart phone [2]. Students' profile or personal data can be revealed through a centralized server. When M-learning personal data is opened for education, it is restricted by the permissions of the centralized server [3].

Blockchain has emerged as an interesting candidate because of its impressive features of decentralization [4]. By leveraging blockchain in the M-learning platform, the network efficiency of the single point server is improved since the growth of the number of learner nodes [5]. Blockchain can reduce the burden of the M-learning network with the number of connecting nodes is increasing [6]. And centralized M-learning system service often break data privacy policies by using data collected from learners for unauthorized purpose [7]. In order to address this issue in privacy related data between online education school and learners, we have designed and implemented a trusted decentralized M-learning platform prototype based on TrustZone device for Fabric Hyperledger. The privacy protection of each user's personal identity key need to be guaranteed through a trusted execution environment, and the decentralized access control system of the blockchain.

However, most blockchain-based platforms use digital pseudonyms [8], allowing users to have multiple pseudonyms, but this approach only provides weaker user identity anonymity [9], the correlation between transactions, and the student or learner's information are exposed on the blockchain, and all public key addresses of a E-learning learner may be inferred if one of the user's addresses is compromised.

Since TrustZone is the domain of trusted computing in the ARM architecture. Such devices like mobile phones and tablets provide a common execution environment (Rich Execution Environment, REE), which will run Android, IOS and other intelligent operating systems in this environment to provide users with a variety of services [10]. Based on the trusted execution environment provided by the ARM TrustZone architecture, this paper analyzes the definition of the trusted platform module TPM specification, and designs its Kernel functions, including integrity measurement, key generation and management, and symmetric asymmetric encryption and decryption. This provides basic security support for trusted services such as trusted startup of upper-level applications and components of the M-learning platform and blockchain network connection, thereby improving the security of students using mobile smart terminals.

In this work we leverage blockchain to reduce the load of network and improve the performance of M-learning platform. We provide a method for secure identity key by trusted execution environment. We have implemented a Trusted M-learning platform prototype on blockchain using Hyperledger Fabric.

The paper is structured as follows. In Sect. 2 we provide technologies on E-learning, M-learning, Blockchain, and TrustZone. In Sect. 3 we discuss the overview of the architecture. In Sect. 4 we describe how we design and implement the decentralized M-learning platform. In Sect. 5 we provide evaluation of the approach. Finally, Sect. 6 we conclude the paper.

2 Technologies

E-Learning

E-Learning often used in online education, also known as electronic learning. It is a way to use Internet technology to disseminate learning resources and quickly learn. It is one of the main ways people acquire knowledge. People can learn online through the Internet, which broadens people's learning channels and improves Learning efficiency, better use of fragmented time for learning. The E-Learning platform has a large amount of behavior data left by user learning, which can more accurately match the learning needs of users after mining and analysis.

M-Learning

M-learning as Mobile Learning, the adoption of Mobile Learning can provide stimulating new possibilities for students, teachers, and school staff through new forms of training and learning innovations [11].

Blockchain

Blockchain, mainly known as the technology for operating Bitcoin encrypted currency [12], is a kind of multi-party participation and joint maintenance of a distributed database. It is based on a peer-to-peer network and uses encryption algorithms and digital signatures in cryptography to ensure the data itself Integrity and immutability and security of access. It uses chain data structure to verify and store data for building the overall structure of blockchain through consensus mechanism. And this kind of distributed accounting has gradually become one of the Internet applications in recent years. An important function. It maintains an ever-growing data block. The data recorded in each block cannot be tampered with or modified. Since there is no central node, all participating nodes can store data. Its decentralized nature provides a viable solution to build security protocols without the need for a third party (Fig. 1).

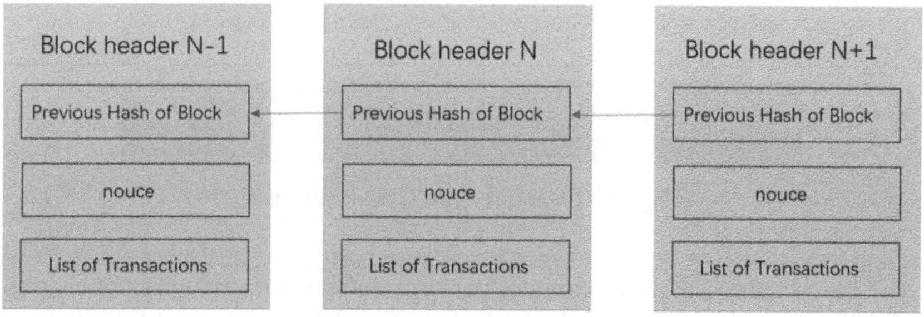

Fig. 1. Blockchain structure

Trusted Execution Environment

The trusted execution environment (Trusted Execution Environment, TEE) provides a completely isolated environment in the CPU, called a safe zone, which can prevent other applications, operating systems, and host owners from tampering to ensure that the code is executed in the TEE. And Data and stars and integrity are protected [13]. Even understand the status of applications running in the safe zone. By using both hardware and software to protect data and code, TEE is more secure than operating systems. We leverage TEE to enhance blockchain performance, efficiency, and security.

TrustZone

ARM proposed a hardware-level mobile platform security technology called TrustZone [14]. The basic principle of TrustZone technology is to virtualize a physical Kernel into multiple Kernels, and use monitors to switch different states, thereby constructing a processor security environment. This technology uses the increased security features in the CPU to cooperate with software and hardware to construct a Trusted execution environment (TEE) completely isolated from ordinary execution environment (REE).

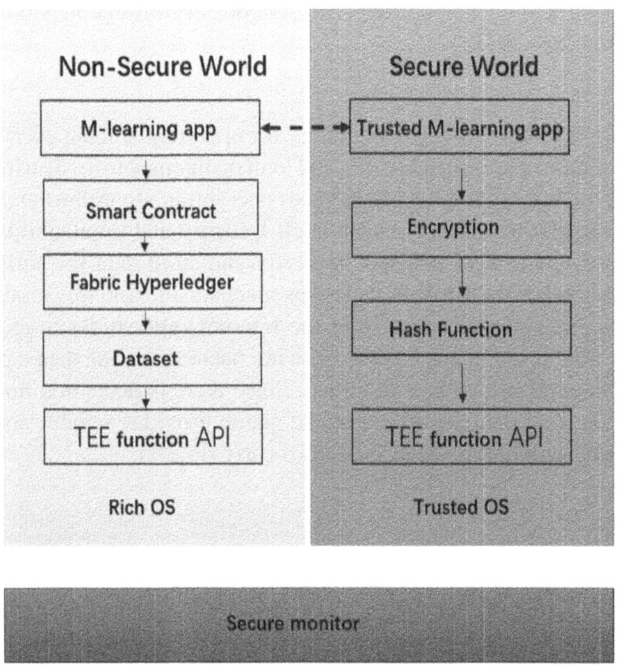

Fig. 2. M-learning TrustZone architecture

The blockchain can store data and perform computation on every decentralized learner all around the world and the hashes of transactions generated from E-learning devices [15]. Fabric Hyperledger is chosen as a local blockchain architecture, which is an open-source fundamental technology WW [16]. For prototyping, the data of M-learning is collected from different learning apps. For each communication between devices or nodes, a transaction is created and stored in the blockchain. As shown in Fig. 2, the ARM TrustZone-enabled application is composed of secure and non-secure world. In secure world, the sensitive operations are called (encryption and hashing).

3 Overview

The proposed M-learning platform consists of three main components which includes arm device client, TrustZone module and blockchain.

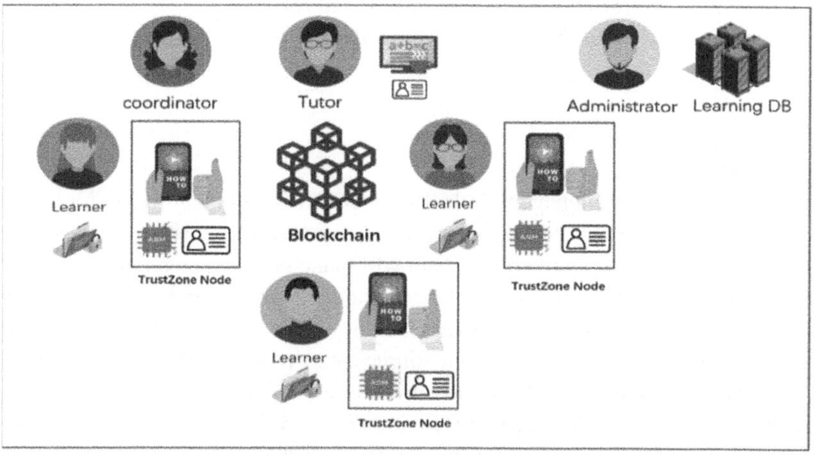

Fig. 3. Decentralized M-learning platform with TEE

All these components are going to solving the problem:

Security of M-Learning Platform with Blockchain
The decentralized and distributed nature of blockchain makes it a promising solution for M-learning security. Mobile phone as a new E-learning device with integration in blockchain enables a higher security level.

Scope and Assumption
The scope of this paper considers the decentralization of data access management using blockchain and data protection using TrustZone. We designed and implemented a security M-learning course platform where user have equal right in managing their data. For this platform, the private data is supposed to encrypted by using asymmetric cryptographic protocols. In this paper we do not consider phishing attacks and denial of service attacks.

Trusted Blockchain M-Learning Platform Components
As shown in Fig. 3, several components are composing the proposed Trust chain M-learning platform:

- Tutor/teacher, the role is to create and upload lessons, after uploading it, this role will release to learners.
- Learner: The learner can register account and download released lessons from tutor. Students can input the course notes in database.

- Coordinator: the role is to disseminate the information to colleagues within the department. Obtain updates and alerts form E-learning group.
- Administrator: Administrator is to manage the E-learning course data and maintain the platform
- Learning Resource Database: The E-learning database is to store E-learning resources include learner's information (course, scores, and records).
- Blockchain: store the hash of the encrypted identity data in the blockchain.
- TrustZone node: the process of encryption is executed in TrustZone.

Trusted Identity Key

M-learning identity key management lacks effective management technology, and key leakage and loss caused by improper use and storage will bring losses to users, and no central node participation in the blockchain will make key management difficult. Using under-chain TrustZone to store wallet-like methods, in an isolated state, the key wallet is executed in this environment to prevent malicious soft attacks and theft of user keys.

Since Fabric Hyperledger is an open-source smart contract platform, the above support can only be contract is public, usually involves multi-user participation, user account information, transactions and status information are exposed in the network, the need to increase privacy protection mechanisms, because most E-learning users are now popular use of smart devices, through arm architecture-based TrustZone to enhance smart contract privacy protection, build a trusted execution environment.

In a processor architecture, each physical processor Kernel provides two virtual Kernels, one non-secure and the other secure Kernels. The mechanism for switching between the two Kernels is called the monitor mode. The non-secure Kernel can only access non-secure system resources, while secure kernel energy accesses all resources. Software in the ordinary world can use Secure Monitor Call (SMC) instructions or through a subset of hardware exception mechanisms to enter monitor mode.

When the user mode of the normal world needs to obtain the services of the secure world, first need to enter the privileged mode of the normal world, call SMC in this mode, the processor will enter the secure monitor mode, monitor mode back up the context of the normal world, and then enter the privileged mode of the secure world, at this time the operating environment is the execution environment of the secure world, and then enter the user mode of the secure world, perform the corresponding security services (Fig. 4).

Decentralized M-Learning Platform Architecture

M-learning is based on the trusted blockchain. The M-learning device indicates that the learner login the M-learning node, and the node number is unique. After students log on, the profile data interacts with user management through the web service interface, while the identification number is verified with the data accessed by the student. The data communicates between the institution and the student. Identity numbers are encrypted using asymmetric encryption algorithms in TrustZone through smart contracts, encrypted identity keys are stored in the blockchain through smart contracts. M-learning users can access their profile data without leaking it since identity key is perform encryption

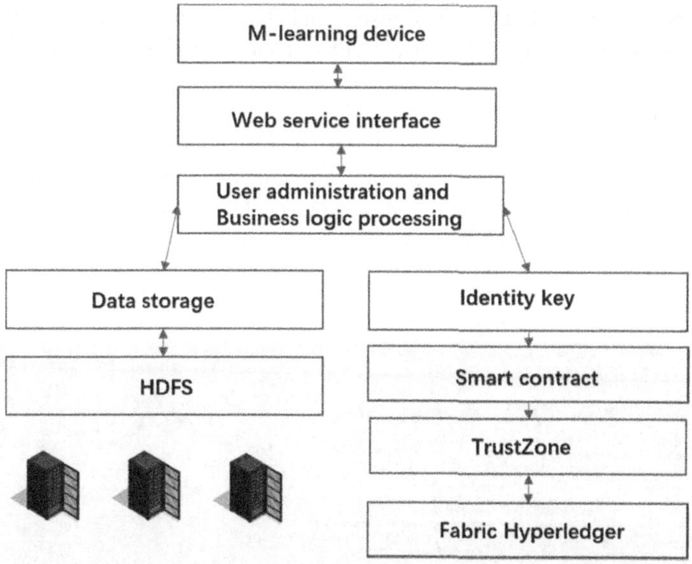

Fig. 4. Decentralized M-learning platform data flow

operations in an isolated environment. This idea adapts to a broader E-learning style and goals. Connections to any new E-learning node are authenticated by blockchain network.

4 Implementation

We used six real processor based on the arm architecture of the smart phone to implement M-learning platform using the Fabric Hyperledger which is a distributed ledger with blockchain as the underlying. The M-Learning platform including the course search engine system and access control management platform, as well as the recommendation module.

Smart Contract Process
Blockchain guarantees that the intra-chain computing process is credible through smart contracts and consensus mechanisms. Here the smart contract is essentially a programmable state machine, and in most blockchains, block time is fixed. It takes to process the business and the latency of M-Learning's network. The solution needs to keep M-learning's business processes out of the blockchain and handle only the state of business initialization and the final state on the chain. This is done by separating business logic from consensus logic and moving the computing portion of performance consumption down the chain for privacy and performance savings.

Data Storage
The data storage layer is mainly responsible for storing and storing the course data generated and collected during the operation of other layers. The system in this paper mainly uses HDFS and MySQL, in which MySQL stores the course information of users,

as well as the structured data of users' historical behavior, such as rating and collection. HDFS is used to store course courseware video resources and other unstructured data.

Web Browser

The web interface is the interactive interface between users and the system, which provides learners with the basic operating functions of the online education platform and supports personalized course recommendation. The browser presents the response results to the user. This layer also generates user behavior data, which can be used by other layers for calculation and analysis (Figs. 5 and 6).

Fig. 5. Trustzone node in fabric hyperledger

Fig. 6. Identity key setup process

Create Identity Key

When the user logs in, the blockchain system will decide whether he or she is a registered user of the platform. The registered user can enter the homepage of the course recommendation system after entering the corresponding user name, password, and verification code. Unregistered users will jump to the registration interface, fill in the registration information, and then log in as registered users (Figs. 7, 8, 9 and 10).

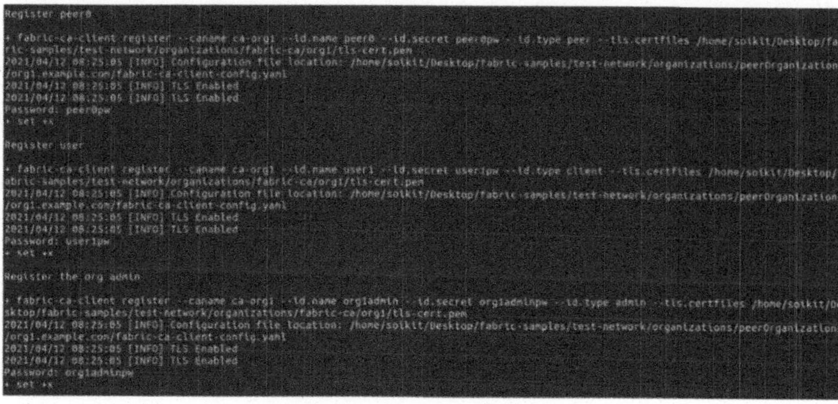

Fig. 7. M-learning role registration

Fig. 8. Educational service frontend user interface

Fig. 9. Student frontend user interface

Fig. 10. Teacher frontend user interface

5 Evaluation

In Fig. 11, it shows the impact of the transaction workload execution on the blockchain. When encryption operations are performed in TrustZone, the write workload is slightly higher than without using TEE. The cryptographic algorithm is performed in an isolated environment when measuring the transaction throughput of the M-learning node. When it is at 600 write workloads, the transaction throughput is 11.17 writes per second. As the write workload increases to 2000, the write throughput stabilizes at 7.82 writes per second. Instead of executing a cryptographic algorithm in an isolated TrustZone, the transaction throughput is 6.24 writes per second at 600 write workloads. At 2000 write workload, transaction throughput drops to 5.61 writes per second.

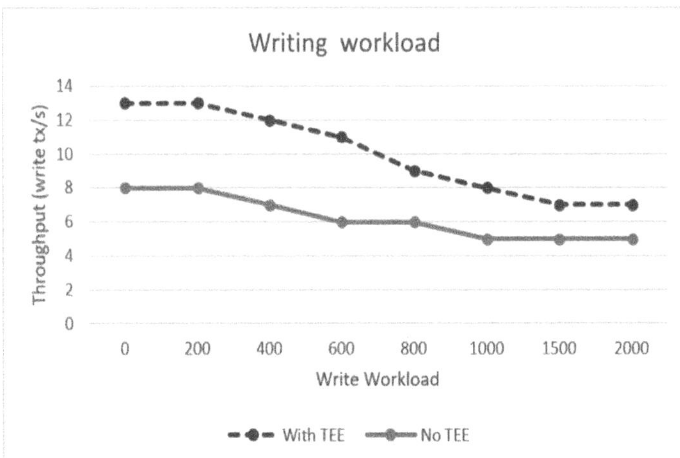

Fig. 11. Throughput and write workload

6 Conclusion

In this research, it introduces M-learning platform in many decentralized nodes that leverage a decentralized network of peers accompanied by a public ledger. However, in terms of blockchain, it encounters some privacy threats, which limit its realistic applications. we have presented a solution that utilizes the combination of TEE and Hyperledger Fabric in M-learning platform. Particularly, for securing identity key, an asymmetric encryption algorithm is used in TrustZone secure world for realizing blockchain privacy demands. Besides, our approach utilizes blockchain to reduce workload. An evaluation revealed that the throughput of our approach is tend to be stable for encryption of the identity key in a trustworthy execution environment, which means, this method protects the user's personal privacy without compromising performance.

Acknowledgments. This research is supported by the: 1. project funded by Zhuhai Industry-University-Research Cooperation Project: Research on Key Technologies of Cross-domain Data

Compliance and Mutual Trust Computing in Zhuhai and Macau (No. ZH22017002200011PWC) 2. Research on knowledge-oriented probabilistic graphical model theory based on multi-source data (FDCT- NSFC Projects: 0066/2019/AFJ) 3. Research and Application of Cooperative Multi-Agent Platform for Zhuhai-Macao Manufacturing Service (0058/2019/AMJ).

References

1. Rodrigues, H., Almeida, F., Figueiredo, V., Lopes, S.L.: Tracking e-learning through published papers: a systematic review. Comput. Educ. **136**, 87–98 (2019)
2. Anwar, M.M., Greer, J., Brooks, C.A.: Privacy enhanced personalization in e-learning, p. 1 (2006). https://doi.org/10.1145/1501434.1501485
3. Zhao, W., Liu, K., Ma, K.: Design of student capability evaluation system merging blockchain technology. J. Phys. Conf. Ser. **1168**, 032123 (2019)
4. Bernabe, J.B., Canovas, J.L., Hernandez-Ramos, J.L., Moreno, R.T., Skarmeta, A.: Privacy-preserving solutions for blockchain: review and challenges. IEEE Access **7**, 164908–164940 (2019)
5. Lam, T.Y., Dongol, B.: A blockchain-enabled e-learning platform. Interact. Learn. Environ. 1–23 (2020)
6. Masud, M.A.H., Huang, X., Islam, M.R.: A novel approach for the security remedial in a cloud-based E-learning network. J. Netw. **9**, 2934 (2014)
7. Anwar, M.: Supporting privacy, trust, and personalization in online learning. Int. J. Artif. Intell. Educ. (2020). https://doi.org/10.1007/s40593-020-00216-0
8. Peng, L., et al.: Privacy preservation in permissionless blockchain: a survey. Digit. Commun. Netw. **7**(3), 295–307 (2020). https://doi.org/10.1016/j.dcan.2020.05.008
9. Zhu, X., Badr, Y.: Identity management systems for the Internet of Things: a survey towards blockchain solutions. Sensors **18**, 1–18 (2018)
10. Muller, C.: Execution of smart contracts with ARM TrustZone, p. 45 (2019)
11. Oakes, K., Green, D.: E-learning. T D, vol. 57, 17–19 October 2003
12. Nakamoto, S.: A peer-to-peer electronic cash system (2008)
13. Van Schaik, S., Kwong, A., Genkin, D., Yarom, Y.: SGAxe: How SGX Fails in Practice (2020). https://Cacheoutattack.Com/
14. Ali, J., Ali, T., Alsaawy, Y., Khalid, A.S., Musa, S.: Blockchain-based smart-IoT trust zone measurement architecture. In: ACM International Conference Proceeding Series, Part F1481, pp. 152–157 (2019)
15. Ubaka-Okoye, M.N., et al.: Blockchain framework for securing e-learning system. Int. J. Adv. Trends Comput. Sci. Eng. **9**, 2933–2940 (2020)
16. Wang, S., Zhang, Y., Zhang, Y.: A blockchain-based framework for data sharing with fine-grained access control in decentralized storage systems. IEEE Access **6**, 38437–38450 (2018)

Scaffolding Teacher Learning During Professional Development with Theory-Driven Learning Analytics

Manisha Khulbe(✉) and Kairit Tammets

Tallinn University, Tallinn, Estonia
{manisha.khulbe,kairit.tammets}@tlu.ee

Abstract. It is claimed that the innovative use of educational technology combined with appropriate pedagogical strategies can lead to improved student outcomes. However, teachers face difficulties in adopting educational technology and novel pedagogical methods as this involves acquiring complex new knowledge. Combined with training, Learning Analytics dashboards – artifacts which mediate teachers' learning in technology-enhanced environments – can aid them in this task. Using student engagement as an example, we present the prototype of a theory-driven dashboard that can help teachers to better understand and implement new instructional methods in technology-enhanced learning environments. We describe here our needs analysis, design, and evaluation process and outcomes, reflecting upon how teachers can benefit from using thoughtfully-designed LA dashboards in professional development scenarios.

Keywords: Learning Analytics dashboard · Teacher-facing dashboard · Theory-driven dashboard · Teacher Professional Development

1 Introduction

In the last decade, access to and use of educational technology have increased significantly. More recently, the pandemic, too, has forced teachers to resort to ICT use for conducting what has been described as "emergency remote teaching" [1]. Therefore, concern has shifted considerably from whether technology is used in schools [2] to how effectively it is used by teachers and students [3, 4]. This effective use, however, is not easy to achieve: while educational technology and constructivist, student-centred pedagogies combined together can lead to improvement in a variety of student outcomes [5, 6], teachers often lack the technological and pedagogical knowledge required to teach in this manner.

Teacher professional development (TPD, or PD) programmes which introduce participants to new technology and accompanying pedagogical methods in an authentic context can be useful in encouraging effective technology integration in K-12 schools [7]. As the teachers are in entirely novel territory and expected to imbibe and then implement complex new technological and pedagogical knowledge, they can stand to benefit from the use of thoughtfully-designed Learning Analytics (LA) dashboards which

W. Zhou and Y. Mu (Eds.): ICWL 2021, LNCS 13103, pp. 14–27, 2021.
https://doi.org/10.1007/978-3-030-90785-3_2

leverage relevant student and classroom data to actively support them in monitoring, understanding, and improving the effects of the new instructional practices and tools on student outcomes. To design such a dashboard, it is important to study teachers' data needs and data use practices in demanding PD environments.

In the context of a PD programme designed to aid teachers in using technology to make mathematics lessons more engaging, we attempted to learn from teachers' experiences with data use to design a prototype for a theory-driven dashboard with a "scaffolding layer" that would help teachers better understand and monitor the new pedagogical methods they were experimenting with in their classrooms. This prototype was then tested with 24 teachers to gauge their perceptions of the usefulness of the scaffolding layer features added to aid interpretation of data and support teachers' pedagogical knowledge.

The questions which guided our work were as follows:

RQ1 What are the obstacles teachers face in using data to understand and improve novel technology-rich pedagogical practices in PD scenarios?
RQ2 What are teachers' perceptions regarding the usefulness of the scaffolding layer?
RQ3 How does teachers' unaided data use compare to what is emphasised and recommended in the scaffolding layer?

Below, we first describe some concerns raised in literature about LA tools and dashboards, followed by recent attempts at addressing the same. After a brief introduction to our research context, we introduce readers to our own analysis of challenges teachers face when working with data in a PD scenario in Sect. 5, and how this informed our dashboard prototype development in Sect. 6. Finally, we present the evaluation study, followed by a short reflection on lessons learnt and future directions.

2 Related Work

While LA tools and dashboards are expected to make the task of monitoring teaching and learning and subsequent decision-making convenient for educators, they have not yet fulfilled their potential due to significant shortcomings which have been pointed out in literature. First, several researchers [8, 9] have warned and recent reviews [10, 11] have confirmed that LA has so far not drawn sufficiently upon established educational theory. Data collected and analysed in the absence of guiding theory is of little use for both teachers and researchers. Second, it has been observed that teachers frequently do not make use of the data made available to them, often due to the data not being relevant to their actual practice [12]. It is suggested that greater weight be given to teachers' opinions and needs when LA tools and dashboards are developed [13, 14]. Third, while developments in technology have allowed the capture of more and varied kinds of data, this volume and complexity of data means teachers may be lacking in the data use skills necessary to draw useful inferences from and act upon the data, making LA tools a burden rather than an aid in the classroom [15, 16].

Informed by this criticism, some steps have already been taken in the right direction. A number of theory-driven LA tools have been described in recent literature, while other researchers have tried various methods to aid teachers in understanding data in varied learning contexts. These are described in some detail below.

2.1 Theory-Driven LA

A significant number of studies involving theory-driven LA have been conducted in recent years, with much focus especially on self-regulation of learning (SRL). For example, a review of LA dashboards for supporting SRL found that nine papers relied on educational theories and models to develop dashboards (Open Learner Models, Automatic Emotion Recognition process, Learning and Study Strategies Inventory, etc.), though none explicitly employed SRL theories [11].

Theory-driven dashboards have also been developed for monitoring constructs other than self-regulation of learning. Recently, Kent and Cukurova [17] drew upon the collaborative cognitive load theory (rather than student learning outcomes) to design LA visualisations for informing instructors of collaboration in a MOOC.

2.2 Aiding Non-technical Users in Data Use

A number of researchers have focused on designing LA dashboards for supporting teachers' sense-making of data. In the field of LA for supporting computer supported collaborative learning (CSCL), especially, researchers have recognised that teachers face difficulties in employing data to effectively orchestrate classroom activities. A distinction is drawn between mirroring and guiding dashboards designed for CSCL scenarios, where mirroring dashboards merely display data collected, with interpretation left entirely up to the teacher, and guiding dashboards indicate struggling groups of students as well as the problems they might be facing [18]. Numerous innovative guiding dashboard prototypes have been described in LA for CSCL literature, such as one involving the use of smart glasses to convey relevant information to teachers [19]. While fewer in number, longitudinal dashboard use studies have also been successfully conducted in authentic settings in recent years [20].

Moving on from CSCL, some authors have differentiated between exploratory and explanatory data visualisations in LA dashboards, with the former "targeted at experts in data analysis in search of insights from unfamiliar datasets", while the latter emphasise the communication of useful insights to teachers and learners who are pressed for time and may also be lacking in data analysis skills [21]. They relied on a "Data Storytelling" approach guided by generic InfoVis guidelines and narrative storytelling principles combined with education-specific information drawn from Learning Designs (LD) to create LA visualisations that highlight aspects of data relevant to teaching. Similarly, there have been attempts at making Multimodal Learning Analytics (MMLA) data from collocated collaboration settings more user-friendly by arranging it into meaningful layers that tell different stories, guiding users' attention to key insights [22].

From the description above, it is clear that there is increasing interest in forging stronger connections between LA, educational theory, and actual practice with the help of carefully designed dashboards. However, so far, most of such research has been conducted in the context of higher education. Further, as far as we are aware, no studies have been conducted in the context of challenging PD programmes which require teachers to learn about and work with unfamiliar pedagogical strategies and ICT tools: with the current study, we hoped to not only aid teachers in interpreting and reacting to data, but also to encourage the development/consolidation of pedagogical knowledge and data use skills.

3 Research Context

We had a first-hand glimpse into the above-mentioned concerns in LA literature as we worked on a design-based research project (DBR, see [23]) that involved the creation of certain interactive Digital Learning Resources (DLRs) followed by PD for mathematics teachers to encourage effective use of the same for engaging students in the classroom. During the PD, teachers were introduced to the DLRs and other online educational resources. Acquisition of pedagogical knowledge was also encouraged, as teachers were required to design, with guidance from university researchers, lesson plans that would make use of available ICT resources to create a more engaging learning environment for students. They were then expected to implement these in their classrooms at least once a month. To monitor and understand how the new instructional methods affected student engagement, teachers had access to students' self-reported engagement data.

Using teacher reflections, we analysed teachers' data use throughout the PD programme in order to understand how LA dashboards could better cater to their data needs in a scenario where they were required to understand and enact novel and complex pedagogical approaches for improving student engagement. Drawing upon this developing understanding of teachers' experiences with data use, we designed a dashboard prototype and later tested it with 24 teachers. In the following sections, we describe in detail these parts of our study.

4 Understanding Teachers' Data Use During PD

We first attempted to understand teachers' data use in PD scenarios. In this, we were guided by RQ1: What are the obstacles teachers face in using data to understand and improve novel technology-rich pedagogical practices in PD scenarios?

4.1 Method

20 high school mathematics teachers (19 female and 1 male, with between 3 and 38 years of teaching experience) participating in the PD programme were encouraged to collect students' reports about engagement twice a month, once after an intervention lesson and once after any conventional lesson. Students replied to a questionnaire adapted from multiple engagement self-report instruments [24, 25] using a 5-point Likert scale, and the tool LAPills was used to collect and visualise their responses. Using these simple visualisations, teachers were asked to monitor whether and how changes in engagement were related to the new instructional methods they used in the classroom. After collecting and reviewing data, the teachers were asked to record monthly responses to two data use questions using an online form provided to them:

- To what extent did you familiarise yourself with the LAPills results (students' engagement data) and what did you learn from them?
- Based on the data, what would you do differently next time?

Over the course of eight months, we received 53 responses to the data use questions, with 17 out of 20 teachers responding at least once. These responses were then analysed using inductive coding to discover obstacles that teachers faced during data use. The authors read and reread the teachers' responses to identify whether and how they struggled with data use. Teachers' issues were independently listed under several categories by both authors, who then reviewed these themes together, and then the writing of results was begun.

4.2 Results

It was found that despite the simplicity of the data visualisations, a few teachers faced difficulties in understanding them. The majority, however, were able to use data to effectively describe students' engagement and disengagement.

When it came to choosing pedagogical actions in response to data, only a couple of specific responses were received about encouraging cognitive engagement, such as, "*... students should be required more frequently to rephrase things. Currently ... some of the students don't rephrase terms and don't perceive the importance of doing so. It should be regarded as ... mandatory...*" Most teachers chose not to respond to this question, while a few mentioned rather general responses such as, *"I should think lessons through even more, but that is very time-consuming"*.

It should be noted that the teachers had received guidance in different aspects of data use: monthly PD sessions devoted time to researcher-led discussion of data from a randomly chosen classroom, including pedagogical responses to engagement problems.

The analysis of teachers' responses showed that choosing pedagogical actions in response to data was difficult for teachers. Some teachers also faced difficulties in distilling information from data visualisations. Our findings were in line with previous research, which found that the most difficult facet of data use for teachers is deciding how to respond to information gleaned from data [26].

These results obtained in an authentic PD scenario indicated that teachers who are learning about and experimenting with new pedagogies can benefit from support in the form of a LA dashboard that scaffolds them in understanding and enacting these instructional practices by providing insights into data and recommending appropriate pedagogical actions. It had been previously proposed that LA reporting systems should diagnose common problems and provide teachers with suggestions about how to handle them [27]. Accordingly, we proceeded with the design of our dashboard prototype, as described next.

5 Designing the Dashboard Prototype

This section briefly describes our design process for developing a LA dashboard capable of scaffolding teachers' understanding and adoption of new pedagogical methods for supporting student engagement in a PD scenario.

In our approach, the scaffolding took place via a "scaffolding layer": notifications and explanations about pedagogically important information and prompts recommending useful pedagogical actions to aid teachers' developing pedagogical knowledge and data use skills. In order to generate this scaffolding layer, we relied on rule-based analysis of data informed by educational theory in the form of peer-reviewed literature about engagement (this included literature about established conceptions of engagement, indicators of engagement, interventions that that have successfully supported student engagement, etc. [e.g., 28, 29, 30]), and also LD created by teachers. Figure 1 illustrates the dashboard structure and how dashboard use supports the goals of the PD programme. Table 1 contains some examples of the link between theory and rules for data analysis and scaffolding layer content generation.

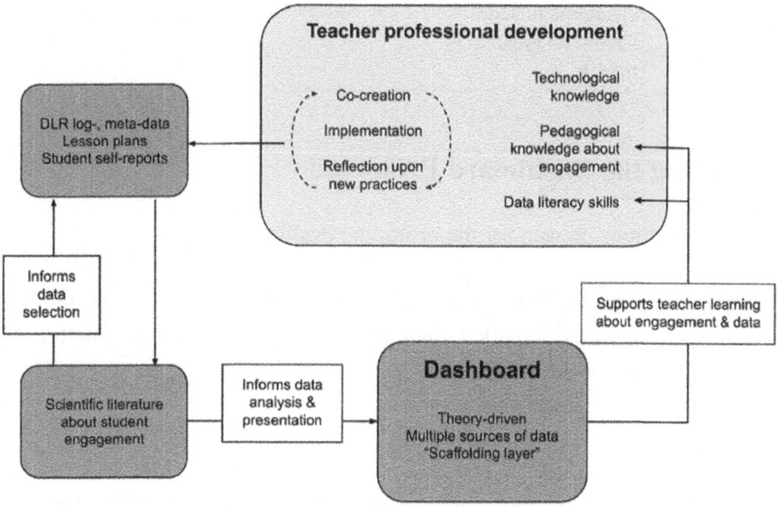

Fig. 1. Dashboard structure, and relationship to the PD programme.

Basic design principles were also kept in mind during the design process. Clutter was reduced, and colours were used judiciously to make certain data stand out and to group similar items together.

Table 1. Examples of theory-based data analysis and presentation rules

Data source	Ideal state	Message displayed in absence of ideal state	Message rationale
Students' collective responses to the engagement questionnaire	Score should be greater than 3 for all types of engagement (cognitive, behavioural, and emotional)	"To support students' cognitive engagement, which appears to be low, you can employ strategies such as helping students connect the current topic to prior knowledge, requiring them to state mathematical concepts in their own words and bringing forth examples from everyday life"	These are research-backed strategies for supporting cognitive engagement
Attendance and individual student responses to engagement questionnaire	Attendance should be higher than 90%, and behavioural engagement score should be greater than 3	"Student x has been missing classes and reports low behavioural engagement"	Student attendance is an indicator of behavioural engagement

6 Evaluating the Dashboard Prototype

The research questions chosen for the prototype evaluation were:

RQ2 What are teachers' perceptions regarding the usefulness of the scaffolding layer?
RQ3 How does teachers' unaided data use compare to what is emphasised and recommended in the scaffolding layer?

6.1 Method

46 high school and middle school mathematics teachers (20 from the PD course analysed above, and 26 from another iteration of the course) were randomly assigned to two groups and requested to complete certain tasks using the dashboard prototype which presented to them actual engagement self-reports from one classroom and fictitious but realistic LD and DLR log data. One group had access to the scaffolding layer of the dashboard, and the other group viewed the dashboard without such enhancements. Table 2 details the tasks and questions assigned to the two groups.

24 teachers responded to the questionnaire, 11 of them from the group with access to the scaffolding layer. Data analysis consisted of drawing up descriptive statistics for RQ1 and inductive coding of teacher responses for RQ2 in order to make possible comparisons with scaffolding layer content.

Table 2. Tasks and questions for evaluation study participants.

Condition	Scenario 1	Scenario 2
Scaffolding layer available	**Task** Reflecting upon usefulness of scaffolding layer content **Question** Do you think the emphasis on some information on the "Task 1" screen is helpful? Choose all options that apply • Yes. It saves time • Yes. I would not have noticed one or both problems on my own • No. The information does not help me teach better • No. I prefer to explore data on my own without external suggestions	**Task** Reflecting upon usefulness of scaffolding layer content **Question** Do you think the suggestion provided on the "questionnaire" screen for improving students' cognitive engagement is helpful? Choose all options that apply • Yes. The/Some strategies mentioned are new to me • Yes. This is a good reminder of engagement-supporting strategies for me • No. I don't think these strategies will help cognitive engagement • No. I don't need the suggestion because I already use these strategies in my class
Scaffolding layer absent	**Task** Interpreting log data about engagement and performance **Question** What information can you draw about class and individual student learning from the data shown on "Task 1" screen?	**Task** Interpreting and responding to students' self-reported engagement data **Questions** Based on the data from the "questionnaire" screen, what kinds of student engagement or disengagement would you choose to address immediately? Based on the data from the "questionnaire" screen, how would you try to improve students' cognitive engagement?

6.2 Results

For RQ2, most teachers reported that for both data navigation/interpretation of log data (Fig. 2) and choosing a response to self-reported engagement data (Fig. 3), the messages displayed were useful in some manner. *Thus, there is some evidence that teachers appreciate having access to the scaffolding layer.*

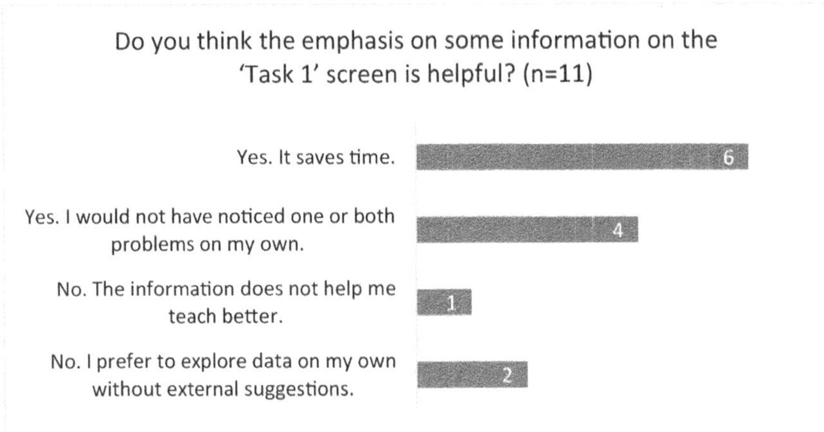

Fig. 2. Teacher perceptions of scaffolding layer usefulness for navigating data.

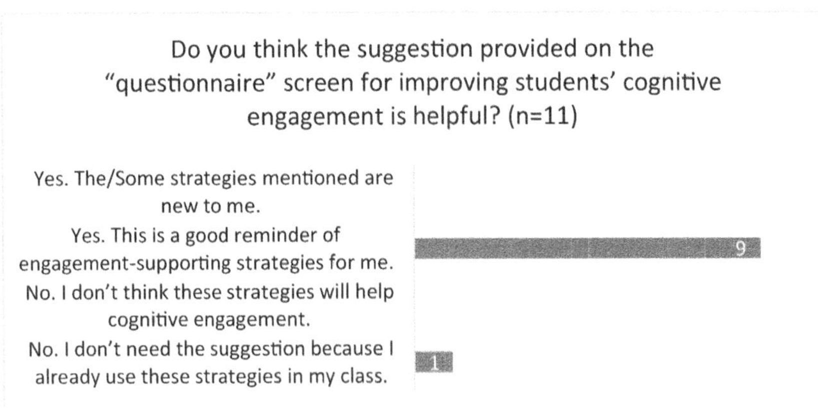

Fig. 3. Teacher perception of scaffolding layer usefulness for responding to data.

For answering RQ3, we compared teachers' responses, categorised by theme, to relevant scaffolding layer messages.

Scenario 1. In the first scenario, the scaffolding layer emphasised most students' struggles with Q3 and how one student might be guessing at answers (Fig. 4).

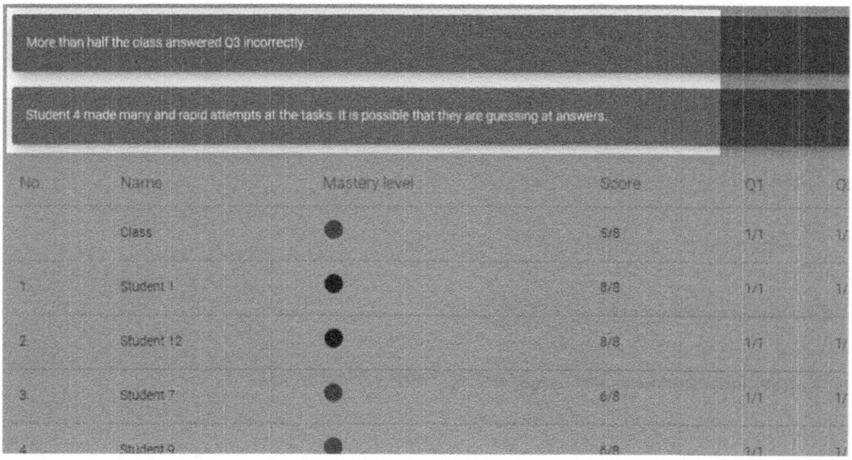

Fig. 4. Providing insights through the scaffolding layer.

Student Struggles with Q3. Out of 13, five teachers responded that they noticed Q3 was challenging and required further discussion. Two others wrote that they would try to improve student understanding, but did not specifically state the problem they noticed. The other five teachers' responses, though interesting, were not quite what we had wanted to elicit here. One teacher wrote, for example, *"If the class is large, then it isn't possible to get information about every student."*

Student 4 and Possible Guessing Behaviour. None of the teachers noticed possible guessing behaviour.

These results show that scaffolding layer content about student performance matched what some teachers noticed in data, and could have made the teachers' task less cumbersome by providing relevant insight. The prompt about possible guessing behaviour could have guided teacher awareness in a desirable direction, and at the very least, could have modelled for teachers a novel way to look at data.

Scenario 2. In the second scenario, the scaffolding layer content indicated that reported cognitive engagement was low and listed some strategies popular in engagement literature for supporting it.

Interpreting Engagement Data. The teachers were first required to infer engagement problems using self-reported engagement data. Using a visualisation embedded in the dashboard (Fig. 5), as expected, 11 out of 13 teachers identified that urgent support was needed for cognitive engagement. Surprisingly, 6 teachers responded that the level of emotional disengagement was concerning for them, with 2 of these 6 choosing emotional disengagement levels as the only immediate problem they noticed.

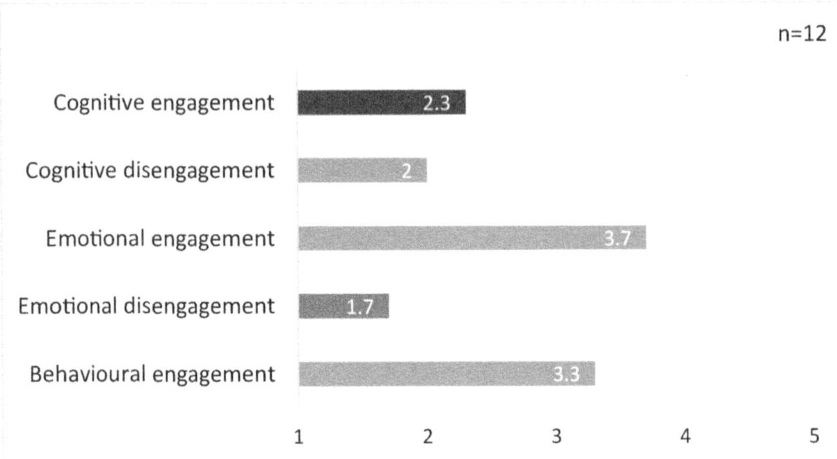

Fig. 5. Students' self-reported engagement data, as displayed in the dashboard prototype.

This result indicates incorrect interpretation of the visualisation, perhaps because of an improper understanding of the term "disengagement". It is interesting that the use of colours – shades of orange and blue – for emphasising data attributes did not aid data interpretation. In this instance, scaffolding layer content could have guided these teachers to focus mostly on cognitive engagement.

Strategies for Supporting Cognitive Engagement. The strategies suggested in the scaffolding layer had been introduced to the teachers during PD, and were each mentioned by at least a couple of teachers. Encouraging students to rephrase concepts in their own words was the most popular research-backed strategy, listed by three teachers. Another proven strategy, eliciting and making connections to prior knowledge was mentioned by two teachers. A third strategy, linking mathematical concepts to real life examples was also listed by two teachers. However, three teachers mentioned only non-specific strategies, such as spending more time on discussion and assigning varied tasks to students. Finally, one teacher wrote that she could not understand the cognitive engagement visualisation.

It is clear that while most of the teachers were familiar with at least one good strategy for supporting cognitive engagement, suggestions/reminders of more strategies could have been useful for all of them and could also encourage the adoption of the pedagogical practices.

7 Conclusion

From the discussion above, we can conclude that our dashboard prototype can scaffold teachers' learning when working with novel instructional methods in technology-enhanced learning environments. Teachers with access to the scaffolding layer perceived it as an aid to their practice. An analysis of the responses of teachers who interacted with data in the absence of the scaffolding layer showed that they would have interpreted data correctly and insightfully, and become aware of numerous suitable instructional methods had they had access to the scaffolding layer.

We also learnt from the prototype evaluation that support for teachers could go further: more explanations about the data visualisations and engagement terminology seem to be required by some teachers. Teacher responses also seem to indicate that the option to hide the scaffolding layer may be useful for some. We had assumed that as teachers learnt more about data interpretation and gained confidence in the use of new pedagogical methods, they would not need some of the scaffolds anymore, while others would still help by making data use more convenient. Finally, strong links between data, theory and LD could be another area to focus on, leading to suggestions of good instructional practices for teachers as they plan lessons.

In the near future, we hope to make the dashboard available, with authentic data, to PD participants as they enact their new pedagogical knowledge in their classrooms. This should help us better understand its applicability to teachers' practice and the ways in which it can assist them in learning about and adopting new pedagogical and data use practices.

References

1. The Difference Between Emergency Remote Teaching and Online Learning. https://er.educause.edu/articles/2020/3/the-difference-between-emergency-remote-teaching-and-online-learning. Accessed 14 Apr 2021
2. Cuban, L.: Oversold and Underused: Computers in the Classroom. Harvard University Press, Cambridge (2001)
3. Keengwe, J., Onchwari, G.: Fostering meaningful student learning through constructivist pedagogy and technology integration. Int. J. Inf. Commun. Technol. Educ. **7**(4), 1–10 (2011)
4. Tunjera, N., Chigona, A.: Teacher educators' appropriation of TPACK-SAMR models for 21st century pre-service teacher preparation. Int. J. Inf. Commun. Technol. Educ. **16**(3), 126–140 (2020)
5. Taber, K.S.: The role of new educational technology in teaching and learning: a constructivist perspective on digital learning. In: Marcus-Quinn, A., Hourigan, T. (eds.) Handbook on Digital Learning for K-12 Schools, pp. 397–412. Springer, Cham (2017). https://doi.org/10.1007/978-3-319-33808-8_24
6. Fullan, M., Langworthy, M.: A rich Seam: How New Pedagogies Find Deep Learning. Pearson, London (2014)
7. van Thiel, L.: Professional learning design framework: supporting technology integration in Alberta. Res. Learn. Technol. **26** (2018)
8. Gašević, D., Dawson, S., Siemens, G.: Let's not forget: Learning Analytics are about learning. TechTrends **59**(1), 64–71 (2015)
9. Wise, A.F., Shaffer, D.W.: Why theory matters more than ever in the age of big data. J. Learn. Anal. **2**(2), 5–13 (2015)
10. Jivet, I., Scheffel, M., Specht, M., Drachsler, H.: License to evaluate: preparing learning analytics dashboards for educational practice. In: Proceedings of the 8th International Conference on Learning Analytics and Knowledge, pp. 31–40. ACM, New York (2018)
11. Matcha, W., Uzir, N.A., Gašević, D., Pardo, A.: A systematic review of empirical studies on learning analytics dashboards: a self-regulated learning perspective. IEEE Trans. Learn. Technol. **13**(2), 226–245 (2020)

12. Rodríguez-Triana, M.J., Martínez-Monés, A., Asensio-Pérez, J.I., Dimitriadis, Y.: Scripting and monitoring meet each other: aligning learning analytics and learning design to support teachers in orchestrating CSCL situations. Br. J. Edu. Technol. **46**(2), 330–343 (2015)
13. Dollinger, M., Lodge, J.M.: Co-creation strategies for learning analytics. In: Proceedings of the 8th International Conference on Learning Analytics and Knowledge, pp. 97–101. ACM, New York (2018)
14. Holstein, K., McLaren, B.M., Aleven, V.: Intelligent tutors as teachers' aides: exploring teacher needs for realtime analytics in blended classrooms. In: Proceedings of the 7th International Conference on Learning Analytics and Knowledge, pp. 257–266. ACM, New York (2017)
15. Mandinach, E.B., Gummer, E.: A systemic view of implementing data literacy in educator preparation. Educ. Res. **42**(1), 30–37 (2013)
16. Marsh, J., Farrell, C.: How leaders can support teachers with data-driven decision making: a framework for understanding capacity building. Educ. Manage. Adm. Leadersh. **43**(2), 269–289 (2015)
17. Kent, C., Cukurova, M.: Investigating collaboration as a process with theory-driven Learning Analytics. J. Learn. Anal. **7**(1), 59–71 (2020)
18. van Leeuwen, A., Rummel, N.: Comparing Teachers' use of mirroring and advising dashboards. In: Proceedings of the 10th International Conference on Learning Analytics and Knowledge, pp. 26–34. ACM, New York (2020)
19. Holstein, K., McLaren, B.M., Aleven, V.: The classroom as a dashboard: co-designing wearable cognitive augmentation for K-12 teachers. In: Proceedings of the 8th International Conference on Learning Analytics and Knowledge, pp. 79–88. ACM, New York (2018)
20. Martinez-Maldonado, R.: A handheld classroom dashboard: teachers' perspectives on the use of real-time collaborative learning analytics. Int. J. Comput.-Support. Collab. Learn. **14**(3), 383–411 (2019). https://doi.org/10.1007/s11412-019-09308-z
21. Echeverria, V., Martinez-Maldonado, R., Buckingham Shum, S., Chiluiza, K., Granda, R., Conati, C.: Exploratory versus explanatory visual learning analytics: driving teachers' attention through educational data storytelling. J. Learn. Anal. **5**(3), 72–97 (2018)
22. Martinez-Maldonado, R., Echeverria, V., Fernandez Nieto, G., Buckingham Shum, S.: From data to insights: a layered storytelling approach for multimodal Learning Analytics. In: Proceedings of the 2020 CHI Conference on Human Factors in Computing Systems, pp. 1–15. ACM, New York (2020)
23. Wang, F., Hannafin, M.J.: Design-based research and technology-enhanced learning environments. Educ. Tech. Res. Dev. **53**(4), 5–23 (2005)
24. Skinner, E., Furrer, C., Marchand, G., Kindermann, T.: Engagement and disaffection in the classroom: Part of a larger motivational dynamic? J. Educ. Psychol. **100**(4), 765–781 (2008)
25. Wolters, C.A.: Advancing achievement goal theory: using goal structures and goal orientations to predict students' motivation, cognition, and achievement. J. Educ. Psychol. **96**(2), 236–250 (2004)
26. Datnow, A., Hubbard, L.: Teachers' use of assessment data to inform instruction: lessons from the past and prospects for the future. Teach. Coll. Rec. **117**(4), 1–26 (2015)
27. Sergis, S., Sampson, D.G.: Teaching and learning analytics to support teacher inquiry: a systematic literature review. In: Peña-Ayala, A. (ed.) Learning Analytics: Fundaments, Applications, and Trends. SSDC, vol. 94, pp. 25–63. Springer, Cham (2017). https://doi.org/10.1007/978-3-319-52977-6_2
28. Fredricks, J.A., Blumenfeld, P.C., Paris, A.H.: School engagement: potential of the concept, state of the evidence. Rev. Educ. Res. **74**, 59–109 (2004)

29. Pianta, R., Hamre, B., Allen, J.: Teacher-student relationships and engagement: conceptualizing, measuring, and improving the capacity of classroom interactions. In: Christenson, S., Reschly, A., Wylie, C. (eds.) Handbook of Research on Student Engagement, pp. 365–386. Springer, Boston (2012). https://doi.org/10.1007/978-1-4614-2018-7_17
30. Pohl, A.J.: Strategies and interventions for promoting cognitive engagement. In: Reschly, A.L., Pohl, A.J., Christenson, S.L. (eds.) Student Engagement, pp. 253–280. Springer, Cham (2020). https://doi.org/10.1007/978-3-030-37285-9_14

ImPres: An Immersive 3D Presentation Framework for Mixed Reality Enhanced Learning

Benedikt Hensen(✉), Lukas Liß, and Ralf Klamma

Advanced Community Information Systems, Chair of Computer Science 5, RWTH Aachen University, Ahornstr. 55, 52056 Aachen, Germany
{hensen,liss,klamma}@dbis.rwth-aachen.de

Abstract. The understanding of three-dimensional structures is an important learning goal, e.g. in anatomy courses or archeology. However, existing 2D slide-based presentation formats are not up to this visualization task as they cannot convey depth and spatial structure well enough. Moreover, a projected slide in a lecture room can be hard to see, depending on the viewer's position and distance from the projection. Mixed reality technology offers an innovative solution for teaching 3D structures with immersive presentations. In this paper, we present the immersive 3D presentation application ImPres. It combines traditional 2D slides with 3D augmented content. With ImPres, students can use their smartphones or tablets to view 3D objects in an augmented reality mode during the presentation. By synchronizing the 3D scene to the currently shown slide by the lecturer, students receive a 3D handout that can be placed individually in each student's environment. Lecturers are able to use the Microsoft HoloLens as a 3D editor to precisely set up the presentation. In combination with a 2D editor for the slide design, existing lecture slides can be imported, reused and augmented for mixed reality. This way, presentations can be held in any use case where 3D content is important for the curriculum. The resulting implementation of ImPres is available as an open-source project and is applicable both in co-located lectures, as well as remote webinars.

Keywords: Mixed reality · Presentation · Learning

1 Introduction

The way how information is presented to students in education is evolving to integrate the abilities and advantages of new media. Replacing blackboards, educators have already adopted digital media using projectors or whiteboards. However, all these presentation forms remain as two-dimensional displays. In order to convey an understanding of a three-dimensional object, lecturers needed to resort to physical 3D sculptures like plastic models of organs or actual dissections in anatomy. The application of such artifacts in education poses challenges

W. Zhou and Y. Mu (Eds.): ICWL 2021, LNCS 13103, pp. 28–39, 2021.
https://doi.org/10.1007/978-3-030-90785-3_3

regarding their availability. In presentations, this leads to difficulties as the lecturer places the object at the front and viewers can only see it from afar or filmed on the two-dimensional projector display. During the COVID-19 pandemic, this challenge is more prominent in remote education as students are only able to view the objects isolated on a screen in video conferences. Mixed reality (MR) enables new possibilities for conveying 3D content in an immersive and intuitive way. For instance, augmented reality (AR) can have a positive impact on education like an increased desire for self-learning, improved memory, and improved spatial understanding [12]. With its ability to embed virtual 3D objects into real-world settings, 3D scans of the physical models can be distributed to a large number of students [8]. Students are able to embed the objects into a real environment and can inspect them from multiple angles by walking around them, gaining an understanding of their true scale and spatial structure. With the introduction of new MR technologies like the Microsoft HoloLens and software libraries like ARCore and ARKit, MR experiences become more available. Especially the mobile libraries enable students to view MR content on their own smartphones, thereby enabling a widespread use in education. This allows them to view the content anywhere and at any time, fitting into their schedules.

In this paper, we elaborate the concept and realization of a MR presentation framework. It is a general-purpose 3D immersive presentation system for lecturers and students. With its collaborative features, synchronous co-located and remote presentations can be supported and mediated. It presents a cross-platform and cross-device approach to combine the advantages of 2D slide editors with the exact placement options in 3D on the HoloLens and the wide distribution of smartphones for AR viewers.

The remainder of this paper is structured as follows. In Sect. 2, we investigate related approaches for MR presentations. After that, we describe our concept for combining the different media for presentations in Sect. 3. Section 4 highlights implementation details and the resulting architecture of the application. With this implementation, we conducted evaluations and the results are laid out in Sect. 5. These results are discussed in Sect. 6. Finally, the paper closes with a conclusion and an outlook on future work in Sect. 7.

2 Related Work

Our work can be classified on Milgram and Kishino's MR continuum in the AR range [10]. The range describes a spectrum between the real world and the virtual reality (VR). Apart from AR, augmented virtuality (AV) defines a second intermediate form. AR and AV are differentiated by the ratio of real objects to virtual elements. In AR, the real world is predominant with some virtual objects integrated into the world. For AV experiences, this ratio is reversed.

In the related work, a series of approaches can be found where augmented reality enhances storytelling and conveys information in presentations. Here, static information systems that augment objects can be distinguished from systems that support a presenter. For instance, Saquib et al. created a video-based presentation system where 2D virtual content can be embedded into a video feed [13]. Using a Kinect camera, the presenter is able to interact with the virtual content on previously set up interaction points. This e.g. allows the presenter to carry a virtual element around or to control a visualization.

Information presentations that do not require a speaker can e.g. be found in museums and exhibitions. For instance, Sommerauer and Müller showed in 2014 in an AR-supported mathematics exhibition that teaching experiences can be improved with AR-compatible smartphones [14]. Results showed that these parts of the exhibition were better understood by visitors. The effects and possible applications of AR have also been further investigated specifically for high-level teaching. This includes, for example, a textbook that was supplemented with 3D content that can be displayed in AR [1]. Alrashidi et al. found that the groups that received AR support outperformed the other groups [2].

The success of these specialized applications has led to the research of generalized cross-discipline systems. Another influence here can be seen in the work of Karsten et al., who have shown that the best learning outcomes can be achieved through a combination of traditional learning practices and AR [9]. In 2018, Antoun et al. created the SlidAR system, which allows lecturers to add AR content to their slides [3]. Students can then view this AR content by scanning the slide with a mobile app. Results showed that both students and professors would like to use the system. The work also shows that the 3D content for the slides needs to be intuitive to set up and place in the 3D environment.

The related work shows that previous concepts for 3D presentations either focus on replacing traditional techniques with AR 3D content or they depend on reference points like slides or physical objects. We did not encounter a related approach that is independent of physical markers on the slides but still integrates slides in the AR content. Our approach has the advantage that it allows teachers to use existing presentations and adds a layer of 3D AR content to them.

3 3D Presentation Concept

Our 3D presentation approach combines the advantages of immersive scenes and 2D presentations. Therefore, we have chosen the following structure for our presentation framework. A presentation consists of *stages* that are arranged sequentially. These give the presentation a structure similar to the slides of a 2D presentation. Each stage can consist of three presentation elements. First, there is the canvas, which can display 2D contents. This element can display existing slides, e.g. imported from traditional 2D presentations. In addition, a stage can contain a *scene* and a *handout*. These two elements can each contain any number of 3D objects that are positioned relative to a starting point. Scenes and handouts can be distinguished by the way how the 3D objects are displayed to the participants and how they can interact with them. Objects in the scene are synchronized in time and space for all participants in a presentation. This allows the presenter to refer to the 3D objects and the entire audience sees them at the same position. The objects from the handout are locally distributed to each participant in a presentation. Thus, each member of the audience can inspect the objects on their own by moving, rotating and scaling them. The handout integrates interactivity into the presentation model as students are motivated to explore the provided 3D objects on their own in the private space.

4 Implemented Presentation System

To gain user experiences and evaluate the concept, we implemented the presentation system ImPres. The resulting implementations are available on GitHub under an open-source license[1].

4.1 System Architecture

The system consists of five parts and each of them is assigned a separate task. They are illustrated in Fig. 1.

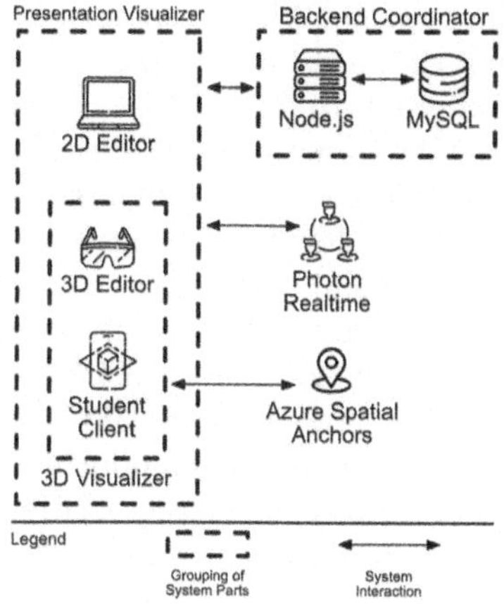

Fig. 1. The system architecture of the ImPres System.

The first element of the system is a 2D editor that runs on desktop PCs and was created using the Windows Presentation Foundation framework (WPF). Complementing this 2D basis, we also implemented a 3D editor in the Unity 3D engine[2] using Microsoft's open-source Mixed Reality Toolkit (MRTK)[3]. The visualization of the presentations for 2D content is handled by the 2D editor and the 3D content is visualized in AR by the 3D editor on smartphones using

[1] https://github.com/rwth-acis/Immersive-presentation---3D-editor, https://github.com/rwth-acis/Immersive-presentation---2D-editor, https://github.com/rwth-acis/Immersive-presentation---Backend-Coordinator.

[2] https://unity.com.

[3] https://github.com/microsoft/MixedRealityToolkit-Unity.

ARCore and on the Microsoft HoloLens[4]. The 3D editor also contains a viewer mode which can e.g. be used by students to follow the presentations. Both the 2D editor and the 3D editor communicate with a backend coordinator. It consists of a Node.js server which e.g. stores created presentations. Moreover, it administers a login system to keep track of users and their activities. Apart from the built-in login system, the presentation framework also supports OpenID Connect login. Access rights are granted via the backend, with which all system parts can communicate via a RESTful API. The synchronization of the presentations consists of two primary tasks which are handled by two services. The temporal synchronization, which allows all clients to get the same state of the presentation in real-time, is implemented with the Photon engine[5]. We integrated Photon synchronization solutions both in our desktop 2D editor and the MR 3D editor to allow them to communicate with each other. For the spatial synchronization in the 3D editor and viewer, Azure Spatial Anchors[6] are used.

4.2 2D Editor

The standard workflow for creating AR presentations starts with the 2D editor where the presenter sets up the slides and defines which 3D content is related to each slide. First, the presenter has to log in using a system-specific account or an OpenID Connect account. The structure of the user interface of the 2D editor is presented in Fig. 2. In the large main view, text and images can be added to the slide. The left slide stack allows for navigating through the set of slides. In order to support existing presentation slides, the 2D editor provides a PDF import option for externally generated LaTeX slides. Alternatively, PowerPoint presentations of already used lecture slides can be exported to PDF and then imported as a basis for the 3D presentations. 3D elements can be added to a presentation by dragging and dropping a 3D model file into the handout or scene panel. While it is possible to already define the position of 3D models in the 2D editor by specifying numeric coordinates, it is more intuitive to switch to the 3D editor at this point to position the model in the 3D environment. To do this, the presentation must first be saved in the 2D editor. It transfers the data to the backend where it is stored in the database.

4.3 3D Editor

The presenter can log in with the same account in the 3D editor as shown in Fig. 3 on the left. Based on the account, the presenter can access the previously created presentations via the backend coordinator. In the 3D view, the slide is presented on a 2D canvas in space and the associated 3D models are also placed in the environment, as can be seen in Fig. 3 in the middle. The presenter can now proceed with the creation process by positioning, rotating and scaling the 3D

[4] Video demonstration: https://youtu.be/HDl6TsrWH5Y.

[5] https://www.photonengine.com/Realtime.

[6] https://azure.microsoft.com/de-de/services/spatial-anchors/.

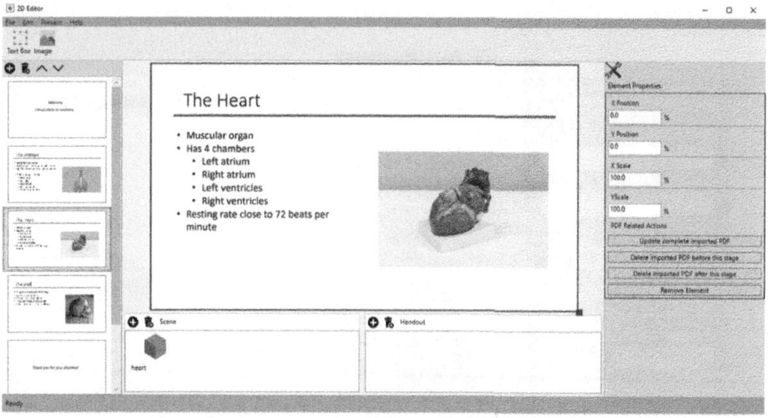

Fig. 2. The 2D editor of the ImPres system.

models precisely. Using a menu, the presenter can navigate through the different stages and thereby edit the 3D content for each slide. The spatial anchor of the scene is presented by a three-dimensional model of an X, shown in Fig. 3 on the right. The objects that belong to the scene are positioned relative to this anchor point. The anchor which is associated with the presentation assures that the presentation content always appears at the defined position in space and with the given orientation and size.

4.4 Conducting Presentations Using the System

The presentation can be started either using the 2D editor or the 3D editor. In a co-located setting, slides from the 2D editor can be projected onto a wall just like traditional PowerPoint presentations. At startup, a short numeric code is displayed. This allows students to join the presentation via the 3D editor on their smartphones. Then, the 3D editor client automatically connects to the Photon engine service. Through this service, the state of the presentation is shared in real-time with all participants of a presentation. In this scenario, we use the Photon engine as a 1-to-n communication channel because only the presenter is allowed to broadcast status updates as only this master client can switch between stages of the presentation. Through this temporal synchronization, the teacher's auditory explanations match the current visual impressions for all students. In order to establish a common spatial understanding where the presenter can walk up to objects and point at them, a spatial synchronization was added to the system. The feature first asks the user to scan the room in the 3D editor by walking around at the start of the presentation. With the HoloLens, its built-in tracking system automatically creates a spatial scan. On smartphones, a visual space reconstruction takes place based on the camera feed of the smartphone's camera. Independent of the used device, a new spatial anchor can be created based on the reference points in the established spatial scan. The anchor is then

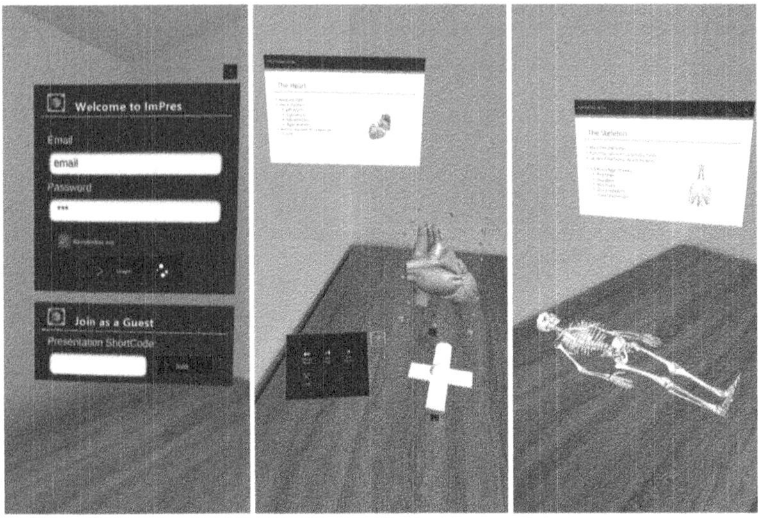

Fig. 3. The 3D editor of the ImPres System. Left: Login menu. Middle: Editor mode. Right: Presentation mode.

stored in the Azure Spatial Anchors service and shared with the students in real-time via the Photon service. Azure Spatial Anchors allow an anchor to be compatible with a variety of devices which enables broader accessibility of the system. This spatial anchor forms a coordinate system that is firmly anchored in space. Students who load the spatial anchor then have the same coordinate system at their disposal as the teacher. This ensures spatial synchronicity and that all 3D objects in the scene are visible in the same place for all participants.

ImPres also supports remote presentations which are especially important during the COVID-19 pandemic. Here, remote participants can establish their own spatial anchor for their local room. In addition, students can also activate the canvas via their 3D viewer in order to see the associated slides directly in AR as shown in Fig. 3 on the right. So, remote learners can follow the entire presentation by using their own smartphones.

5 Evaluation

We conducted three evaluations at different stages of the project, following the "iterative cycle of human-centered design" [11]. In this method, user evaluations are carried out within the smallest possible iterations. The fidelity of the used prototypes increases with each iteration. The feedback from each iteration is then used as input for improvements for the next prototype. We performed two iterations to collect user impressions, first using a paper prototype and then, in the second user evaluation, we used the implemented software prototype of ImPres. Finally, a technical evaluation was conducted.

5.1 Paper Prototype

The paper prototype was created directly after the initial concept for immersive 3D group presentations was ideated. It consists of paper elements that represent both the 2D user interface and the 3D user interface elements. In a Wizard of Oz experiment, we simulate the behavior and functionality by positioning the paper elements in the room according to the user's inputs [6].

We have vertically limited our paper prototype and restricted ourselves to the 3D editor functionalities. We have chosen this limitation since the layout of the 2D editor follows other slide creation tools and is therefore already well-known by users. Moreover, the main goal of the evaluation is to inspect the concept of the 3D presentation. The paper prototype was used in a user evaluation with five users. Only one had previous experience with MR applications. During the user evaluation, the users were given two tasks in succession. First, a prepared presentation was to be opened and presented. The goal of this task was primarily to observe how the users interact with the given menu elements to control the presentation. In the second task, the users were asked to enter the edit mode. Here, they should navigate to a specific slide in the presentation and they should rotate an object. The goal of this task was to evaluate whether the planned interactions to place 3D content could be used intuitively. During the evaluation, we observed the users, noting their steps. We also obtained additional insights about the user's thoughts by letting them fill out a qualitative questionnaire afterward. The questionnaire contained the following questions:

- Was there a time during your use when you felt uncertain about how to perform the task? If so, then please tell me about that situation.
- What aspects of the user interface do you remember positively?
- What aspects of the user interface do you remember negatively?
- What improvements do you want to see in future versions?

The most dominant result of the paper prototype evaluation was that all users understood the structure of the 3D presentations quickly. According to their statements, they already felt confident in presenting and dealing with 3D content in the presentation. The placement method was also positively evaluated by the users and therefore the concept was further included in the development of the ImPres system. The aspect that bothered the users the most was the input of text to sign in or to join a presentation. For the software prototype, we focused on reducing the text input to a minimum. Presentations can now be joined with a short numeric code and it is no longer necessary to enter the complete presentation name and a password. Moreover, this validated the importance of the 2D editor in the system as users can type on conventional desktop keyboards to produce the text for the 2D slides. In addition, the paper prototype evaluation revealed several user interface improvements that streamlined the menu structure. Since these improvement requests were noticed so early, we were able to integrate them directly into the software prototype.

5.2 Software Prototype

The software prototype is a fully functional software solution that realizes all features of the described system in Sect. 4. We evaluated the resulting ImPres system with 16 students. Since the underlying concept was already examined in the previous evaluation, the focus of this evaluation was to examine its usability. Users were able to try out the 2D and 3D editor in order to create new presentations and to view existing ones. To enable comparability with other systems, we used two questionnaires. The System Usability Scale (SUS), which was created by Brooke, provides a score with which the usability of the system can be quantified [5]. However, the given score does not allow a linear comparison, since a doubling of the score does not correspond to a doubling of the usability, but Bangor et al. has already divided the scale into blocks with adjective ratings [4]. When averaging the computed scales, the evaluated software prototype of the ImPres system achieved an SUS score of 86.5, which indicates good usability.

In order to gain detailed insights into how demanding the system is, we also used the NASA-Task Load Index (NASA-TLX) questionnaire [7]. In addition to an overall score, the NASA-TLX questionnaire also provides individual ratings for the categories "Mental Demand", "Physical Demand", "Temporal Demand", "Overall Performance", "Effort" and "Frustration Level". The participants were asked to rate the workload in each category on a scale from 0 to 100 in steps of 5 after performing a given set of taks. Those tasks contained the editing of a presentation by adding new 3D objects and changing their position and scale. In the task set, participants were also asked to hold a presentation and to join an existing one by the instructor using the ImPres system. After performing the tasks, they had to rank the NASA-TLX categories in terms of their importance for the user. Categories received five points each time they were selected as the most important and one point less for each position behind the first one. Therefore, a category got zero points if it is considered least important. By normalizing this score we created the weight for each category. The scores and weights for the individual dimensions of the questionnaire are laid out in Table 1.

Table 1. The individual scores and their weight of the NASA-TLX questionnaire evaluation.

Dimensions	Score	Weight
Mental demand	23.67	0.21
Physical demand	12.33	0.03
Temporal demand	14.33	0.21
Performance	27.33	0.24
Effort	44	0.12
Frustration	24.33	0.19

We observed that the perceived workload was the lowest for the physical demand, directly followed by the temporal demand. Combined with the low weight of the physical demand, this shows that participants were not bothered by holding the smartphone or wearing a Microsoft HoloLens. The low temporal demand is a good indication that lecturers are able to create an immersive presentation in a time-efficient manner with ImPres. The weight of 0.21 for the temporal demand shows that the users perceive the time perspective as crucial. Noticeable is the relatively high value for the effort dimension. Compared to the other categories this value is significantly higher with a value of 44. One possible reason for this could be that most of the users that participated in the evaluation had not been in contact with MR applications or devices before. Therefore, they had to learn the interaction paradigms for immersive applications while participating in our user study. We believe that this additional learning curve can lead to a higher perceived effort. We plan to investigate this further with future iterations of the ImPres system. Nevertheless, participants assigned a lower weight to this dimension, thereby rating it as less important. The individual scores in the categories were combined into an overall NASA-TLX score of 24.81. Since this score is in the lower quarter of the score that stretches from 0 to 100, it can be deduced that the workload was perceived as fairly low by most users. The NASA-TLX helped us to get a better estimation of the workload. This value can also serve as a benchmark for future iterations and improvements of the ImPres system.

Furthermore, we also subjected the system to a technical evaluation. We used a computer with 8 GB RAM and a 2.50 GHz Intel(R) Core(TM) i5-6300U processor. The 2D editor runs continuously at 60 frames per second (fps) with a CPU utilization of 5%. Only when saving the presentation, the CPU load briefly increase to about 30%. The 3D editor also runs at stable 60 fps. The only drops in the framerate can be observed if a presentation is loaded. To improve the user experience here, load indicators were added to indicate to the user that the system is working on a background task. Overall, the technical analysis showed that ImPres provides users a smooth interaction that supports usability in MR.

6 Discussion

ImPres provides students access to 3D models during presentations. Especially its remote support has potential for remote teaching. Students can use their own smartphones to gain access to interactive 3D content independent of their location. This way, education that used to be conducted with physical 3D models can be maintained during the pandemic and is enhanced by digital models.

Regarding the conducted studies, the initial focus is on the usability and perceived task load of users. We plan on conducting further studies that have a closer look at other aspects of the system, e.g. regarding its learning effect.

The cross-platform support for the Microsoft HoloLens and smartphones opens up suitable use cases. Since the Microsoft HoloLens is less available than smartphones which can even be provided by the students themselves, the

HoloLens is mainly for the lecturer's use. As the lecturer has to author the presentation content, the HoloLens can be beneficial because of its intuitive in-air interactions for placing the 3D models. Smartphones only provide interactions on the touch screen which require a bit of practice to master the 3D placements. Hence, it is fitting that smartphones predominantly serve as viewers for the audience. Thus, the lecturer can prepare the 3D content which is then accessible for students anywhere and anytime.

7 Conclusion and Future Work

In this paper, we introduced ImPres, an immersive presentation framework for MR. It enhances traditional 2D slides with 3D content. On a conceptual level, we extended the slide-based structure of a presentation to stages. Each stage contains the slide, a 3D scene for displaying spatially anchored 3D objects and a handout. With the handout, students can inspect designated 3D models in their personal space. The implemented cross-platform solution is available as an open-source project. It runs on the Microsoft HoloLens and smartphones. During the development, we followed an iterative design approach where we started with a paper prototype that was evaluated first in a Wizard of Oz study. Based on the results which e.g. showed that typing in MR should be avoided, we created the fully functional prototype. In a user evaluation that focused on the usability of the prototype and a technical evaluation, its practicability was investigated. The SUS questionnaire yielded an average value of 86.5 and the NASA-TLX showed also an adequate average value of 24.81.

We plan on using the developed presentation system in our lectures and our MR software lab. Especially in the MR lab, where we teach the fundamentals of MR development, 3D visualizations can be beneficial to visualize coordinate systems and geometric operations to students. Moreover, they can gain an impression of a MR application and it is also possible to convey different 3D interaction metaphors using 3D visualizations. Regarding the features, we plan the extension of the system by animations. Animations can e.g. be applied to 3D objects like a beating heart. Alternatively, the scene itself can be animated by recording the movement of objects in the anchored space. This would allow objects to appear and move into a highlighted zone at the click of a button during the presentation. Currently, the audio itself is not transmitted using ImPres but a separate audio call is still necessary. Thus, we plan on including an audio stream in the presentation where the built-in microphones of the MR devices record the presenter's voice.

All in all, the presentation framework ImPres enables new opportunities to enhance traditional presentation slides by adding 3D content to them. It offers a new approach that combines existing slide-based practices with interactive 3D models both for co-located and remote presentations in formal learning.

Acknowledgment. We thank the German Federal Ministry of Education and Research for their support within the project "Personalisierte Kompetenzentwicklung durch skalierbare Mentoringprozesse" (tech4comp; id: 16DHB2110).

References

1. Aliev, Y., Kozov, V., Ivanova, G., Ivanov, A.: 3D augmented reality software solution for mechanical engineering education. In: Rachev, B., Smrikarov, A. (eds.) Proceedings of the 18th International Conference on Computer Systems and Technologies, pp. 318–325. ACM, New York (2017). https://doi.org/10.1145/3134302.3134306
2. Alrashidi, M., Alzahrani, A., Gardner, M., Callaghan, V.: A pedagogical virtual machine for assembling mobile robot using augmented reality. In: Schmidt, A., et al. (eds.) Proceedings of the 7th Augmented Human International Conference 2016 on - AH 2016, pp. 1–2. ACM Press, New York (2016). https://doi.org/10.1145/2875194.2875229
3. Antoun, S., Auda, J., Schneegass, S.: SlidAR. In: Abdennadher, S., Alt, F. (eds.) Proceedings of the 17th International Conference on Mobile and Ubiquitous Multimedia - MUM 2018, pp. 491–498. ACM Press, New York (2018). https://doi.org/10.1145/3282894.3289744
4. Bangor, A., Kortum, P.T., Miller, J.T.: An empirical evaluation of the system usability scale. Int. J. Hum.-Comput. Interac. **24**(6), 574–594 (2008). https://doi.org/10.1080/10447310802205776
5. Brooke, J.: SUS: a quick and dirty usability scale. In: Jordan, P.W., Thomas, B., Weerdmeester, B.A., McClelland, I.L. (eds.) Usability Evaluation in Industry, pp. 189–194. Taylor & Francis (1996). http://www.itu.dk/courses/U/E2005/litteratur/sus.pdf
6. Dow, S., MacIntyre, B., Lee, J., Oezbek, C., Bolter, J.D., Gandy, M.: Wizard of Oz support throughout an iterative design process. IEEE Perv. Comput. **4**(4), 18–26 (2005). https://doi.org/10.1109/MPRV.2005.93
7. Hart, S.G.: Nasa-task load index (NASA-TLX); 20 years later. Proc. Hum. Fact. Ergon. Soc. Ann. Meet. **50**(9), 904–908 (2006). https://doi.org/10.1177/154193120605000909
8. Hensen, B., Koren, I., Klamma, R., Herrler, A.: An augmented reality framework for gamified learning. In: Hancke, G., Spaniol, M., Osathanunkul, K., Unankard, S., Klamma, R. (eds.) ICWL 2018. LNCS, vol. 11007, pp. 67–76. Springer, Cham (2018). https://doi.org/10.1007/978-3-319-96565-9_7
9. Karsten, S., Jörg, D., Hornecker, E.: Learner versus system control in augmented lab experiments. In: Proceedings of the Interactive Surfaces and Spaces on ZZZ - ISS 2017, pp. 354–359. ACM Press, New York (2017). https://doi.org/10.1145/3132272.3132276
10. Milgram, P., Kishino, F.: A taxonomy of mixed reality visual displays. IEICE Trans. Inf. Syst. **E77-D**(12), 1321–1329 (1994)
11. Norman, D.A.: The Design of Everyday Things: Revised and Expanded Edition, expanded Basic Books, Philadelphia (2013)
12. Radu, I.: Augmented reality in education: a meta-review and cross-media analysis. Pers. Ubiquit. Comput. **18**(6), 1533–1543 (2014). https://doi.org/10.1007/s00779-013-0747-y
13. Saquib, N., Kazi, R.H., Wei, L.Y., Li, W.: Interactive body-driven graphics for augmented video performance. In: Proceedings of the 2019 CHI Conference on Human Factors in Computing Systems, CHI 2019, pp. 1–12. Association for Computing Machinery, New York (2019). https://doi.org/10.1145/3290605.3300852
14. Sommerauer, P., Müller, O.: Augmented reality in informal learning environments: a field experiment in a mathematics exhibition. Comput. Educ. **79**, 59–68 (2014). https://doi.org/10.1016/j.compedu.2014.07.013

Designing a Virtual Learning Environment Based on a Learner Language Corpus

Kaisa Norak(✉) and Hans Põldoja

Tallinn University, Narva mnt 25, 10120 Tallinn, Estonia
{kaisa.norak,hans.poldoja}@tlu.ee

Abstract. Learner language corpora which contain examples of written texts have been invaluable for research on second language acquisition and the development of corpus-based learning resources. However, building a learner corpora can be a slow process and the resources based on these corpora often do not directly benefit the language learners who provided their texts for analysis. One way to solve these problems is to combine a learner corpus with a virtual learning environment so that the learners can submit examples of their language use to the corpus and gain from online learning resources developed by teachers and researchers with the help of corpus analysis. Using participatory design methods, a prototype of an integrated learning environment was designed based on Estonian learner language corpus. Findings from the participatory design process helped us to understand learners' motivation for using a corpus-based virtual learning environment and to identify necessary support structures. Integrating a virtual learning environment with a learner language corpus opens up new opportunities for language technology research. While this study has been carried out in the context of Estonian learner corpus, the same design principles can be transferred to other language corpora.

Keywords: Learner language corpus · Virtual learning environments · Participatory design · Technology-enhanced language learning · Data-driven learning

1 Introduction

Learner corpora have several applications in language teaching such as developing second language curricula [1], language level tests [2] or interactive exercises [3]. Based on their application, these corpora can be divided between delayed pedagogical use (DPU) or immediate pedagogical use (IPU) [4]. The difference is that DPU corpora are mostly used by researchers or teachers to create new learning resources, while IPU corpora, often containing learners' own recent texts, are more often used by the same learners to explore their typical language patterns and errors. The corpus is therefore also a digital learning resource. The latter stems from the definition of corpus as "a large, principled collection of naturally occurring examples of language stored electronically" [5], even

W. Zhou and Y. Mu (Eds.): ICWL 2021, LNCS 13103, pp. 40–51, 2021.
https://doi.org/10.1007/978-3-030-90785-3_4

though IPU corpora can be small in size, and often stored only in teacher's own computer. Regardless, both IPU and DPU corpora contain digitally-born or digitized texts that can be used for language learning.

Corpus as a learning resource is a central concept in data-driven learning (DDL), where the learner becomes a language researcher, creating their own language model through exploration [6]. This applies especially to IPU corpora. However, we must not diminish the value of DPU corpora. While learner corpora can be used as a learning material on their own, they are also invaluable in creating learner grammars, language exercises with automatic feedback and improving learner language analysis tools [7]. Therefore, it makes sense to combine a DPU and IPU corpus and benefit from both [4].

Since IPU corpora are used directly in the classroom, they can already be considered as digital learning resources. Using the learner corpus as a DPU corpus and creating new exercises and learning resources from this data means that the corpus analysis environment could also contain a virtual learning environment. This would allow the system to host the learning resources and make them accessible for the learners, whether or not the resources are created from the analysis of their own texts or not.

In addition, the development of a classical DPU corpus can be slow. Taking the work of Hana et al. [8] as an example, we see that creating a corpus can take a long time because the texts are often written by hand, they need to be transcribed and annotated with relevant metadata, not to mention, this process should be done by several researchers to ensure valid results. The same can be seen with the Estonian Interlanguage Corpus (EIC), which also contains written exam texts that have to be digitized and annotated with metadata [9]. Considering that IPU corpora are created relatively fast, since the texts are already digital, it could be possible to apply similar methods to DPU corpora and have the learners supply the corpus with their own digitally-born texts.

Our goal is to create a platform for Estonian context that combines both a language corpus and a virtual learning environment. Meanwhile, the corpus can be both IPU or DPU and the virtual learning environment can benefit from the corpus and also replenish the corpus with its results. In order to create such a multi-faceted system, it is imperative to know what the learners, teachers and researchers expect from language learning and/or corpus platforms. Thus, we formulated two research questions:

RQ1: What do researchers, teachers, and language learners need from an online platform combining virtual learning environment and text corpora?
RQ2: What are the opportunities and drawbacks of such a platform based on the results of testing the digital prototype?

Section 2 discusses the potential benefits and hindrances of a language corpus and a language learning environment. Section 3 describes the methods used to design a corpus-based language learning environment. These methods are applied in Sect. 4, which first answers RQ1, defining the users needs as a starting point. RQ2 is answered through an iterative participatory design process, in which scenarios and prototypes are tested with various stakeholders. Section 5 discusses the results of the study and compares our findings with previous research. Section 6 summarizes the conclusions and provides directions for future research.

2 Corpora and Virtual Learning Environments in Language Learning

Learner corpora and virtual learning environments often exist separately. However there are examples that a corpus can still have ties to a learning environment, especially as a source of data. Write and Improve [10] uses Cambridge Learner Corpus data to provide automatic writing feedback for different tasks. In Swedish Lärka [11] exercises are automatically created for the learner, using the data from the Korp corpus. They can also be combined the other way – the learning environment itself can contribute to the corpus. An example of this is IWiLL [12], where the learners' essays and teachers' feedback are moved directly to the Taiwan Learners' Corpus.

Both corpora and virtual learning environments positively affect the learning process. As described before, corpora can be used as a source for data-driven learning. Virtual learning environments also have an important role in learning. According to [13] and [14], learners are more motivated to learn in a virtual learning environment. They especially enjoy the diversity and the autonomy it offers. Al-Zahrani [15] has pointed out that learners often want to immerse themselves in a language by using subtitles when watching videos, listening to radio, having conversations with other students and translating texts which they do not understand.

On the other hand, [15] has also mentioned that the lack of use of such environments could stem from insufficient technical competence. The same has been found with corpora. Several authors [16, 17] point out that while corpus has a potential as a learning resource, students need a significant amount of training to start using them and the knowledge of existing corpora can be low. In addition, curriculum design might not allow for something new to be integrated into classroom activities and teachers might need more support from others in order to implement new technology [18]. Furthermore, [19] and [20] have found that students also need different support structures when learning virtually. They often miss the social interaction and require immediate teacher feedback.

From these findings we can derive that corpora and virtual learning environments are indeed beneficial to learning, but there are still several drawbacks that need to be handled in order to fully implement them in classroom activities. To help solve the problems at hand, we turned to the users.

3 Methods

Creating a corpus-based virtual learning environment requires an interdisciplinary research approach combining language technology, educational technology, and human-computer interaction. Therefore we approached the problem with the design-based research methodology where new research knowledge is created through the design process [21]. Furthermore, we applied the improved Double Diamond model described by Santos Ordóñez et al. [22] to create an iterative process. The model is diverging and converging, where the divergence allows us to collect as much data as we can and then define key knowledge at the convergence. The iterative aspect of this model allowed us to revisit previous results and the design artifacts created based on them in order to further improve and validate what has been learned so far.

Since users' needs and their knowledge were vital to us, we also applied different participatory design methods in our process. In participatory design, the designer works with the users to fit the design to their existing knowledge [23]. Initially we conducted a series of interviews to better understand users' needs and a context in which the platform is going to be used. Since the environment was created in Estonian context, we chose to interview Estonian language researchers, Estonian language teachers, foreign students as well as adults and high-school students who either spoke Estonian natively or had Russian as their mother tongue. The latter were chosen to include the biggest ethnic minority group in Estonia. Based on these interviews we created personas of archetypical users. Then we moved on to write scenarios which were discussed with the stakeholders in the participatory design sessions. The prototyping involved both low-fidelity paper prototypes and a high-fidelity click-through prototype created on Figma platform, which were tested with the users. The way we adapted our process to the aforementioned Double Diamond model is described on Fig. 1.

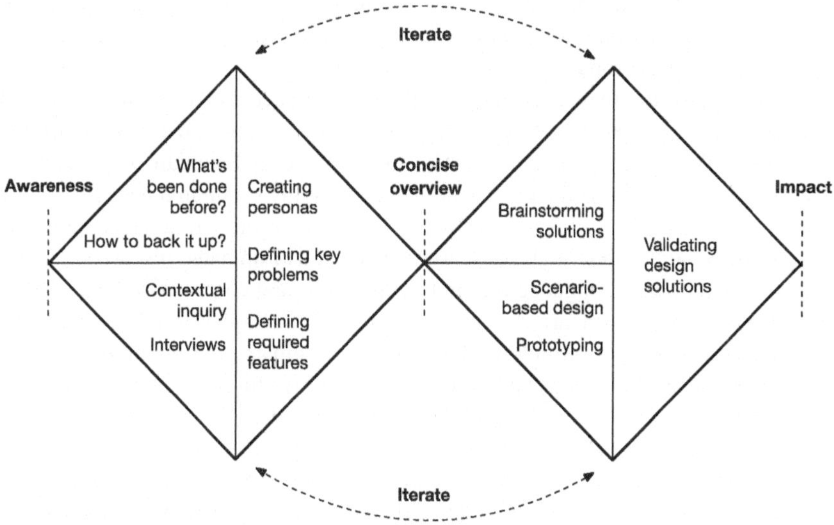

Fig. 1. Double Diamond model applied to the design of a corpus-based virtual learning environment (adapted from [22]).

The design process took place from spring 2020 to spring 2021. We involved 23 interviewees, 11 participants for scenario-based design sessions, 10 users for testing paper prototypes and 5 for testing digital prototypes. All-in-all, 49 persons participated in the design study. Every interview and design session was recorded and notes were taken on missing features, important aspects and discovered problems. We used inductive qualitative analysis to come to conclusions based on the data received from the design sessions and interviews.

4 Results

In order to answer RQ1, a set of personas was developed based on the insights from the interviews. We discovered that language researchers were alike to the language teachers, since they also taught Estonian on different proficiency levels, but they had more knowledge of corpora than the latter. Hence two different personas were derived: Estonian language teacher persona with a goal to find printable worksheets and listening exercises as well as seeing their students progress and a researcher persona with a goal to analyze language use and create new learning resources.

We could also differentiate between three language learner personas. Two of them were independent learners, one of whom was a self-paced learner, more intrinsically motivated, the other a competitive learner, who found gamified solutions and comparing their learning progress with others very motivating. We also identified a third language learner persona, a high-school student with Russian mother tongue, who was not very highly motivated to learn Estonian and found teacher feedback and learning in a classroom highly important. The rest of the interviewees formed an additional persona, whose goal was to check their texts for language errors, whether using dictionaries or automatic correction tools. That last persona, mostly Estonian native, is not trying to use the platform for language learning, but rather uses it for practical reasons such as correcting their writings. This persona covers also lifelong learners.

Based on personas, their goals and problems, we created and tested scenarios, paper prototypes and digital prototypes, each containing more details and enhanced after testing sessions. We wrote 13 scenarios. The first 5 were in Estonian for teachers and researchers to assess: 1) Language teacher creates a study group in a new virtual learning environment; 2) Language teacher shares exercises in the virtual learning environment; 3) Language teacher analyzes learners results; 4) Language researcher analyzes the corpus material; 5) Language researcher creates a new corpus-based exercise. The second 5 were written for learners and they were both in English and Estonian, so that language learners at every proficiency level could participate: 6) Student joins an online study group in a new language learning environment; 7) A foreign student starts to learn Estonian on his own; 8) A foreign student is learning Estonian regularly; 9) Student submits an exercise several times; 10) Student wants to produce a text with proper use of Estonian. The last 3 scenarios, written in Estonian, were meant for Estonian natives: 11) Estonian happens upon an environment with Estonian text correction; 12) Estonian uses the text corrector to analyze her writing; 13) Estonian uses the environment regularly to improve her language use. Discussing these scenarios in participatory design sessions helped us prioritize offered features and allowed us to start creating prototypes.

The final prototype was named ELLE – Estonian Language Learning, Teaching & Research Environment. Through integrating a corpus with a virtual learning environment, it offers valuable features for language researchers, teachers or learners of any kind. As a result of the design sessions, we combined user needs based on their personas in Fig. 2.

Based on the results of the design sessions, we could derive two primary user profiles: one for teachers and researchers and the other for language learners. Since Estonians do not usually want to log in to the environment, there was no need to create a separate user interface for them – everything they need can be accessed without logging in.

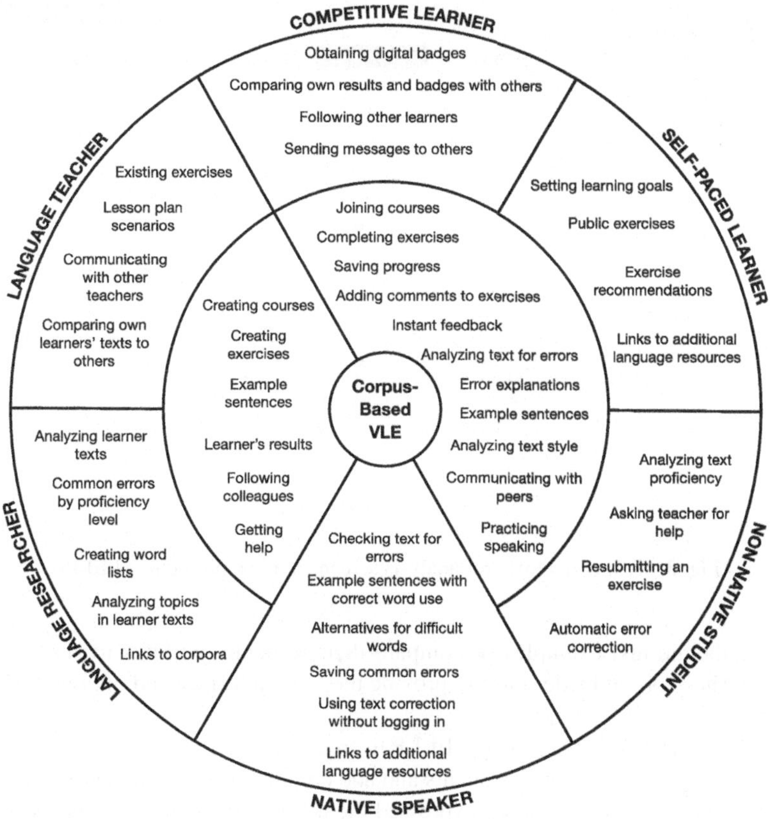

Fig. 2. User needs in a corpus-based virtual learning environment.

The ELLE platform allows analyzing corpus texts with various analysis tools. To make this analysis easier for users without a corpus analysis background, we offered the option to use a text corrector (Fig. 3) with some of the analysis features, especially the ones mentioned by different learners and Estonians as well. In addition to text analysis, teachers and researchers can create courses and new interactive exercises and share them with their own students or with the general public. Independent learners can also learn outside of a language course with public exercises or browse the collection of links to find texts or podcasts in the target language.

To motivate the learners, the environment offers several support structures such as digital badges. Learners can earn badges for uploading and publishing their writings, completing interactive exercises or being an active learner in general. For support, they can ask for help privately from their teacher, post to a forum in a language course or send messages to fellow students.

Since the researchers and teachers have common needs, they share the same user interface. That got further validated after testing the scenarios. It was found that while language teachers have not had contact with corpora before, they would also like to use some of the offered corpus analysis features. For example they would use the corpora

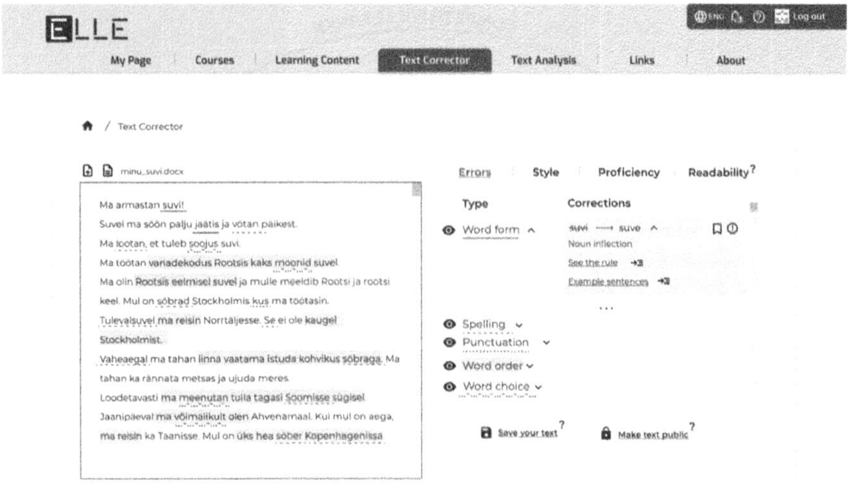

Fig. 3. Text corrector error analysis screen from the prototype of ELLE.

to find authentic text examples or compare their students' writings to similar corpus material. Therefore, it made sense to provide the same interface and options for both of these users.

Teachers and researchers can use ELLE to create new learning resources, analyze the corpus, create courses for their students and add comments to the exercises to help their students along. Not every teacher expressed the need to create new resources, but they often chose to find existing exercises from the site, based on its topic and rated quality. If however they were to create an exercise, they might occasionally want to share it with their own coworkers, keep it private or share it publicly with everyone – the opinions on that matter varied. Furthermore, some teachers also mentioned the need to follow other teachers' profiles and talk with them to get additional support either applying new techniques in class or on how to use the materials or exercises they had created.

Insights into using corpus analysis tools on the site were gained mostly from the researchers. They valued the most the error and readability analysis, but also occasionally wanted to create word lists, use keyword analysis as a tool for comparison or see concordances. As a drawback however, they did not see themselves leading their students to the corpus and its analysis tools, for fear that they get confused or learn from incorrect contexts, since we're dealing with mostly learner corpus data. In addition, since the researchers themselves were also language teachers of different proficiency levels, they focused more on what the site offers for teachers and gave less detailed feedback on the corpus analysis tools functionality.

All of ELLEs users were also offered a chance to find additional virtual learning or corpus websites from the collection of useful links. The teachers had mentioned that it is difficult to find some learning resources, that there are many sites and they cannot remember them all. Also, it was pointed out that since the ELLE website contains a learner language corpus, teachers might want to use an Estonian native corpus for finding good example sentences. Estonian natives wanted to find links to translators and dictionaries or to a short collection of Estonian grammar or formatting rules. The foreign students wanted to find texts to read in Estonian, radio shows and podcasts to listen to as well as to explore other Estonian language learning environments and apps. Thus, the collection of links is quite extensive and leads users to various other web sites, not contributing directly to the improvement of the learner language corpus. However, if our goal is to improve Estonian language learning and teaching, it is an important aspect to consider.

For the language learners, whether they were independent learners or not, it was important to join language courses and to find public courses. They also mentioned the need to have conversations with other learners via forum or private messages so that they could feel as part of a group and get help with their learning. The learners appreciated the ability to add comments to their exercises to ask the teacher for help, but also wanted to turn to their coursemates in case their teacher does not respond fast enough.

In addition to doing exercises as part of ELLE's courses, some students wanted to do additional exercises or find new learning resources on their own. The most popular exercise types for learners were multiple choice, flashcards, fill in the blanks or listening exercises. Longer writing tasks did not appeal to the students, however an independent learner on a higher language proficiency level noted that he would occasionally also like to write essays or other kinds of writings to polish his knowledge. Most other students preferred shorter tasks. It is worth noting however, that the learners wanted to have conversations with others – their coursemates, teachers or even Estonian natives – meaning that they prefer to write in a more organic manner, not just for the sake of an exercise. Therefore, when a language learning environment is combined with a corpus, it should also take into account that learners are not always essay writers and that the data in this corpus or any kind of database should reflect that.

To make ELLE even more practical for the learners, we also offered the chance to assess their own writings, should they want to write in Estonian in any aspect of their daily lives. That was a favorable feature for Estonians as well. Learners as well as Estonians appreciated most the possibility to analyze their text for various errors. They noted that it is not enough to just highlight the mistaken word or phrase, but they also want to see why the system recognizes it is a mistake and have some example sentences with the correct use that would help them along. Some of the test users, especially learners, found that they would allow all manner of texts to be imported directly to the corpus from this text corrector. Estonians were the most reserved, since they would use it to correct important emails, not wanting private correspondence to end up in a public corpus. Although they added that if the text was not sensitive and making it public was straightforward, they would sometimes allow even some of their writings to move to the corpus.

While error analysis was the highlight of the text corrector, the users found that they would sometimes even use some of its other features. The learners said that they would see their text proficiency level and find out how to improve their text to get to a higher proficiency level. They also wanted occasionally to check their text style, to make it more suitable for the writing situation they had in mind. Readability analysis, also offered as part of the text corrector, was not that important for most learners. However, it was something that some of the Estonians, and some learners, would use to improve their text even more, to simplify their sentences or change repeating words.

ELLE also offers several incentives for learners to publish their writings to the corpus or to continue doing exercises. Competitive learner types were more motivated from the digital badges they would receive for their activity on the site. They also found that they want to compare their results to that of their friends, coursemates or other similar learners. Competitive learners would also opt to receive daily notifications to do exercises and keep up their streak, however most learners are not interested in this and would come to ELLE and do exercises when they feel like it. All learners were interested in seeing their progress on their dashboard, telling them what is their proficiency level, what kind of errors they do most and how they can improve.

Analyzing the user needs and feedback to the scenarios and prototypes helped us to design the prototype for an online platform which combines a learner language corpus with a virtual learning environment. This is, however, a snapshot of the process, since design is never final and further improvements based on the recommendations still need to be accounted for.

5 Discussion

The article describes the prototype of ELLE – Estonian Language Learning, Teaching & Research Environment. To create and test this prototype, we formulated two research questions. RQ1 helped us find the users needs to start off the design process. RQ2 allowed us evaluate the final prototype at the end of the current design process. In this discussion, we'd like to point out how our findings from RQ1 and RQ2 correspond to the existing research.

From user testing we found, similar to [13] and [14], that learners appreciate the autonomy that a virtual learning environment offers. They also want to find exercises to test themselves, especially the case with independent learners. In order to support learner autonomy, ELLE offers the option to evaluate one's text with the text corrector, find exercises with automatic feedback and discover new language learning resources from the collection of useful links.

Language learners are hence also more motivated to learn (e.g. [13–15]) using a virtual learning environment. Test users found that interactive exercises enhance in-class learning. There were also users who appreciated gamified elements, especially digital badges and a possibility to compare their own results with others. However, it was noted that doing exercises is not enough. It was also important for learners to practice speech and they found that they can not often do it in online language learning environments. The design of ELLE has not currently tackled the problem of adding means to practice speech and communicate with peers. It was currently left out due to the corpus behind ELLE being a written text corpus and not a speech corpus. However, in the future it is worth considering the possibility to integrate speaking exercises to the platform and to link their data directly to the speech corpus.

During the design sessions it was also found that learners (e.g. [19, 20]) as well as teachers [18] need additional support structures. For learners we offered the option to chat with their coursemates in a forum, send private messages or add comments to their teacher in a shared exercise. Offering the chance to ask help from other learners is also catering to their need for more autonomy, but might also be less stressful. Furthermore, allowing learners to help each other reduces the teachers workload. The teachers themselves can find support from their colleagues using the site, either looking up some public exercises, not having to create one from scratch, or asking for additional support with private messages. The teachers pointed out, however, that most of the support structures still exist offline and face-to-face meetings are more helpful than asking for help online.

In addition, some learners and teachers are not using a virtual learning environment or a corpus due to the lack of technical knowledge (e.g. [16, 17]). The researchers and teachers we interviewed pointed out that they have not used corpora much and they often do not use virtual learning environments either. They still use available digital resources occasionally, but most of the exercises are on paper or based on oral communication. Corpora have been the tool for some researchers, but to find example sentences for the exercises they are creating. Hopefully, using ELLE, corpora are more accessible and easier to use. In order to increase the usability, we simplified the terms used, offered immediate explanations with popups and planned short videos explaining the use of the platform. Some further limitations remain: changing teaching and learning habits, to include corpora more into classroom activities and promoting awareness about different virtual learning environments and Estonian corpora. Those issues could be tackled with offline activities, such as workshops in schools and universities.

6 Conclusions and Future Work

While the resulting prototype depicts an online platform bringing together teachers, learners and researchers in one corpus-based virtual learning environment, it is still a work in progress. We still need to have additional design sessions with language researchers who work with corpora on a daily basis, such as lexicographers. This would allow us to focus specifically on corpus analysis tools and to investigate how the data from the use of a learning environment provides input for the language technology research.

The prototype of ELLE was designed for a desktop platform, since the users said that when working with texts, they use their computers more often. However, learners pointed out that they use their mobile devices when learning languages online and that these devices are always with them. Therefore we also need to consider which features can be transferred to a mobile platform. We can assume that text writing and text correction will be uncomfortable on a small device. However, most of the exercises and learning resources would be easily accessible. We also need to think about the corpus and how much of it will be accessible on a mobile device or would the exercise results moving back to the corpus be the only connection with the mobile version.

While ELLE has been designed with the Estonian learner corpus in mind, the same design principles can be transferred to the development of other similar corpus-based virtual learning environments. More work on ELLE's design and development still lies ahead. Combining language corpus with a virtual learning environment is a promising approach which opens up new opportunities both for language learning and for language technology research.

Acknowledgements. This work has been supported by Tallinn University research grant TF2621 ELLE: A language technological resource to support Estonian language learning.

References

1. Staples, S.: Using corpus-based discourse analysis for curriculum development: creating and evaluating a pronunciation course for internationally educated nurses. Engl. Specif. Purp. **53**, 13–29 (2019). https://doi.org/10.1016/j.esp.2018.08.005
2. Díez-Bedmar, M.B.: Fine-tuning descriptors for CEFR B1 level: insights from learner corpora. ELT J. **72**, 199–209 (2017). https://doi.org/10.1093/elt/ccx052
3. Vinogradova, O., Login, N.: The Design of Tests with Multiple Choice Questions Automatically Generated from Essays in a Learner Corpus. Higher School of Economics Research Paper No. WP BRP 60/LNG/2017 (2017). https://doi.org/10.2139/ssrn.3087215
4. Granger, S.: The contribution of learner corpora to second language acquisition and foreign language teaching: a critical evaluation. In: Aijmer, K. (ed.) Corpora and Language Teaching, pp. 13–32. John Benjamins Publishing (2009). https://doi.org/10.1075/scl.33.04gra
5. Bennett, G.R.: Using Corpora in the Language Learning Classroom. University of Michigan Press (2010). https://doi.org/10.3998/mpub.371534
6. Boulton, A.: Integrating corpus tools and techniques in ESP courses. Asp La Revue Du Geras., 113–137 (2016). https://doi.org/10.4000/asp.4826
7. Meunier, F.: Learner corpora and pedagogical applications. In: Farr, F., Murray, L. (eds.) The Routledge Handbook of Language Learning and Technology, pp. 376–387. Routledge, New York (2016)
8. Hana, J., Rosen, A., Štindlová, B., Jäger, P.: Building a learner corpus. In: Calzolari, N., et al. (eds.) Proceedings of the Eighth International Conference on Language Resources and Evaluation (LREC 2012), pp. 3228–3232 (2012)
9. Eslon, P.: Eesti vahekeele korpus. Keel ja Kirjandus, 436–451 (2014)
10. Andersen, Ø.E., Yannakoudakis, H., Barker, F., Parish, T.: Developing and testing a self-assessment and tutoring system. In: Tetreault, J., Burstein, J., Leacock, C. (eds.) Proceedings of the Eighth Workshop on Innovative Use of NLP for Building Educational Applications, pp. 32–41. Association for Computational Linguistics (2013)
11. Alfter, D., Borin, L., Pilán, I., Tiedemann, T.L., Volodina, E.: Lärka: from language learning platform to infrastructure for research on language learning. In: Skadina, I., Eskevich, M. (eds.) Selected papers from the CLARIN Annual Conference 2018. Linköping University Electronic Press (2018)
12. Wible, D., Kuo, C.-H., Chien, F., Liu, A., Tsao, N.-L.: A Web-based EFL writing environment: integrating information for learners, teachers, and researchers. Comput. Educ. **37**, 297–315 (2001). https://doi.org/10.1016/s0360-1315(01)00056-2
13. Dayag, J.D.: EFL Virtual learning environments: perception, concerns and challenges. Teach. Engl. Technol. **18**, 20–33 (2018)
14. Fandiño, F.G.E., Muñoz, L.D., Velandia, A.J.S.: Motivation and E-Learning English as a foreign language: a qualitative study. Heliyon. **5**, e02394 (2019). https://doi.org/10.1016/j.heliyon.2019.e02394
15. Al-Zahrani, A.S.: Smartphones wandering at the mall : a case study investigating the use of smartphones on English oral learning skills in a collaborative mobile-assisted language learning environment (2015)
16. Cheng, W., Warren, M., Xun-feng, X.: The language learner as language researcher: putting corpus linguistics on the timetable. System **31**, 173–186 (2003). https://doi.org/10.1016/s0346-251x(03)00019-8

17. Chambers, A., O'Sullivan, Í.: Corpus consultation and advanced learners' writing skills in French. Recall. **16**, 158–172 (2004). https://doi.org/10.1017/s0958344004001211
18. Vrasidas, C., et al.: Teacher use of ICT: challenges and opportunities. In: Dirckinck-Holmfeld, L., Hodgson, V., Jones, C., de Laat, M., McConnell, D., Ryberg, T. (eds.) Proceedings of the 7th International Conference on Networked Learning 2010, pp. 439–445 (2010).
19. Ozudogru, F., Hismanoglu, M.: Views of freshmen students on foreign language courses delivered via e-learning. Turk. Online J. Distance Educ. **17**, 31–47 (2016). https://doi.org/10.17718/tojde.18660
20. Trajanovic, M., Domazet, D., Misic-Ilic, B.: Distance learning and foreign language teaching. In: Balkan Conference in Informatics (BCI 2007), pp. 441–452 (2007)
21. Faste, T., Faste, H.: Demystifying "design research": design is not research, research is design. In: Proceedings of the IDSA Education Symposium, 15 August 2012. IDSA (2012)
22. Ordóñez, A.S., Lema, C.G., Puga, M.F.M., Lema, C.P., Vega, F.C.: Design thinking as a methodology for solving problems: contributions from academia to society. In: Petrie, M.M.L., Alvarez, H. (eds.) Global Partnerships for Development and Engineering Education: Proceedings of the 15th LACCEI International Multi-Conference for Engineering, Education and Technology (2017). https://doi.org/10.18687/laccei2017.1.1.256
23. Spinuzzi, C.: The methodology of participatory design. Tech. Commun. **52**, 163–174 (2005)

Is This Fake or Credible? A Virtual Learning Companion Supporting the Judgment of Young Learners Facing Social Media Content

Farbod Aprin[1](✉), Sven Manske[1], Irene-Angelica Chounta[2], and H. Ulrich Hoppe[1]

[1] RIAS – Rhein-Ruhr-Institut für angewandte Systeminnovation e.V, Bürgerstr. 15, 47057 Duisburg, Germany
{fa,sm,uh}@rias-institute.eu
[2] Department of Computer Science and Applied Cognitive Science, University of Duisburg-Essen, 47057 Duisburg, Germany
irene-angelica.chounta@uni-due.de

Abstract. Today's young generation uses a variety of social media as part of their everyday life. This can be seen as an enrichment, but it is also the source of various threats: Filter bubbles and echo chambers are general phenomena that counter-balance free communication and exchange and can lead to toxic radicalization confirmation bias and polarization. Conspiracy theories, fake news are two phenomena that can change the social media user perspective about the facts. This paper reports on the development of a web-based learning environment that includes a dedicated "learning companion" to help students in raising their understanding, resilience, and critical thinking related to such social media threats. The point is not to protect young people from such threats through a type of censorship but to help them develop their own strategies to identify and counteract such influences. The web-based learning environment mimics Instagram as a well-known social medium. The actual companion is realized as a browser plugin with an underlying architecture that supports xAPI logging as well as the connection to intelligent backend components.

Keywords: Learning companion systems (LCS) · Intelligent tutoring system · Recommendation · Resilience · Increase awareness · Fake news · Social media · AI-based learning support systems · Chatbot · xAPI

1 Introduction

Besides positive aspects of social media like facilitating the exchange of information and opinions, young people have some general issues, mainly because of toxic content like cyberbullying, hate speech, fake news, and conspiracy theories. Cyberbullying has become increasingly common using social media channels like WhatsApp, especially among teenagers [1, 2]. Near half of the teachers stated that students face harassment

W. Zhou and Y. Mu (Eds.): ICWL 2021, LNCS 13103, pp. 52–60, 2021.
https://doi.org/10.1007/978-3-030-90785-3_5

through their mobile phones and the Internet, and some teachers were themselves victims of cyberbullying [3].

Fake news is presented as real news, and because dis/misinformation, and even blatant propaganda continue to spread, it can undoubtedly distort one's worldview. The most common fake news narratives were more broadly shared on Facebook than the most popular mainstream news stories. Most US Americans who see fake news stories report that they believe them [4]. Coupled with "deep fake" videos and other manipulated images and audio files, the truth is not so easy to identify independent of user's age groups.

Other issues originate from the social media companies' goal to retain users on their platforms. To increase user engagement social platforms present and filter the posts that are in line with prevailing opinions to draw them more into their platform [5]. Eli Parisier calls this phenomenon "filter bubble" [6]. Parisier explains that recommendation algorithms may create a situation where users increasingly receive information that confirms their previous beliefs and leaves no space for doubt. The "echo chamber" phenomenon is a similar issue in social media where users only face opinions that indicate and reinforce their argument, leading to distancing themselves from contradicting beliefs and allowing extreme views to be amplified [7]. As a result, users become isolated from information that opposes their perspectives.

The spiral of silence theory indicates that if people realize that their private opinion differs from the perceived majority, they are less likely to comment publicly [8]. Although the spiral of silence theory has been discussed controversially for traditional media, there is some evidence for the effects in the context of social media [9].

A serious mini-game platform and information booklet have already been prepared and distributed to help teenagers critically reflect on digital advertising by Media Awareness Network (MNet) [10]. MNet made available various free games for teenage users, some of which are specifically aimed at petitioning the question of cyberhate through exploring bias and prejudice and supporting critical thinking skills. The aim is to encourage teenagers to check information and look for alternative viewpoints to increase their awareness [11]. In the Reality Check game[1], students will discover how to find evidence, like finding where a story initially came from and matching it to other sources, plus, how to use tools like fact-checking websites and reverse image searches.

There are two main strategies to control toxic content in social media. The first one is to detect and eliminate postings of poisonous content ("censorship"). This strategy is currently applied in social media. On the other hand, some threats like hate speech are laborious to track and control their distribution since nuances in cultures and languages make it hard to present a well-defined distinction between hate speech and dangerous speeches. The detection is not an easy task for social media providers [6]. The second strategy is to help users develop their own mechanisms to identify and counteract such influences.

[1] Reality Check: The Game https://mediasmarts.ca/digital-media-literacy/educational-games/reality-check-game, 2021.

In this paper, we present an approach that aims to increase the resilience and awareness of social media users within the European project Courage[2] funded by Volkswagenstiftung.

The Courage is characterized by providing games and an educational platform to simulate social media environments with inherent challenges. In this paper we report on the development of a virtual companion that supports and educates young learners in the prepared environment. The main focus is on strengthening self-protection through analytical/critical thinking, empathy, and ultimately resilience rather than providing external protection through censorship.

2 Learning Companion Systems and ITS

As a specific version of intelligent tutoring systems (ITS), learning companion systems (LCS) personalize the support and adaptive feedback through an explicit, and possibly human-like agent interacting with the learner [12]. The agent or companion guides the learner step by step and typically adopting a non-authoritative role. The interface may be composed of multimedia, interactive buttons, menus, text, voice, animation, diagrams, virtual reality, or other interactive techniques.

LCS interfaces usually include natural language processing (NLP) to facilitate communication between LCS and the student. Tracing the student's interactions with an LCS is used as a part of student modeling. For example, the LCS may ask the student to explain the reasons behind their answers as a reflective question for each step during their task, which might consequently lead to more robust learning, in line with work on self-explanation at the time. Learners might generate many explanations and articulate the reasons behind their answers that refine their understanding (self-regulated learning strategies) [13].

According to the definition of an adaptive system, one of the key points for a tutoring system that includes LCS to be adaptive is to respond to learner actions flexibly depending on the context and history. This response can be implemented in the conversation as feedback to the user textual input or give proper response to the user interaction in various ways, like suggesting a multimedia instruction as a recommendation [14]. Student modeling as a basis for adaptive feedback in LCS tutorial dialogues can significantly increase learning gains in low and high prior knowledge students [15]. A LCS can play many roles in an instructional context. For instance, the role of an executive, suggesting new ideas for the learners to consider, or a critic, challenging the learner's proposals [16].

For answering the question "how knowledgeable should the companion agent be to reach the learner's expectation and motivate the student to continue collaborating with the agent?", Hietala and Niemirepo [17] found that the learners lose their motivation if they use a strong and knowledgeable companion all the time. Especially in the beginning, a companion that makes mistakes like humans is more effective. Still, for a challenging task or for dealing with a new issue, both introvert and extrovert learners prefer knowledgeable and robust learning companions.

[2] A social Media Companion Safeguarding and Education Students couragecompanion.eu.

Our virtual learning companion (VLC) supports features such as role-playing for the users, gives adaptive feedback based on previous user interaction, judges the answers, and asks knowledge activation questions. In addition, providing analysis and recommendations, comprising receiving input and displaying the information, are core features of the VLC system.

3 System Environment and Implementation

3.1 Conceptual Architecture

To meet the objectives to help learners develop strategies to counteract the negative influences social media, we provide a virtual companion that will work with two different environments. First, in a controlled social network environment, where the scenario controls the content and reaction of the participants. Second, the companion should also provide basic support in real, open environments like Instagram as an example that is frequently used by the target age group.

Currently, the interaction is situated in a controlled environment that is implemented using the PixelFed[3] framework. PixelFed is an open-source social media network, like Instagram, that is suitable for multimedia. Our PixelFed version has been enhanced with a logging component to archive user actions for analytical purposes.

In conjunction with PixelFed, the VLC is developed as a Chrome browser plugin. It intervenes with questions and suggestions while the student interacts with the environment's artifacts. Learners will interact with the social media environment guided by the tasks they receive from the companion as a chatbot (cf. Fig. 1).

To prepare and enable such scenarios, educational designers identify example cases and materials by creating new cases from harvested real-world examples. We designed a companion scenario for the controlled environment that includes fake news and conspiracy theory samples mostly related to the pandemic for the first trials.

3.2 PixelFed and Browser Plugin

To create a companion that can interact with simulated social media independently, we developed a Chrome extension as a plugin to detect the user's interaction with the social media environment. The closed environment is an Instagram-like environment enriched with images and their captions. The user can right-click on images or highlight the image caption to send them to the Chrome extension and activate the companion to respond to it.

As depicted in Fig. 2, the companion has two main sections: first, a frontend with a Chrome extension communicating with the PixelFed environment; second, backend microservices with a middleware mediating the frontend communication. WIT.AI[4] in the backend is responsible for managing the companion conversation via chatbot and detecting the user's intent for each conversation step. In the frontend, ReactJS[5] allows

[3] PixelFed is a decentralized open-source Instagram-like photo-sharing network based on the Activity Pub protocol, making it suitable for applying it in research experiments, https://pixelfed.social/. (2021).

[4] WIT-AI is a tool to Build Natural Language Experiences https://wit.ai, 2021.

[5] React JS is A JavaScript library for building user interfaces https://reactjs.org, 2021.

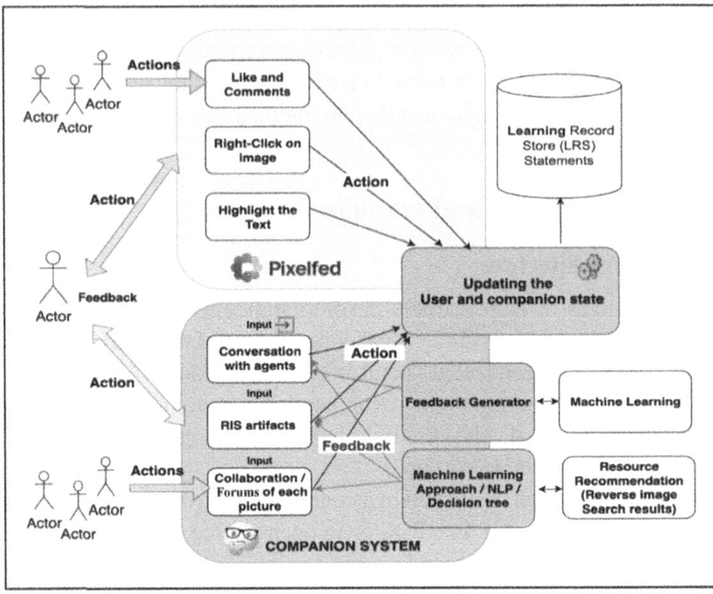

Fig. 1. User Interaction with companion and controlled environment architecture (focused on a single actor).

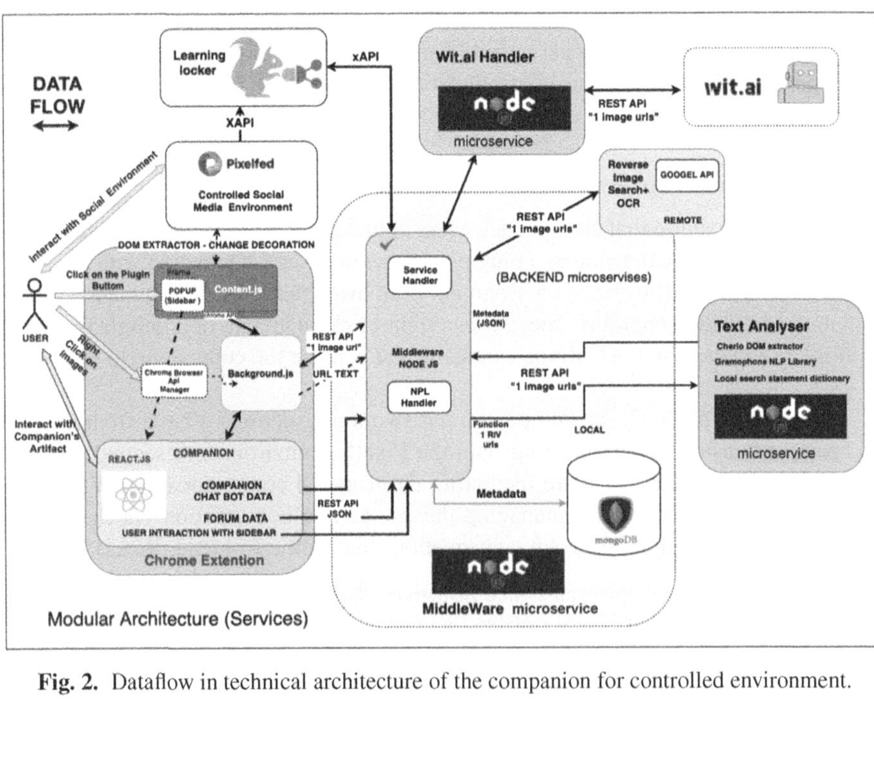

Fig. 2. Dataflow in technical architecture of the companion for controlled environment.

for a modern, responsive web design with flexible and reusable UI components in the standard structure of Chrome extension[6].

The image-link is accessed from the frontend via a REST API to the backend middleware (NodeJS express[7]) modules. The reverse image search (RIS) API, applied to find similar images the user interacts with the environment from the external resources. Via, text analyzer module, we can extract the semantic keywords and the important section of text behind each RIS-link associated with retrieved extracted semantic keywords. We create and enrich the metadata for each image and store it in the document-oriented database (MongoDB[8]). We use Learning Locker[9] as Learning Record Store (LRS) to store action logs in the standard Experience API (xAPI) format.

4 Example Scenario

The experimental trials are carried out on desktop computers running Chrome browsers. The user has access to PixelFed environments enriched with limited numbers of images and captions containing fake/fact news. Also, the setup includes the Chrome extension that represents the virtual learning companion system in the browser.

4.1 Example Walkthrough

When users visit the PixelFed environment via a provided web link they will first see a short guide on how to open and use the browser plugin (Courage Chrome extension). After that, they log in to the companion system by clicking on the provided anonymous user-token link. Next, they will see a user-guide video on the sidebar equipped with the virtual tutor that explains how to interact with the environment artifacts to activate the companion.

The companion starts to communicate automatically with a chatbot-style conversation (e.g., "How are you?") and asks some general introductory questions (sex, age). After a few steps, the companion will ask to right-click on one of the images followed by knowledge activation questions and asks for the user's opinion about the selected image in the social media environment. After the response, the learner needs to answer some reflective questions that explain why they chose that specific answer. In the conversation, the companion asks if the user thinks it is fake news or fact, considering an image in social media and the caption text behind it. The user is limited to choose one of the provided choices. Then, the companion applies to stimulate reflection questions (e.g. "How sure are you?") according to a predefined decision tree.

Next, the companion will unlock a "Recommended" tab that contains reverse image search (RIS) links from the web. In these places, the same image is shown in a different context. The learners can visit these links and compare the keywords, metadata and

[6] Standard Chrome extension consists of three main modules: 1. Background and content script – https://developer.Chrome.com/docs/extensions/mv3/getstarted, Manifest file 2021.

[7] NodeJS is a JavaScript runtime built on Chrome's V8 JavaScript engine, 2021.

[8] MongoDB, document-based, distributed database built for modern application, 2021.

[9] Learning-Locker used to store learning activity statements generated by xAPI compliant learning activitieshttps://docs.learninglocker.net/welcome/, 2021.

abstract texts of each RIS link for the selected post. In this step, the learner can freely continue the instructions and come back to the conversation. Then, the user writes down their opinion as demanded in the chat and answers. Then chatbot will give new (adaptive) feedback. Next, the system will unlock the collaboration chart option Analysis Tab for the selected artifact. After interacting with metadata for around each image, the companion can give an alert or feedback as a pedagogical intervention. For example, if they judge or answer promptly in a short time without checking the recommended RIS or had poor participation in collaboration sections in comments.

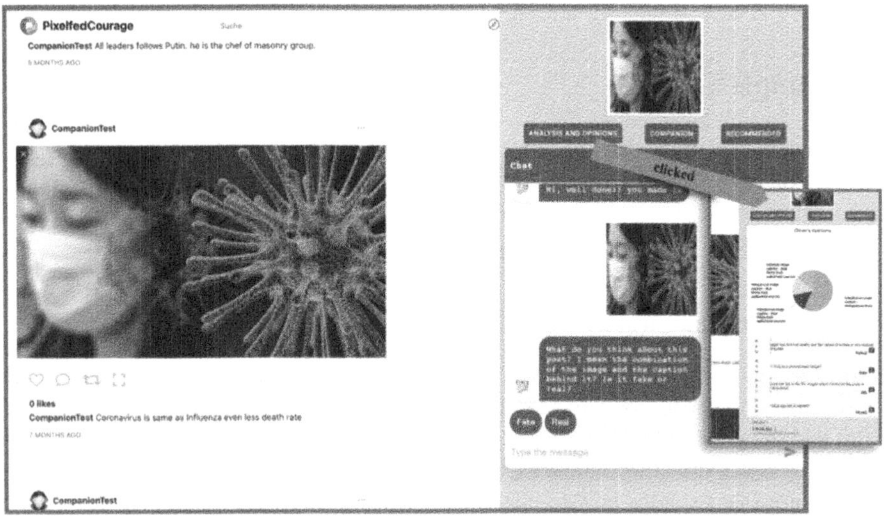

Fig. 3. Left: right-click on a Picture, then the companion will activate to react (ask their opinion about the selected picture). Right: companion unlocks the collaboration tab and ask if the user changes their mind after observing comments and others votes in the diagram.

Figure 3 shows how learners can see others' opinions in a collaborative forum and compare the answers. The best answers according to the user's votes goes to the top. For example, if the image is manipulated (fake) or real news. In the provided forum, the learner can find a better link from the comments. Via a pie chart, users can compare the answers of others to themselves. After observation of recommended metadata, the companion asks if learners would like to reconsider their judgments.

As researchers, it is interesting to know if learners change their minds after each step or if their direction of thinking and judgment changes after receiving feedback from the companion and interacting with recommended learning instructions? Therefore, we log all-important user interactions along with time stamps. Thus, we need the log for the answers, companion chats responses, interactions with an environment's artifacts.

One possible pedagogical intervention of the companion could be to warn or encourage learners. For example, the artifact has a clear orientation and status, and the user's initial opinion changes in contrast with their first judgment, when the learner observes that the majority has another mindset. In this case, the companion warns the users about the "spiral of silence" phenomenon and encourages them to think again, and the companion present a small tutorial video (pedagogical intervention).

In the first scenario that we consider applying for the following school trials, we will select four pictures for the PixelFed environment related to pandemic situations. Pictures may include fake news and conspiracy theories, used to teach critical thinking as a skill or to increase their awareness. At the end of interacting with four pictures, the companion will ask the overall user's opinion and feedback.

4.2 Preliminary User Study

A first informal study was carried out with a small group of participants confronted with a controversial report on the coronavirus that included a picture shared on social media. The participants had to complete the classification "fake" or "real" for this item based on their assessment of credibility. After that, they wrote a few lines about their reflection on this task. The goal of the study was to check how users understood and handled the task and to identify possible misunderstandings. Fourteen participants aged 19–35 with varying cultural backgrounds contributed actively to the study. The education level ranged from bachelor students to postdoc.

As a result of the study, we found that more than half of the participants mentioned that they were unsure about their answers and would have preferred a broader range of answers reflecting levels of uncertainty, such as "probably fake," "not sure," "probably fact" in addition to just "fake" and "fact". Only three of the participants used external fact check tools or search engines to determine the truth. None of the participants was aware of Reverse Image Search tools to find a similar topic which is considered in the VLC tool and scenario. We envision that a real-time VLC can support learners in making more correct judgments and better usage of web resources.

5 Conclusion and Outlook

This paper presents our work to design and implement a virtual learning companion in a simulated social media environment. This companion assists learners in coping with the threats and toxic content of social media like Fake news. The companion is implemented as a browser plugin that can be added to Instagram-like social media environments for orchestrating the controlled tests. This companion interacts with learners via chat and triggers the user's action with the artifacts of the environment. The presented companion utilizes interactive multimedia to give learners feedback and intervene with a pedagogical reflection. The companion encourages the learners and provides knowledge according to a pre-defined decision tree.

In the next version, the companion will work with artifacts on open social media platforms such as Instagram, possibly repeated in the closed environment (with identical artifacts). Via interaction with the same metadata for the repeated artifact, the expert and other users can indicate their opinion around the unique conversion about controversial content and represent their different mindsets and backgrounds. This feature will give the users the power to view other parties' opinions without biased pre-filtering.

References

1. Sprugnoli, R., Menini, S., Tonelli, S., Oncini, F., Piras, E.: Creating a Whatsapp dataset to study pre-teen cyberbullying. In: Proceedings of the 2nd Workshop on Abusive Language Online (ALW2), June 2019, pp. 51–59 (2019). https://doi.org/10.18653/v1/w18-5107
2. Aizenkot, D., Kashy-Rosenbaum, G.: Cyberbullying in WhatsApp classmates' groups: evaluation of an intervention program implemented in Israeli elementary and middle schools. New Media Soc. **20**(12), 4709–4727 (2018). https://doi.org/10.1177/1461444818782702
3. Eden, S., Heiman, T., Olenik-Shemesh, D.: Teachers' perceptions, beliefs and concerns about cyberbullying. Br. J. Edu. Technol. **44**(6), 1036–1052 (2013). https://doi.org/10.1111/j.1467-8535.2012.01363.x
4. Silverman, C., Singer-Vine, J.: Most Americans who see fake news believe it, new survey says. BuzzFeed (2016)
5. Bucher, T.: The algorithmic imaginary: exploring the ordinary affects of Facebook algorithms. Inf. Commun. Soc. **20**(1), 30–44 (2017). https://doi.org/10.1080/1369118X.2016.1154086
6. Rowland, F.: The filter bubble: what the internet is hiding from you. Portal: Lib. Acad. **11**(4), 1009–1011 (2011)
7. Colleoni, E., Rozza, A., Arvidsson, A.: Echo chamber or public sphere? predicting political orientation and measuring political homophily in twitter using big data. J. commun. **64**(2), 317–332 (2014). https://doi.org/10.1111/jcom.12084.
8. Schmidt, R.E.: Legacy of Elisabeth Noelle-Neumann: The spiral of silence and other controversies. Eur. J. Commun. **30**(3), 353–363, https://doi.org/10.1177/0267323115589265
9. Ross, B., Pilz, L., Cabrera, B., Brachten, F., Neubaum, G., Stieglitz, S.: Are social bots a real threat? an agent-based model of the spiral of silence to analyse the impact of manipulative actors in social networks. Eur. J. Inf. Syst. **28**(4), 394–412 (2019). https://doi.org/10.1080/0960085X.2018.1560920
10. De Jans, S., Hudders, L., Herrewijn, L., Van Geit, K., Cauberghe, V.: Serious games going beyond the call of duty: Impact of an advertising literacy mini-game platform on adolescents' motivational outcomes through user experiences and learning outcomes. Cyberpsychology **13**(2) (2019). https://doi.org/10.5817/CP2019-2-3.
11. Titley, G., Keen, E., Földi, L.: Three studies about online hate speech and ways to address it (2014)
12. Chou, C.Y., Chan, T.W., Lin, C.J.: Redefining the learning companion: the past, present, and future of educational agents. Comput. Educ. **40**(3), 255–269 (2003). https://doi.org/10.1016/S0360-1315(02)00130-6
13. Chi, M.T.H., Bassok, M., Lewis, M.W., Reimann, P., Glaser, R.: Self-explanations: how students study and use examples in learning to solve problems. Cogn. Sci. **13**(2), 145–182 (1989). https://doi.org/10.1016/0364-0213(89)90002-5
14. Aleven, V., Beal, C.R., Graesser, A.C.: Introduction to the special issue on advanced learning technologies. J. Educ. Psychol. **105**(4), 929–931 (2013). https://doi.org/10.1037/a0034155
15. Katz, S., Albacete, P., Chounta, I.A., Jordan, P., Mclaren, B.M., Zapata-Rivera, D.: Linking dialogue with student modelling to create an adaptive tutoring system for conceptual physics. Int. J. Artif. Intell. Educ. **31**(3), 1–49 (2021)
16. Goodman, B., Linton, F., Gaimari, R.: Encouraging student reflection and articulation using a learning companion: a commentary. Int. J. Artif. Intell. Educ. **26**(1), 474–488 (2015). https://doi.org/10.1007/s40593-015-0041-4
17. Hietala, P., Niemirepo, T.: The competence of learning companion agents. Int. J. Artif. Intell. Educ. (IJAIED) **9**, 178–192 (1998)

Online Learning Environment with Tools

Extending Narrative Serious Games Using Ad-Hoc Mini-games

Víctor M. Pérez-Colado(✉), Iván J. Pérez-Colado, Iván Martínez-Ortiz, Manuel Freire-Morán, and Baltasar Fernández-Manjón

Department of Software Engineering and Artificial Intelligence, Complutense University of Madrid, C/ Profesor José García Santesmases, 9, 28040 Madrid, Spain
victormp@ucm.es

Abstract. Narrative games have proven their effectiveness as serious games in different domains and for different purposes, such as promoting learning or increasing user awareness. However, there are many situations where the narrative model falls short and can benefit from being extended with puzzles or mini-games to afford more flexibility or explore non-narrative mechanics more adequate to the task at hand. In our uAdventure game authoring environment, a narrative serious game provides support for the driving narrative, managing stories, conversations, and other narrative elements, together with an integrated game learning analytics support. We present how we have extended uAdventure to support the inclusion of mini-games within a host narrative game, while allowing hosted mini-games to access uAdventure services through a streamlined interface. As a case study, we describe how this extension has been used by students learning serious games development to create narrative games with ad-hoc puzzles that use alternate mechanics to achieve game-specific goals.

Keywords: Serious games · Narrative games · Mini-games · Game authoring · Game analytics

1 Introduction

The use of video games in teaching has attracted great interest from teachers and researchers for their ability to improve the interest and retention of players by keeping them motivated [1, 2]. As their primary goal is not that of entertainment, such games are often called serious games; for example, players may face a series of challenges to improve knowledge or cognitive skills [3]. Genres such as action games allow players to improve their dexterity and reflexes, while simulation games use realistic environments where players can test and apply their knowledge without being exposed to the risks of real environments [4].

Due to the different characteristics of serious games, for example to their genre, the requirements for their design and development also vary. For example, simulation games, which are very effective for specific learning, are also very costly to develop due to the high level of detail required to emulate the target domain. Therefore, when

W. Zhou and Y. Mu (Eds.): ICWL 2021, LNCS 13103, pp. 63–74, 2021.
https://doi.org/10.1007/978-3-030-90785-3_6

developing a serious game, the genre chosen is key for both its effectiveness and educational applicability as well as for its development feasibility in terms of requirements and costs. While development costs can sometimes be reduced by using pre-built assets (such as those available at Unity's Asset Store), such assets will require significant effort and expertise to customize for any sufficiently-specific domain.

Among the different types of games, narrative games offer a good balance between simplicity and flexibility, as they allow players to play roles and perform meaningful tasks in an environment not excessively expensive to create, but rich enough to achieve immersion. In particular, the "point and click" subgenre of narrative games [5] often relies on interactive conversations to deliver content, using characters who play different roles in the story; together with different objects and interactions to solve logical puzzles where players can apply their knowledge and learn from their mistakes [6]. For this reason, narrative games have been applied in very different domains and with very different purposes (e.g., learning, awareness).

However, narrative mechanics also have limitations. For example, they are not suitable for the development of other types of cognitive skills, such as pattern recognition, reflexes, or physical skills in general, which can be taught through mechanics present in other genres (e.g., action games to develop reflexes) [7]. Despite the possibility of simulating the mechanics from other genres, the adaptation needed to implement them is complex and costly. For example, developers that intend to use a narrative engine to develop a visual puzzle would need to manually analyze the different states of the puzzle and configure a series of narrative elements (and their corresponding graphical representations) to represent the state of the puzzle. This is impractical, complex and, above all, unnatural for a game developer; and is the case of commercial narrative content authoring tools such as Adobe Captivate[1], Articulate 360[2] and ITyStudio[3].

We describe an extensible model that allows enriching narrative games with other mechanics, such as puzzles; and an implementation of this model in a tool to demonstrate the feasibility of this approach. For the integration of mini-games in narrative games we have taken as a basis uAdventure [8], an open-source authoring tool for serious narrative games built on the Unity game platform. The challenge is to incorporate other mechanics into uAdventure's narrative game model, which increases its versatility and allows new capabilities to be addressed, all without significantly increasing the difficulty of game creation. However, the inclusion of these new mechanics through the mini-games requires game creators to know how to program the mini-games. This approach has been tested in two case studies with students within the serious games course of the Videogame Development degree at Complutense University of Madrid.

The following sections of this article describe the mini-game integration model, the use cases of this integration model, lessons we have learned from our experiences, and finally conclusions and future lines of work.

[1] https://www.adobe.com/es/products/captivate.html.
[2] https://articulate.com/360.
[3] https://itystudio.com/.

2 Extending the uAdventure Narrative Model Through Ad-Hoc Mini-games

uAdventure is a tool that simplifies the prototyping and development of games for non-experts, such as most teachers, as no programming is required. The authoring metaphor with uAdventure is based on creating a series of scenes, where the author will use the narrative for the player to develop a role through the game. Players learn new content or develop additional awareness by interacting with other players, participating in in-game conversations, or solving logical puzzles. For situations where it is too complex to adapt the content to the narrative model, uAdventure also provides other types of scenes where it is possible to include videos and interactive animations that can be interspersed with the main narrative content [8].

Furthermore, uAdventure includes other educational-specific features, such built-in assessment of learners and the capability to deploy and integrate games with other educational platforms by means of widely used educational standards [9]. In addition, player actions can be recorded and used internally in the game (through a mechanism of variables and conditions to change game behavior), as well as externally through the built-in learning analytics mechanism. Use of built-in learning analytics allows creators to not only access the final results at the end of the game (e.g. score, completeness, progress), but also to analyze the full sequence of actions that each player took to achieve that score, with minimal work required from game authors [10, 11].

Despite the benefits of uAdventure for most developers, the point-and-click narrative model it implements may fall short of the requirements of some games. For example, the narrative model ill-suited for puzzles with a very large number of states. For example, in a Rubik's Cube representation, where pattern recognition and spatial recognition skills can be learned, a direct three-dimensional representation would be much simpler than a representation through narrative elements. Our proposal provides support for including self-contained, alternate game mechanics that are more appropriate for the type of skills to be worked on in those parts of the serious narrative game that require it. The challenge is to achieve the integration of those alternate mechanics within the narrative game model of uAdventure, therefore increasing its versatility and allowing new skills to be addressed while avoiding a large increase in the difficulty of creating such games. While the integration of these new mechanics would certainly require a programming effort, once created, our goal is for the mechanics to be freely reusable by other authors without needing to program them themselves.

The process of adding new mechanics is done by programming mini-games integrated into uAdventure [12, 13]. The mini-games are launched from uAdventure, which delegates full control of the game execution to them (Fig. 1). With this model it is possible, for example, to develop an action mini-game that can read the state of the game to adapt its difficulty to the narrative moment in which it is found and use conversations during the mini-game itself to explain it or as part of its operation. The mini-games are developed as new components integrated with uAdventure, so mini-game authors must know how to program for the Unity platform. In this regard, mini-games can exploit all the capabilities of Unity to create the new mechanics, but they must also be integrated with the services offered by uAdventure: the core of the game; the narrative engine, and the learning analytics engine.

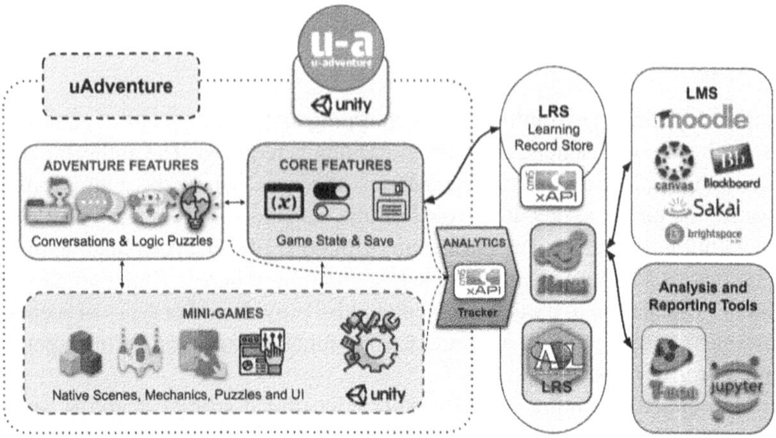

Fig. 1. Mini-game integration into the uAdventure game authoring tool. Mini-games allow additional game mechanics to be added to uAdventure, and can make use of uAdventure-provided features such as conversations, persistence, or xAPI-SG analytics.

The core game system is the system in charge of maintaining and managing the global state of the game. Using it, the mini-game can inspect the current state of the main game as a result of the previous actions that the player has carried out up to this moment. This allows the mini-game to adapt to its context of use within the current session; for example, by adjusting its own difficulty, or the style or visibility of certain features. In addition, mini-games can also save significant actions performed by players to the game state. In summary, through the game state, it is possible to communicate bidirectionally with uAdventure and thus read the different parameters that will define the configuration of the game; and write in uAdventure those parameters that are relevant once the main narrative game resumes.

uAdventure's narrative engine provides support for narrative content and interaction as well as corresponding visual effects. Through the narrative engine it is possible to launch conversation sequences and customizable options without leaving the mini-game. The mini-game developer has access to this uAdventure functionality, for example, to show tutorials or to pause the mini-game when it reaches a milestone, displaying a conversation at that moment. In addition, it allows scenes to be changed, and different events to be triggered once the mini-game ends, continuing with the flow of the game while taking into account the results of the mini-game. Finally, the learning analytics engine provides mini-game developers with a means to generate logs of the player's progress through the mini-game, which can be stored locally or sent to a remote storage location for further analysis. The main component of the analytics engine is the xAPI tracker [14] which provides a high-level interface to hide the details of the xAPI-SG specification and allows developers who are not experienced in analytics to generate traces to analyze the player's progress through the mini-games. Using this feature, a mini-game developer can, for example, generate traces that describe the interactions of the player with the interactive elements present in the mini-game.

From a more technical point of view, the uAdventure mini-game feature is based on Unity's scene mechanism. The developer of a mini-game must create a Unity scene into which to place the mini-game. In it, by means of the various features available in Unity (such as the physics engine, lighting, or its user interface system) and its scripting interfaces, the scene and its behavior will be shaped, thus defining its concrete mechanics and the layout of the mini-game. For example, in a serious game involving perception evaluation, the user could use the physics engine to create a realistic environment in which different particles move more naturally. Once the scene is created and an identifier is assigned, the developer will be able to reference the scene from the main game as any other native uAdventure scene, thus allowing the application of the uAdventure's authoring metaphor that does not require programming.

This trade-off allows advanced users (programmers) using uAdventure to use native Unity scenes without great effort; while offering non-expert users the possibility of reusing previously-developed mini-games within their own uAdventure games. Thanks to this extensibility model, it is possible to create an ecosystem where programmers and teachers can collaborate to improve the educational experience through the resulting game. In addition, thanks to uAdventure's built-in services provided to the mini-game, it is possible to create parameterized mini-games so that the experience is not unique to specific games and can be customized by teachers using uAdventure's visual editor.

Because this integration architecture is quite flexible, it can be adapted to all kinds of situations with different requirements. Although mini-games do not need to comply with any particular structure, Fig. 2 describes our recommended structure for mini-games, focusing on allowing the mini-game to be executed in a subrogated way to the host game, thus allowing the game to be decoupled from the main game and thus promoting a simpler distribution of roles in its development. In order to establish an independent execution of the mini-game, the input and output parameters must be defined beforehand. The input of parameters should be defined before launching the mini-game through the visual programming system of uAdventure, and will be read at the beginning of the execution of the mini-game through the core; while the output of parameters will become available at the end of the mini-game, to be incorporated into the state of the game for later use.

While the mini-game is running, it should not manipulate game variables, thus avoiding collateral effects. In order to return control from the mini-game to the main game, we have introduced a new special command that returns to the previous scene, available using uAdventure's visual programming system. Although mini-games have access to the narrative engine, and can execute conversations and provide other visual feedback, it should rely on this command to switch scenes. Finally, in terms of learning analytics, the mini-game should generate its specific traces by calling the analytics tracker directly. Mini-games developed following these recommendations act as uAdventure components and thus are reusable across games.

3 Pilots of uAdventure and Ad-Hoc Minigames

The mini-game integration model in uAdventure has been tested with students in two case studies within the Serious Games course of the Video Game Development Degree at the Faculty of Computer Science of the Complutense University of Madrid. In other words,

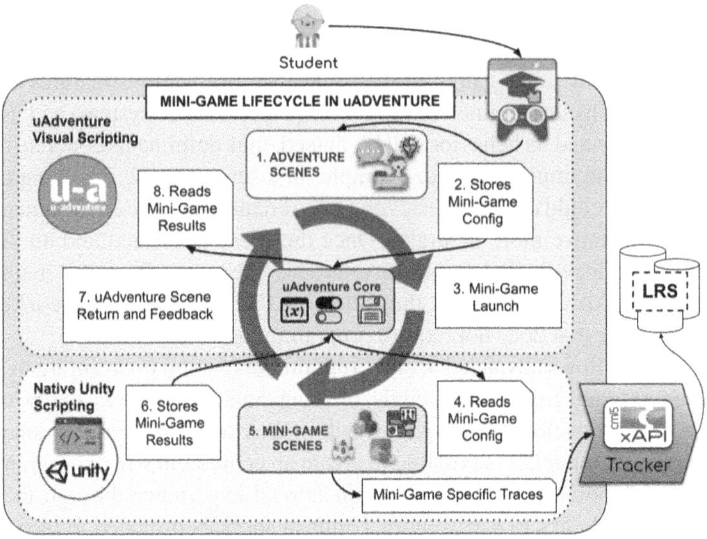

Fig. 2. Mini-game lifecycle within uAdventure. The transition between the uAdventure and mini-game scenes allow exchange of inputs and outputs, as well as the use of the tracker for analytics. The launching process of the mini-game is customizable through uAdventure's visual editor. The actual mechanics of mini-games must be developed using Unity scripts

it has been tested with students who know how to program games, although they have limited experience in the creation of narrative games. The first case was a pilot test with the objective of addressing a need for a more flexible environment in uAdventure; and analyzed the strengths and weaknesses of the proposed integration model. The second case is more complex in terms of educational goals and narrative depth, using multiple mini-games as part of an escape room-like narrative game whose objective is to teach competencies related to computational thinking.

3.1 Pilot: Serious Game for Airport Protocols Training

In the 2019–20 academic year, students used uAdventure to prototype and create narrative games, but since they knew how to program with Unity, they were also asked to enhance these games with other mechanics and visual effects. To do so, they used the proposed mini-game system, which provided them with the flexibility of the Unity engine without losing the advantages of uAdventure.

One of the games designed by the students aimed to teach different protocols typically found in air travel (Fig. 3). More specifically, it had three educational objectives: to learn to differentiate between the objects that can be carried in the flight cabin and those that must be carried in the cargo hold; to examine the different pieces of documentation required on a flight and the different problems associated with these documents; and to remind flyers of the different safety rules that must be followed during flight.

To address the first objective, the students chose to develop a mini-game in which, through the use of "drag and drop" mechanics, players had to overcome the challenge of

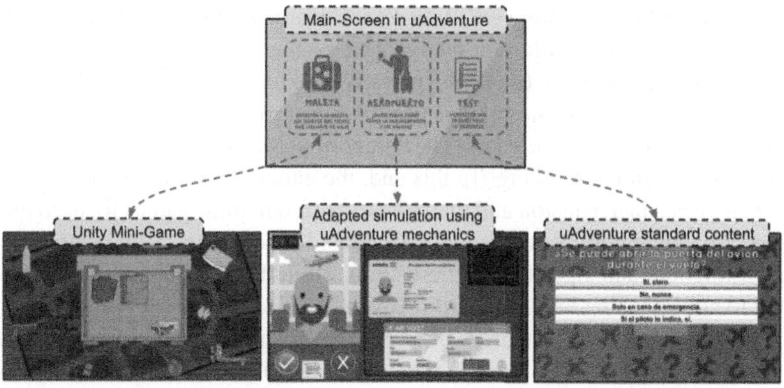

Fig. 3. Integration of different mechanics in uAdventure in the serious game "Vuela" (Fly) to teach flying protocols

being able to make the most of the space in the suitcase, by including only the essential (and valid) objects for cabin carry-ons. In this case, the mini-game not only taught players to differentiate objects by their visual appearance, but also took advantage of the limited space mechanics to infer which objects should actually travel in the checked luggage due to size constraints.

Regarding the educational goal of teaching the rules related to documentation, the developers opted, utilizing the different narrative resources of uAdventure, to create a simulation in which players temporarily take on the role of an officer who must review the different documents of would-be passengers. This mechanic is particularly interesting, as it represents the case in which the mechanics of a narrative engine are used to develop a limited simulation that is at the limit before being necessary a mini-game due to the complexity of its development and the large number of elements involved in its different states. In this case, the uAdventure mini-game used a simulation in which the face and shoulders of passengers are visible to one side and, to the other side, the passenger's documentation appears. Players must then decide whether or not each passenger can board the plane, identifying possible errors or contradictions in the documentation and thus favoring deductive learning. Finally, the educational objective related to safety rules was addressed through a questionnaire built using uAdventure's conversation system.

Despite being a first proof of concept of mini-game integration, the students were able to successfully use mini-games to develop their own mechanics extending uAdventure's narrative model. Additionally, during development, multiple shortcomings were identified, including lack of details regarding the different APIs to take advantage of uAdventure's mechanics, the communication flow between the mini-game and the main game, and the integration of analytics from the mini-games. As a result, documentation was significantly improved in time for the second round of testing.

3.2 Developing an Escape Room Game for Promoting Computational Thinking

During the 2020/2021 academic year, the enhanced version of uAdventure was used to create narrative games, while placing more emphasis on the importance of learning analytics. Unlike the previous year, as a lesson learned, students received additional guidance on the use of the different uAdventure systems within mini-games, including two-way communication, the use of the narrative engine, and the use of the tracker.

The uAdventure mini-games model allowed a group of students to develop an escape room-themed narrative game named "The Paranormal Mansion", teaching competencies related to computational thinking. To this end, the game focuses on the investigation of paranormal events in a mansion and intersperses different mini-games focused on developing specific computational thinking skills, including decomposition, pattern identification, abstraction, and algorithms. These skills would have been either not possible or practical to convey using only standard uAdventure mechanics.

The mini-games (Fig. 4) address different topics and visual styles and use Unity's three-dimensional capabilities, visual effects, and user interfaces. Also, all mini-games have three levels of difficulty. The implemented mini-games are: shapes and colors (3), which develops abstraction by representing numbers using geometric shapes and debugging by requiring players to use shapes to create a specific sequence of numbers; ethical hacking (4), where players must combine a set of cards with color bars to generate a new card with a specific pattern of color bars, by first identifying how cards combine their patterns and later using trial and error until they achieve the correct pattern; crazy rings (5), where players must rotate several groups of rings until the colored flags of each ring are aligned, by identifying the rotation patterns and decomposing the problem into smaller problems associated with each ring; electrician (6), where players illuminate a series of boxes by abstracting the pattern of changes that occur when interacting with each box, exercising both pattern identification and abstraction; and finally number maze (7), where payers must input a path of numbers that connects the blue box to the red box by following a series of rules, while both developing both algorithms that adhere to the rules and abstraction by representing the path with numbers.

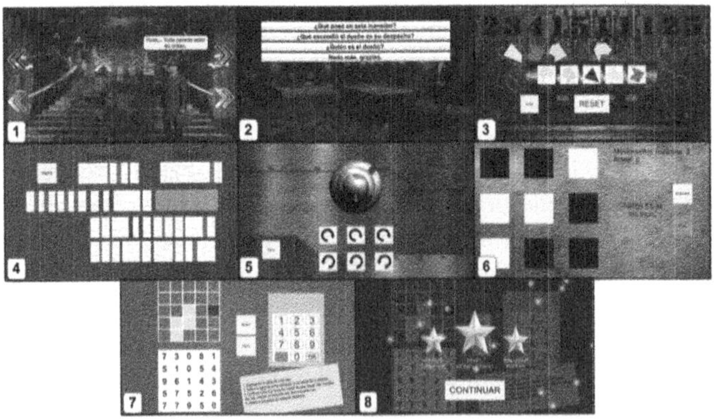

Fig. 4. "The Paranormal Mansion", a narrative game with integration of mini-games for the development of computational thinking skills. Images (1) and (2) show game scenes created with uAdventure in the point and click style with conversations and options. The rest of the images are mini-games: (3) shapes and colors (4) ethical hacking, (5) crazy rings, (6) elec-trician, (7) number maze. The image (8) shows the score obtained from one to three stars.

The interaction mechanisms used in the puzzles and their high number of states (and steps) needed to solve them, were the motivations for the students to develop them as mini-games. For example, in the crazy rings game (5), due to the large number of buttons and turning possibilities, the titular rings can reach a large number of different configurations, making it extremely complicated to simulate this behavior exclusively through narrative mechanics.

In this case, in addition to using its capabilities as an engine, the students take advantage of the different uAdventure systems so that, at the end of the execution of the mini-games, they can store a score which ranges from 1 to 3 stars. This score is then used in the credits screen and in the different analytics that the game generates. In addition, each time a mini-game ends, students made use of uAdventure's narrative engine to create appropriate conversations.

During the development of this game and its associated mini-games, students used uAdventure's learning analytics system to create and send traces that would allow the progress of players through mini-games to be examined. Their goal was to detect possible problems in the difficulty of the games and the progress of levels, and to find possible improvements for future iterations. To this end, the students sent enough traces from the mini-games to be able to recreate the players' actions during the completion of the mini-games; as well as to measure the progress/completeness of the mini-games themselves.

After the game was played by 8 users, all the traces generated by the mini-games were analyzed in order to compare their complexity based on the number of steps required to complete each of them. In Fig. 5, we can observe how the electrician mini-game was particularly complex, closely followed by the crazy rings mini-game and the one on ethical hacking. These results corroborate feedback from the players, who had already pointed out that these mini-games could be too complex. In addition, an unexpected result that was not pointed out by the players was that the complexity in the levels was

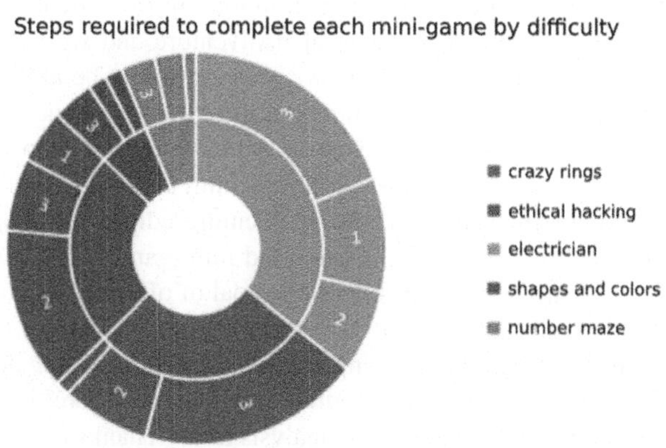

Fig. 5. Comparison of the number of steps required to pass a difficulty level in one of the mini-games. The legend shows the different mini-games names. In the graph, the inner layer represents each mini-game, while the outer layer represents each difficulty level in each mini-game.

not progressive in all cases, for example in the electrician mini-game, level 1 requires on average more steps than level 2.

4 Conclusions and Future Work

The extension model based on mini-games presented in this article increases the flexibility of the narrative model implemented in uAdventure. This versatility allows, on the one hand, to include new game mechanics to address skills that were previously very difficult to address within the narrative model. On the other hand, this approach enables a new development model where game developers can benefit from narrative aspects while, at the same time, making greater use of the full capabilities of the Unity platform.

The mini-games are built using uAdventure's native capabilities, such as the narrative engine or learning analytics. In particular, the use of the learning analytics capability is especially relevant for the evaluation of the capabilities and skills to be trained in the mini-games, in line with uAdventure's philosophy of providing analytics by default and with little effort. As seen in the case studies, easy access to analytics also facilitates the development and validation of the mini-games.

The proposed extension model has been validated in two case studies with game development students, where two serious games have been developed in which mini-games have played major roles. In these two serious games, the mini-games allowed cognitive skills to be addressed such as space management or computational thinking, which would have been difficult to tackle using pure narrative elements. We consider that these two case studies validate our proposal, but do not fully exploit its potential. Some of the mini-games developed in the case studies could, with minimal modifications, be reused in other games as new uAdventure game components.

Currently, uAdventure games can be reused (i.e. it is possible to reload a game into the uAdventure editor), with the aim of customizing the educational experience. For example, by adapting the resources or texts to the group of students who will use it. This has been one of the notable features of uAdventure and we believe it can also be applied to mini-games. As future work, we are working to be able to package and exchange mini-games (Fig. 6) through Pumva, a repository of games and mini-games created with and for uAdventure. For ease of use, a mini-game will be packaged together with a descriptor of the input and output variables configuration, as well as its different analytics traces. Using this descriptor, the uAdventure editor will display a friendly interface through which to configure the imported mini-game. On the other hand, we also want to improve learning analytics, with the goal of offering default analytics also for mini-games; and to offer templates for the xAPI traces generated by the mini-games, thus complying with xAPI's goal of keeping traces/statements self-contained. The traces will also include information about the context in the game where the mini-game has been integrated, further simplifying certain analysis tasks. Thanks to this new extension model, the separation of responsibilities between game and mini-game developers will allow educational experts to create games in uAdventure using mini-games in an even simpler way.

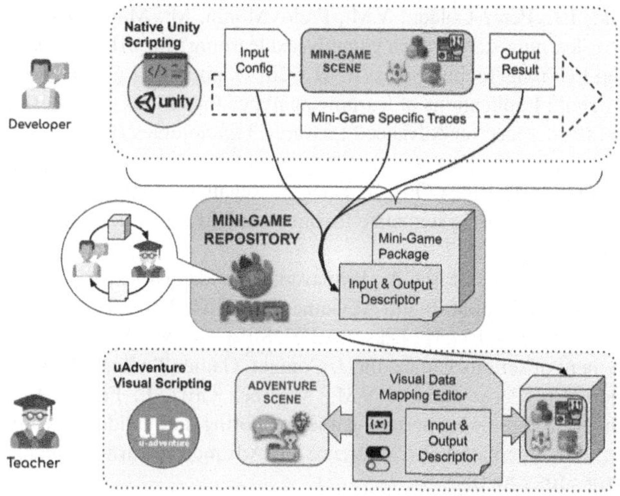

Fig. 6. uAdventure mini-game exchange model through Pumva. The mini-game must be packaged together with a descriptor that identifies its input and output parameters and ana-lytics traces.

Acknowledgements. This work has been partially funded by Regional Government of Madrid (eMadrid S2018/TCS4307, co-funded by the European Structural Funds FSE and FEDER), by the Ministry of Education (TIN2017–89238-R, PID2020-119620RB-I00), by MIT-La Caixa (MISTI program, LCF/PR/MIT19/5184001) and by the Telefonica-Complutense Chair on Digital Education and Serious Games.

References

1. Susi, T., Johannesson, M., Backlund, P.: Serious games – an overview. Elearning **73**(10), 28 (2007)
2. Michael, D.R., Chen, S.: Serious Games: Games that Educate, Train and Inform. Thomson Course Technology (2006)
3. Mitchell, A., Savill-Smith, C.: The Use of Computer and Video Games for Learning: a Review of the Literature, Learning and Skills Development Agency, London (2004)
4. Center for Technology Implementation in Education: Learning with Computer Games and Simulations. American Institute Research (2014)
5. Dickey, M.D.: Game design narrative for learning: appropriating adventure game design narrative devices and techniques for the design of interactive learning environments. Educ. Technol. Res. Dev. **54**(3), 245–263 (2006)
6. Amory, A.: Building an educational adventure game: theory, design and lessons. J. Interact. Learn. Res. **12**(2), 249–263 (2001)
7. Baptista, R., Coelho, A., Vaz de Carvalho, C.: Relation between game genres and competences for in-game certification. Significance **13**(6), 28–35 (2016)
8. Pérez-Colado, V.M., Pérez-Colado, I.J., Freire-Morán, M., Martínez-Ortiz, I., Fernández-Manjón, B.: Simplifying the creation of adventure serious games with educational-oriented features. Educ. Technol. Soc. **22**(3), 32–46 (2019)

9. Pérez-Colado, I.J., Pérez-Colado, V.M., Freire-Morán, M., Martínez-Ortiz, I., Fernández-Manjón, B.: e-learning standards in game-based learning? In: 21th International Conference on Advanced Learning Technologies (ICALT 2021), pp. 81–82 (2021)
10. Hauge, J.B., et al.: Implications of learning analytics for serious game design. In: IEEE 14th International Conference on Advanced Learning Technologies (ICALT 2014), pp. 230–232 (2014)
11. Serrano-Laguna, Á., Martínez-Ortiz, I., Haag, J., Regan, D., Johnson, A., Fernández-Manjón, B.: Applying standards to systematize learning analytics in serious games. Comput. Stand. Interfaces **50**, 116–123 (2017)
12. Bellotti, F., Berta, R., De Gloria, A., Primavera, L.: Adaptive experience engine for serious games. IEEE Trans. Comput. Intell. AI Games **1**(4), 264–280 (2009)
13. Barbosa, A.F.S., Pereira, P.N.M., Dias, J.A.F.F., Silva, F.G.M.: A new methodology of design and development of serious games. Int. J. Comput. Games Technol. **2014**, 1–8 (2014)
14. Perez Colado, I.J., Perez Colado, V.M., Martinez Ortiz, I., Freire Moran, M., Fernandez Manjon, B.: Simplifiying serious games authoring and validation with uadventure and SIMVA. In: 21th International Conference on Advanced Learning Technologies (ICALT 2020), pp. 106–108 (2020)

Supplemental Mobile Learner Support Through Moodle-Independent Assessment Bots

Alexander Tobias Neumann(✉), Aaron David Conrardy, and Ralf Klamma

RWTH Aachen University, Aachen, Germany
{neumann,conrardy,klamma}@dbis.rwth-aachen.de

Abstract. Conducting assessments is necessary to evaluate student performance. Online tests offer a scaling solution over traditional tests administered by examiners. However, these online tests come with the drawback of losing the interactivity that one has with examiners, as online tests mostly take the form of self-correcting tests which expect students to answer all available questions in a survey-like manner with feedback that may be given at the end. In this work, we present the implementation and evaluation of social bots capable of performing online tests. These bots are implemented as chatbots that can access and evaluate existing tests from learning management systems. With these bots, we enhance mobile learning support for students. Students can perform assessments anytime, anywhere using their favorite messenger application such as Rocket.Chat, Slack or Telegram. Furthermore, the activity data in the chat flows into learning record stores which can be aggregated and visualized there. These types of bots can be used as additional learning opportunities in university courses. As before, instructors can create their tests in their regular environment and make them automatically accessible to the bot, so that students can take the quiz in their learning management system, but also in a familiar chat environment. Our evaluation shows that assessment chatbots are an attractive and accessible self-assessment opportunity for students on a mobile device.

Keywords: Chatbots · Learning management systems · Assessments

1 Introduction

With the rapidly increasing use of technology in our society, comes the role of technology in e-Learning, and with social bots being a part of technology, comes their use in education. Although social bots did not start with the best reputation due to controversies on social media [24], they still show a lot of other benefits, especially in education. Nowadays, Learning Management System (LMS) play a big role in higher education by creating Virtual Learning Environments (VLEs) for students [8]. These provide students with numerous educational content, seemingly course overviews, learning material, discussion forums, online tests,

W. Zhou and Y. Mu (Eds.): ICWL 2021, LNCS 13103, pp. 75–89, 2021.
https://doi.org/10.1007/978-3-030-90785-3_7

and more. Thus with the relevancy of bots, comes the goal of further improving online education and LMSs with bots. A bot should not replace a teacher, but rather, ease the teacher's job while enhancing the student's learning experience. Such bots were already shown to be beneficial in the context of Massive Open Online Courses (MOOCs) [3]. As of now, most of the bots used in education are only used to help teachers take care of Frequently Asked Questions (FAQs) or inform students about certain events. But what if bots could also help students learn by completing assessments with them? Another important aspect is the fact that currently, the number of people using mobile messaging apps exceeds 2.52 Billion[1], thus concluding that most people are familiar with them. This in turn leads to the student having a friendly learning partner, which is constantly available and that on a trusted platform. The ongoing tech4comp project[2] aims at improving mentoring in higher education through creating scalable and personalized mentoring processes with the help of digitalization and using data from LMSs. In light of this, chatbots that can conduct assessments could play a role to reach the goal of this project. This allows a variety of existing past quizzes from the LMSs to be linked to an existing chatbot is conceivable so that students can test themselves on desired topics where they see room for improvement. Thus, taking over some of the basic mentoring tasks, and relieving them of redundant work. Scalability is given by the use of chat platforms, as they are available on smartphones. This in turn offers an arbitrary number of students the opportunity to perform the previously mentioned queries without being tied to location, which is not the case when using a computer, leveraging the potential of mobile learning. In this paper, we want to address the following research questions:

RQ1: How can quizzes from LMSs like Moodle be automatically incorporated into dialog systems?
RQ2: How do students perceive chat assessments in terms of motivation for self-assessment and usability compared to LMS-based solutions on mobile devices?

Therefore we created Assessment Bots with our Social Bot Framework (SBF) [19], which can create bots that access Web services with a REST API, react to user actions, run routine actions, and possesses a bidirectional chat interface to communicate with users [20]. We also present an empirical study in which we test the use of assessment bots on students.

The following part of the paper is structured as follows: The next section (Sect. 2) describes related work. After that, we describe our use case (Sect. 3) followed by the implementation (Sect. 4). In (Sect. 5) we present our evaluation and conclude with a summary and outlook (Sect. 7).

2 Related Work

2.1 Technology-Mediated Learning

Having a social bot that can do assessments with students fits in the category of Technology-Mediated Learning (TML). In this context, we use the definition of

[1] https://www.statista.com/statistics/483255/.
[2] https://tech4comp.de/.

TML as "an environment in which the learner's interactions with learning materials (readings, assignments, exercises, etc.), peers, and/or instructors are mediated through advanced information technologies" [26]. Mobile learning which is a subset of TML gained popularity among the students and education as it allows to complete everyday tasks comfortably and flexibly due to not being limited by the location [1], with studies suggesting that both students and instructors have a positive attitude towards mobile learning. Another reason to consider mobile learning is the number of students possessing a mobile device [6]. Mobile learning showed positive results when used for language learning [15], which can be seen in a study where two groups of students took part in an English course with one group using a special English learning app, which they were prompted to use outside their courses. The final test resulted in the group having used mobile learning ending up with an average grade 20% higher than the group without mobile learning, thus mobile learning showing benefits in the language learning domain.

2.2 Assessments in E-learning

Traditionally, assessments were done by students, where teachers would assess the work of the student to be able to grade them/their work [23]. Furthermore, there is a learning experience for the assessed student, and the quality of the assessment should be based upon how well of a learning experience the assessment proves to be. Online assessments are essentially the same as before, only now over the Internet and by using available web technologies [11]. A major aspect of online assessment is the fact that they can take place anywhere with an unlimited number of participants [2]. As we are now in an age where almost everyone owns a computer and has access to the Internet, the scalability of online assessments opens new doors in terms of education. Additionally, if it is an assessment that auto-corrects after being over, it removes the teacher's burden to correct the assessments by themselves, thus easing their job. We differentiate between *Formative Assessments* and *Summative Assessments* [13]. The latter is described as an assessment that takes place at the end of an educational program to measure one's capabilities, whereas formative assessments take place during the teaching-learning process with the main goal of enhancing the students' learning experience by always optimizing the said process. Within this paper, we concentrate on assessments in chat environments. Therefore, we limit our focus on the formative type, as the content of summative assessments is not fit to be handled in chat form due to its size. The most common type of formative assessment comes in form of an online quiz [10]. Studies suggest that good quizzes increase the students' performance for summative assessments [27]. Quizzes consist mostly of the following types of questions:

- *Multiple-choice questions*, where one receives a list of answers to a question and has to choose one or more right answers.
- *Drag and drop questions* consists of having multiple possible items that one has to place in the right position. This is viable for either a text with missing

words or a background image with missing pieces of either descriptive text or image components.
- *True/false questions*, where one has to decide whether a given statement is true or false, hence the name.
- *Matching questions* work similarly to the previous type, only that now there is only one central question that asks to match one data-set to another.
- *Numerical questions*, which essentially consists of answering with a single number with the possibility to allow a certain margin of error
- *Short-answer questions*, where the user is expected to write an answer consisting of one or more exact words.

Multiple-choice questions tend to get criticized due to them exposing students to wrong answers [16]. Going as far as proclaiming that even if the student picks the right answer, reading the wrong ones may lead to confusing the student. Yet compared to short-answer questions, which only tend to test basic-knowledge facts, well-made multiple-choice questions can push students to think about a certain problem and use their knowledge to understand each entry for said problem. The shown question types all possess the property of auto-correction, which we already defined as important for scalability, hence making online assessments attractive. There are multiple ways of timing the feedback, differentiating between immediate feedback (also called item-by-item feedback) and delayed feedback (or end-of-test feedback) [5]. The latter is implemented by the Moodle quizzes, which lets users respond to every question, review their answers, submit and then get feedback. For the immediate feedback type, users receive feedback upon answering a question. For student self-assessment, we use the direct feedback type since studies have shown that it has benefits such as *remembering*, *understanding*, and *applying* [25]. Under self-assessment, we refer to Brown and Harris' definition that "self-assessment is a descriptive and evaluative act carried out by the student concerning his or her own work and academic abilities" [4].

2.3 Assessment Bots

In the context of this work, we consider assessment bots as a subclass of social bots, since we use them in the context of chatbots. Under social bots, we refer to the definition of Ferrara et al. [9] which states that a social bot "automatically produces content and interacts with humans on social media". We are concentrating here on chatbots in the domain of education that especially perform assessments. It has also been shown that these are already being used to a greater extent and can contribute to the success of individual student learning [18,26]. Peirera [21] presented *@dawebot*, a Telegram chatbot asking multiple-choice questions. The bot was evaluated by Computer Science students who stated that this kind of bot is a good idea for quiz preparation and should be used in general. A comparison with other bots showed that generally more than just natural language processing is required [22]. For our bot, we use a modeling framework with a template system and propose the automatic transfer of quizzes from the LMS, which also eliminates technical hurdles for teachers. In the area of foreign language learning, Clarizia et al. [7] also used multiple-choice questions. A separate app was developed for this and offered in the Playstore. The bot was designed with a low depth, so students broke out of the conversations and the bot could no longer meet the requirements. We rely on existing messengers so there is no need to install a new app [21]. Our bot also expects short answers and also offers possibilities to shorten answers, while explicitly pointing out the possible answers so that outbursts are avoided. Huang et al. [12] used IBM Watson for a flipped classroom scenario. They created three chatbots, one of which was a multiple-choice question bot that included three multiple-choice questions with scaffolding (giving the student another chance) questions. Evaluations showed that this type of bot was well suited for self-assessment before moving on to a graded assignment. We endorse this statement with our work and also offer a way to encourage students to self-assess. As previously mentioned, our approach makes it easy to scale and facilitate the creation of the bot through the automatic transfer of quizzes and is not limited to multiple-choice questions.

3 Assessment Chatbot for Computer Science Lectures

In the following, we describe the use of an assessment chatbot as a mentoring measure, so that, it provides additional material for beginners or difficult subjects in computer science studies. A teacher decides to create a chatbot to practice for upcoming exams, where students can assess themselves on different topics. The teacher opts for the chatbot as they believe that chat platforms are convenient for smartphones and the students might be motivated to use a known platform with an interactive learning partner. The teacher is a member of several Moodle courses and decides to map existing quizzes to the bot, which conducts them as chat assessments. For this, the teacher accesses the bot framework [19] and uses the template for the assessment bot. Here, the instructor just needs to customize a few parameters like the URL of the Moodle instance, the authentication token and the course ID so that the quizzes of the course can be automatically extracted from the Moodle instance. This is a straightforward task for the teacher, as they can read the required parameters from the URL of the course on Moodle. The *Bot Model* also possesses a default vocabulary, which the teacher can extend. He can still customize the messages so that the messages are appropriate for his course. The teacher then uploads the *Bot Model*, which is deployed on Rocket.Chat with the name "techbot".

One of the students, Bob, now wants to be assessed by the bot to test his math logic knowledge. He first greets techbot, which greets Bob back and asks him if he would like to start a Moodle quiz. Bob agrees and receives a numbered list of available quiz topics from the bot. Bob chooses one of the math logic quizzes by responding with the corresponding list number. The bot correctly recognizes this and starts the respective quiz. Bob is first presented with the True/False question: "If $\phi \rightarrow \psi$ is a tautology, then $\neg\phi \rightarrow \neg\psi$ is also a tautology." Bob answers with "True". The bot immediately tells him that his answer was wrong and gives the following feedback: "For example choose ϕ unsatisfiable." After a bit of thinking, Bob understands the errors in his reasoning. After the feedback, the bot followed up with a multiple-choice question, where Bob is prompted to choose between *a*, *b* and *c*. Bob unintentionally writes "d" as an answer. The bot warns Bob to only choose between the given answers and lets Bob choose again. After the last question, the bot gives Bob additional feedback, consisting of the marks from the Moodle quiz, and also provides him with a list of the wrongly answered questions. This gives Bob a certain idea of his current capabilities, while also pushing him to look for the answers himself and thus engaging himself with the assessed subject. Bob wants to start another quiz but unintentionally starts the same one. In this case, Bob tells the bot that he wants to stop the current quiz, which the bot understands through Natural Language Understanding (NLU) and stops the quiz.

Figures 1 and 2 show the implemented version of such conversations with techbot.

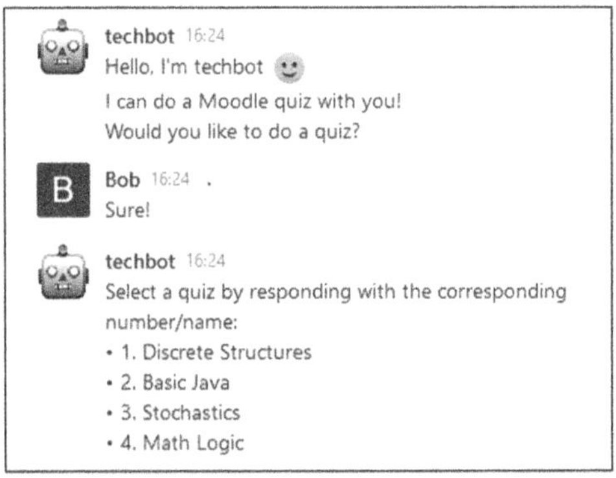

Fig. 1. Bot presenting a list of available topics.

4 Assessment-Handler-Service

Concept of Assessment on Chat Platform. For assessing the chat platform, the assessment needs at least a name, a set of questions, and the fitting correct answers. Additionally, a special quitting intent is needed, which if recognized, lets the bot know that the user wants to stop the assessment. To first start an assessment, the user first receives a list of available topics from which he or she can choose. After the selection, the assessment begins with the first question. During the assessment, the bot asks a question and expects an answer. To make the bot more communicative, it immediately informs the user of the correctness of his or her answer. If additional feedback is available, the bot also gives the feedback to the user after telling them if they were right or wrong and then follow up with the next question. The bot thus implements the immediate feedback type of feedback. Depending on the feedback, the user receives a larger quantity of text. Therefore, the question itself is written in bold, to make it clear

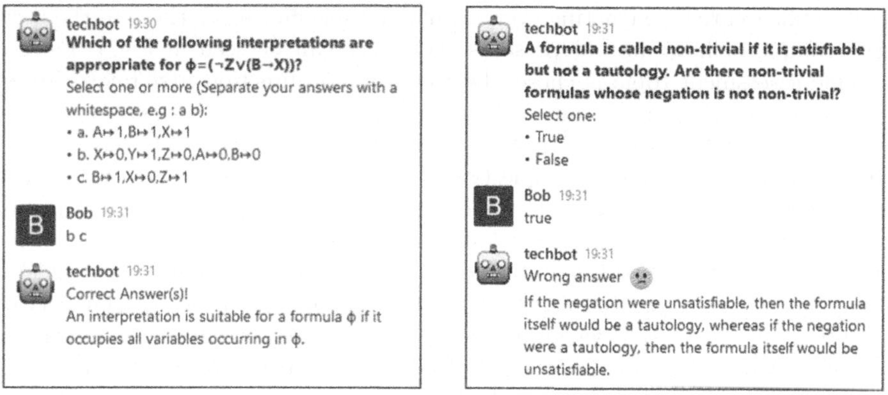

(a) Student answering multiple-choice question.

(b) Student answering true/false question.

Fig. 2. Student completing math logic quiz.

to the user where the question is. The questions themselves also need some sort of grading, which is added to a total mark every time the user answers correctly. In the end, the user receives the total mark and the wrongly answered questions as was described in the use case. The Assessment-Handler-Service takes care of setting up the assessment content and conducting the assessment. It accesses the available RESTful API provided by the Moodle platform in order to extract quizzes. We chose this approach over manually exporting and importing questionnaire files, as it allows us to fetch the latest quiz version without manual intervention in case of an update. The service works for every Moodle instance, given the right parameters during the modeling, thus being Moodle-independent.

Creation of the Service. The Assessment-Handler-Service was created for handling the content of the assessments, this includes preparing the content and handling the course of the assessments. The service itself was written as a RESTful microservices based on las2peer [14]. The service can currently handle two types of assessments, the NLU Assessments, and the Moodle quizzes. An abstract *Assessment* class was created, which is used to store general information about an assessment, as described in the previous section. Concrete assessments such as a Moodle quiz build upon this class, adding attributes that are unique to the type of assessment. The *Assessment* class contains some basic attributes and methods that can be used for any type of assessment. There is also the possibility to create classes for assessments from other LMSs, which would also build upon the *Assessment* class. The idea of creating an abstract class that was specific for LMSs was not possible, as there is currently no generalization of how a quiz should look on such a platform. This leads to each LMS having quizzes that possess different attributes, making it difficult to pick out specific attributes that are present on every LMS. For both types of assessment, the service takes care of extracting every available topic and sends these to the user. An example of how the bot presents the topics can be seen in Fig. 1. Once a specific assessment topic is chosen by the user, the function first takes care of preparing the assessment. This includes creating the specific *Assessment* object and setting Boolean variables in the service to make it aware of the assessment that will take place. For each question, the service creates and sends a JSON object containing the question to the bot which takes care of forwarding them to the user. Similarly, the user's answers are forwarded to the service by the bot for checking. The service additionally checks if the extracted intent corresponds to the quitIntent. The quitIntent is an expected parameter in the assessment service that represents an intent which once recognized, stops the current assessment.

After completing a quiz, the absolved quiz data is additionally sent to a Learning Record Store (LRS), which allows for the aggregation and visualization of all the quiz data from all participants.

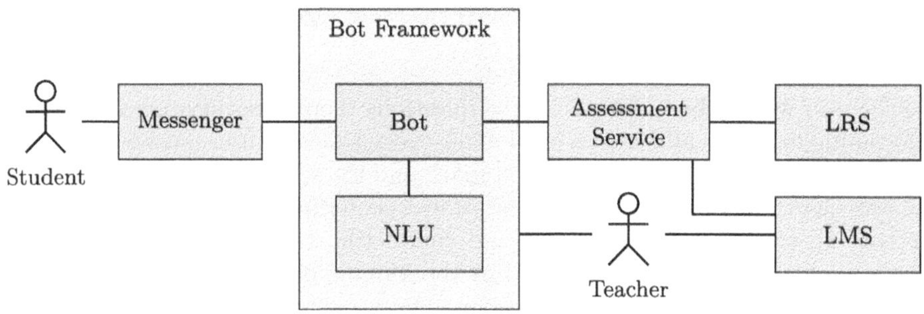

Fig. 3. Architecture with relationships between components.

Figure 3 shows the overall architecture and the integration of the assessment service. Deployed within a cloud infrastructure, the microservices can be easily scaled up and can serve a large number of users.

5 Evaluation

The main goal during this evaluation was to find out about the participants' thoughts on mobile chat assessments with a bot in terms of usability and as a mobile self-assessment possibility. Thus, attempting to answer our second research question. We focused on the students' perspective and how they perceived the novelty. Specifically, if they felt the interactivity improved their experience and motivated them to make use of the mobility to learn in unconventional places. The results from both during the evaluation and from the survey are presented. The questions which expected an answer between 1 and 5, the mean value and standard deviation can be found in Table 1.

5.1 Participants

The evaluation took place with university students, which were part of the chair's Slack workspace. Participants constituted a voluntary response sample [17], as an evaluation call was made with deliberate participation and no incentives. We chose this sampling method as it was easy to organize and it excluded subjects who would feel forced to participate. Overall, there were 24 participants, which were between the age of 18–24 and three exceptions being 25–34. All participants except one were male. There were 19 computer scientists, one maths student, one engineering student, one mechatronics student, one data science student and one student studying both computer science and engineering.

5.2 Materials and Procedure

Single sessions were done in an online context and the participants shared the screen of their mobile device. This allowed us to carefully monitor the participants' experience and help us figure out usability problems. After an introduction to some concepts and the used platforms, Moodle and *Rocket.Chat*, the participants were first asked to go to our Moodle platform using their mobile device. There, they were greeted with several available quiz topics, ranging from computer science to mathematics. The participants were then prompted to choose two topics to do a quiz on, with the first goal being to see every possible question type that could be done by the bot. After having completed the quizzes, the participants switched to the *Rocket.Chat* platform with their mobile device. There, they first started by greeting the available bot. The bot would then lead the participants to start a quiz and choosing a quiz topic from a list. The presented list contained the same topics that were also available on the Moodle platform from the previous task. The users then started one of the previously done topics and another one of their choice. After each quiz, the bot asked the user if they wanted to do another quiz and upon confirmation presented the topics list again. The evaluation was complete once the participants experienced every possible question type with the bot. Post-evaluation, a survey was made available to the users. The survey consisted of demographic questions, questions about the concept relating to the tasks, and an optional comments field.

5.3 Results and Discussion

This group of statements focuses on the participants' experience during the evaluation when absolving the quizzes with the chatbot. Starting a quiz with the bot seemed to have been no issue at all. The bot explicitly told users how to start one of the available quizzes. Some participants even proclaimed that starting the quiz with the bot was more straightforward than doing the same on the Moodle platform. Concerning how the bot presented the quizzes' content, the participants did not seem to have had any form of trouble. As the question itself was always written in bold, participants always figured out where the question was in the bot's message. The same can be said about the answer choices for a

Table 1. Results of the questionnaire. Score is an ordinal scale where 1 ≙ "strongly disagree" and 5 ≙ "strongly agree" (n = 24).

Question	Avg	SD
I understood how I can start a quiz with the bot	4.96	±0.2
During a quiz, it was always clear which part of the bot's message was the question	4.63	±0.58
The bot presented the possible answers for a multiple-choice question in a readable way	4.75	±0.44
I had the feeling that the bot responded well to inappropriate answers during the quiz	4.63	±0.58
I understood how I can answer multiple-choice questions during the quiz with the bot	4.75	±0.44
I always understood when I had to answer with a number/word for the numerical/short-answer question	4.54	±0.59
Doing a Moodle quiz on a chat platform on a mobile device went better than expected	4.29	±0.75
Performing assessments with a bot without switching pages or platforms makes the bot more interesting	4.54	±0.78
I could imagine if I only had a mobile phone with me doing the same quizzes with the bot rather than going to the Moodle website and doing them there	4.29	±1
While traveling I would take advantage of the accessibility of the chat platform to do quizzes with the bot to learn	4.21	±0.98
I find the idea of a learning partner that is available at all times would motivate me to interact with it outside my learning time	3.71	±1.23

multiple-choice question, which were always presented in form of a list with each item having a corresponding letter/number like the participants were used to from the Moodle platform. The multiple-choice questions presentation was thus already familiar to the students, which made absolving quizzes with the bot more appealing. The participants quickly understood how to answer multiple-choice questions, as the bot explicitly explained how to. The participants also had no problem differentiating between a multiple-choice question or true/false question with a numerical or short-answer question. The bot did not give any form of answer possibility, which immediately made the participants understand that they had to come up with an answer.

While the previous statements were about the quiz function itself and how well the bot can do the quizzes with the user, the following statements are generally about doing quizzes on a chat platform and also about the mobile aspect of doing these on your smartphone. Most participants were quite satisfied after having done the Moodle quizzes they already knew on a chat platform. One participant even claiming they were quite skeptical at the beginning, saying they could not picture how a Moodle quiz should work on a chat platform but left the evaluation with a positive experience. This shows that interactivity with the bot plays an important role in motivating the students to do these quizzes. The participants also liked the idea of having the possibility to review their quizzes by simply scrolling up in the conversation, thus not having to reload and switch between pages for each quiz to review their quiz attempts. This allows the users to quickly reread important questions, especially with the search function that is included in messaging apps. Participants generally enjoyed the bot's communication aspect, as well as the accessibility of the mobile device in terms of the chat platform. Some participants even proclaimed that they would even rather do the quizzes with the bot on their computer/laptop instead of going to the Moodle platform, for self-assessment purposes. This fact shows that the communication aspect, which is missing when doing these quizzes on the Moodle platform, plays a big role in motivating the students to complete the quizzes and thus learn. Most participants agreed on the fact that they would take advantage of the accessibility of the chat platform to do quizzes with the bot while traveling. This could thus lead to students spending additional time to learn while not at home but in unconventional places, as in a bus for example. Especially since chat platforms are easily accessible on such already flexible devices. A lot of participants shared the thought that chatting with the bot was intuitive and that they quite enjoyed the responsiveness of the bot regarding their messages. Some mentioned that the "chatting" aspect was more engaging than going through the Moodle page. One participant said that a chatbot would motivate them to do these quizzes. The argument being that chatting gives the illusion of not being alone, which makes it more social. Therefore, motivating people to learn, as they do not feel as lonely as when learning alone. Compared to doing quizzes on Moodle, for example, there is much more interactivity at hand here. Another appeal for some participants was the fact that the bot immediately informed the user of the correctness of their answer, while also giving the general feedback if provided. This made the participants immediately aware of their success/failure for each question, thus putting more emphasis on each question's correctness. In contrast, during the quizzes on the Moodle platform, most participants simply flew over the feedback page. Our results related to the second research question indicate promising success. There did not seem to be any experience-breaking usability problems and the easily accessible chat platform combined with the interactivity of the bot proved to be good motivational factors. We believe these factors could lead to users being motivated to self-assess more while only having their mobile device at hand.

6 Limitations and Future Work

The first limitation we would like to mention is the voluntary preliminary evaluation. Here, the number of participants does not allow us to make any claims in terms of learning success. In this paper, we focused more on the novelty and tried to improve the accessibility and usability of mobile learning. To this end, further evaluation will take place in university courses. Students could participate voluntarily with the use of incentives, which would lead to extrinsically motivated participants. However, this could lead to less interest in the actual novelty, giving participants a different perspective. Another limitation was the fact that we did not take the participant's screen size into account. This may have affected the overall enjoyment of the interaction. Taking this factor into account a future evaluation could result in identifying a correlation between screen size and enjoyment. Another limitation is the use of chat platforms, which reduce the user's input possibilities to textual answers. Therefore, question types depending on some form of drag and drop interaction were excluded.

7 Conclusion

In this paper, we tackled the concept of bots in education and asked ourselves if bots capable of doing chat assessments would encourage students to learn more, especially in a more mobile-oriented fashion. From this, we derived two research questions. The first focused on the question of how Moodle quizzes can be automatically integrated into dialog systems, which we answered by creating the *Assessment-Handler-Service*. The service itself is written as a RESTful microservice and is used to let bots conduct assessments with users. These assessments include quizzes extracted from the *Moodle* platform by using the provided RESTful API. After absolving a Moodle quiz with a bot, the data from the absolved quiz is sent to an LRS. Our second research question focused on the usability of our tool and if it possibly led to a higher motivation to self-assess. For this purpose, we conducted an evaluation where the students' perspective was taken into account. The preliminary study yielded positive feedback and bears promising potential, but further evaluations are needed to cover learning outcomes. We found out that the communication aspect and the mobility of the chat platform both made for great attributes speaking in favor of mobile self-assessment.

In conclusion, chat-assessment bots provide an accessible way of self-assessment on a mobile device. Not only that, but the communication aspect of a learning partner could further motivate the students to complete these assessments, as can be extracted from the evaluation's results. The bots now having basic abilities such as FAQ answering, accessing Web services, and setting routine actions could become a powerful learning tool with the newly added chat-assessment feature.

Acknowledgments. The authors would like to thank the German Federal Ministry of Education and Research (BMBF) for their kind support within the project "Personalisierte Kompetenzentwicklung durch skalierbare Mentoringprozesse" (tech4comp) under the project id 16DHB2110.

Appendix

A Extracting Content of Quizzes From Moodle

Moodle currently possesses a variety of RESTful API function calls which allows for content to be extracted. To extract the quiz content, following API calls are made with JSON as the content format (in calling order):

1. core_course_get_contents: Used to get the quizzes for a given course.
2. mod_quiz_start_attempt: Used to start a quiz on the Moodle platform.
3. mod_quiz_process_attempt: Used to stop the quiz attempt.
4. mod_quiz_get_attempt_review: Used to get HTML code of the review page.

Note that for each call an authentication token called *wstoken* is needed, which is provided by an admin of the moodle instance. The first function call returns every activity or resource contained in a course based on the given course id. The *Assessment Handler* then uses the response to find out the id for the chosen quiz topic. The second function call is used to choose and start a quiz attempt on the Moodle platform. As *wstokens* are linked to a specific account, the attempt starts on the respective account. The last two calls allow us to stop the started attempt and retrieve the HTML code of the final review page of the quiz. This review page contains every question that is in the quiz, the question types, the corresponding correct answers to each question, the optional feedback, and the marks corresponding to the questions. The *jsoup* library was used to parse the retrieved HTML code in Java and thus extract the quiz information using DOM methods provided by the library.

References

1. Al-Emran, M., Elsherif, H.M., Shaalan, K.: Investigating attitudes towards the use of mobile learning in higher education. Comput. Hum. Behav. **56**, 93–102 (2016)
2. Alruwais, N., Wills, G., Wald, M.: Advantages and challenges of using e-assessment. Int. J. Inf. Educ. Technol. **8**(1), 34–37 (2018)
3. Bozkurt, A., Kilgore, W., Crosslin, M.: Bot-teachers in hybrid massive open online courses (MOOCs): a post-humanist experience. Australas. J. Educ. Technol. **34**(3), 39–59 (2018)
4. Brown, G.T.L., Harris, L.R.: Student self-assessment. In: SAGE Handbook of Research on Classroom Assessment, pp. 367–393. SAGE Publications Inc., Thousand Oaks (2013)
5. Buzhardt, J., Semb, G.B.: Item-by-item versus end-of-test feedback in a computer-based PSI course. J. Behav. Educ. **11**(2), 89–104 (2002). https://doi.org/10.1023/A:1015479225777
6. Cheung, S.K.S.: A case study on the students' attitude and acceptance of mobile learning. In: Li, K.C., Wong, T.L., Cheung, S.K.S., Lam, J., Ng, K.K. (eds.) Technology in Education. Transforming Educational Practices with Technology. CCIS, vol. 494, pp. 45–54. Springer, Heidelberg (2015). https://doi.org/10.1007/978-3-662-46158-7_5

7. Clarizia, F., Colace, F., Lombardi, M., Pascale, F., Santaniello, D.: Chatbot: an education support system for student. In: Castiglione, A., Pop, F., Ficco, M., Palmieri, F. (eds.) CSS 2018. LNCS, vol. 11161, pp. 291–302. Springer, Cham (2018). https://doi.org/10.1007/978-3-030-01689-0_23
8. Coates, H., James, R., Baldwin, G.: A critical examination of the effects of learning management systems on university teaching and learning. Tert. Educ. Manag. **11**(1), 19–36 (2005). https://doi.org/10.1007/s11233-004-3567-9
9. Ferrara, E., Varol, O., Davis, C., Menczer, F., Flammini, A.: The rise of social bots. Commun. ACM **59**(7), 96–104 (2016)
10. Govindasamy, T.: Successful implementation of e-learning. Internet High. Educ. **4**(3–4), 287–299 (2001)
11. Gray, K., Thompson, C., Sheard, J., Clerehan, R., Hamilton, M.: Students as web 2.0 authors: implications for assessment design and conduct. Australas. J. Educ. Technol. **26**(1), 105–122 (2010)
12. Huang, W., Hew, K.F., Gonda, D.E.: Designing and evaluating three chatbot-enhanced activities for a flipped graduate course. Int. J. Mech. Eng. Robot. Res. **8**(5), 813–818 (2019)
13. Ibabe, I., Jauregizar, J.: Online self-assessment with feedback and metacognitive knowledge. High. Educ. **59**(2), 243–258 (2010). https://doi.org/10.1007/s10734-009-9245-6
14. Klamma, R., Renzel, D., de Lange, P., Janßen, H.: las2peer - a primer. https://doi.org/10.13140/RG.2.2.31456.48645
15. Klimova, B.: Impact of mobile learning on students' achievement results. Educ. Sci. **9**(2), 90 (2019)
16. Marsh, E.J., Roediger, H.L., Bjork, R.A., Bjork, E.L.: The memorial consequences of multiple-choice testing. Psychon. Bull. Rev. **14**(2), 194–199 (2007). https://doi.org/10.3758/BF03194051
17. Murairwa, S.: Voluntary sampling design. Int. J. Adv. Res. Manag. Soc. Sci. **4**(2), 185–200 (2015)
18. Neumann, A.T., et al.: Chatbots as a tool to scale mentoring processes: individually supporting self-study in higher education. Front. Artif. Intell. **4**, 64–71 (2021). https://doi.org/10.3389/frai.2021.668220
19. Neumann, A.T., de Lange, P., Klamma, R.: Collaborative creation and training of social bots in learning communities. In: 2019 IEEE 5th International Conference on Collaboration and Internet Computing (CIC), pp. 11–19. IEEE (2019). https://doi.org/10.1109/CIC48465.2019.00011
20. Neumann, A.T., de Lange, P., Klamma, R., Pengel, N., Arndt, T., et al.: Intelligent mentoring bots in learning management systems. In: Pang, C. (ed.) SETE/ICWL -2020. LNCS, vol. 12511, pp. 3–14. Springer, Cham (2021). https://doi.org/10.1007/978-3-030-66906-5_1
21. Pereira, J.: Leveraging chatbots to improve self-guided learning through conversational quizzes. In: García-Peñalvo, F.J. (ed.) Proceedings of the Fourth International Conference on Technological Ecosystems for Enhancing Multiculturality - TEEM 2016, pp. 911–918. ACM Press, New York (2016)
22. Pereira, J., Díaz, Ó.: Chatbot dimensions that matter: lessons from the trenches. In: Mikkonen, T., Klamma, R., Hernández, J. (eds.) ICWE 2018. LNCS, vol. 10845, pp. 129–135. Springer, Cham (2018). https://doi.org/10.1007/978-3-319-91662-0_9
23. Roberts, T.S.: Self, peer, and group assessment in e-learning. IGI Global Research Collection. IGI Global, Hershey (2006)
24. Shao, C., Ciampaglia, G.L., Varol, O., Yang, K.C., Flammini, A., Menczer, F.: The spread of low-credibility content by social bots. Nat. Commun. **9**(1), 4787 (2018)

25. van der Kleij, F.M., Feskens, R.C.W., Eggen, T.J.H.M.: Effects of feedback in a computer-based learning environment on students' learning outcomes. Rev. Educ. Res. **85**(4), 475–511 (2015)
26. Winkler, R., Söllner, M.: Unleashing the potential of chatbots in education: a state-of-the-art analysis. In: Academy of Management Annual Meeting (AOM) (2018)
27. Zhang, N., Henderson, C.N.R.: Can formative quizzes predict or improve summative exam performance? J. Chiropr. Educ. **29**(1), 16–21 (2015)

Exploring the Innovative Blockchain-Based Application of Online Learning System in University

Liang Xue[1,2](✉), Renxuan Fu[3], Dan Lin[1], Kailan Kuok[1], Chufeng Huang[2], Junyu Su[1], and Wei Hong[1]

[1] Institute of Data Science, City University of Macau, Macau, China
[2] Guangdong University of Education, Guangzhou, China
[3] School of Mechanical and Electrical Engineering, Guangdong Polytechnic of Industry and Commerce, Guangzhou, China

Abstract. With the prosperity of the Internet, online education has entered a period of rapid development. However, the online learning systems in universities still have some problems, such as the quality of teaching resources are monotonous and uneven, lack of sharing and insufficient education evaluation standards. Therefore it is difficult to motivate students to sustain their interest in learning, leaving educators with little confidence on online education. This paper analyses how to combine blockchain technologies with online learning system in order to design innovative applications, and proposes the establishment of university education chain to promote the sharing of high-quality online resources, protection on the copyright of online resources, establishing the Ethereum token-based incentive mechanism for participants, tracking and recording of the learning behaviour of students to prevent forgery of learning certificates, and creating a fair and reasonable learning evaluation.

Keywords: Online learning · Blockchain · Education chain · Smart contract · Learning evaluation

1 Introduction

As a new form of education, "Internet and Education" has developed rapidly and is welcomed by the public. It is geographically unrestricted, flexible in format, and can be live or recorded for convenience. The video playback function also makes it easy for learners to review. During the Covid-19 pandemic, online education became even more indispensable as a form of teaching or meeting in schools, businesses and other institutions. Online learning has numerous advantages such as lower cost, accessibility, and flexibility [1], but it still suffers from some drawbacks described as below:

W. Zhou and Y. Mu (Eds.): ICWL 2021, LNCS 13103, pp. 90–101, 2021.
https://doi.org/10.1007/978-3-030-90785-3_8

1) Inconsistent standards among many online learning platforms

   Nowadays many online education platforms are springing up in the world like MOOC (Massive Open Online Courses) and SPOC (Small Private Online Course). Furthermore, Udemy, edX, Linkedin Learning, Coursera, Khan Academy, Tree-House, SkillShare and etc., are all well-known online learning platforms. Many universities in China broadcast live or video online through online platforms such as China University MOOC, Wisdom Tree, Chaoxing Learning, Tencent Conference and Classroom, Zoom and etc. However, inconsistent standards across the Universities' platforms, widely varying operational processes and poorly maintained systems lead to pedagogical problems.

2) Online education resources are difficult to share and the quality of resources varies

   Most online courses at universities are only available to students within the university and are rarely open to students outside the university or shared with other universities. Different universities have commonalities in curriculum development and talent training methods, and many teaching or curriculum resources can be shared. However, at present, there is nearly no sharing of course resources between universities, and a platform for mutual resource sharing is lacking. University teachers have to spend a lot of time designing and organising teaching resources for online courses. There is a lack of a professional and sound quality assessment system and the low quality of some online resources.

3) Difficult to protect the copyright of teaching or result of scientific research

   In some platforms, the teaching resources such as videos and documents, may be cracked, causing them to be downloaded at will due to the lack of protection of intellectual property rights. Some individual students may also disseminate or tamper with those teaching resources at will, so that teaching resources would spread to the Internet, leading to copyright infringement. In addition, on the Internet, the possibility exists that the research results or patents of teachers and students could be illegally stolen, tampered with or plagiarised. As intellectual achievements are difficult to prove and defend [2], the copyright issues have restricted the sharing of online education resources to a certain extent.

4) Absence of a scientific and sound evaluation system of teaching quality

   The form of online learning is relatively free, allowing the teachers to check the attendance of students by means of roll call, check-ins, and questions. However, those forms do not provide a true picture of how students are learning, i.e. whether they are taking the course seriously and whether they have mastered the knowledge of the course. The current assessment methods of online learning are mostly in the form of tests and quizzes and the teacher's evaluation on the work of student is still the decisive factor. Some online education systems only incorporate indicators like student's learning process and the length of study into the grading reference, but often teachers do not use this reference when grading and still grade students based on the completion of uploaded assignments, which can potentially result in the existence of humane marks.

5) Short of incentives for online education

Currently, online education is mostly the recorded courses and the real-time interaction between the learners and educators is not enough. Students often rely on self-study, which can lead to a gradual loss of interest and motivation in the long run. A mechanism to motivate learners to continue learning is expected.

Therefore, the novel methods are required to solve the above problems and blockchain is one of the expected technology. As a cutting-edge information technology, blockchain has its unique advantages in data sharing and dissemination, e.g. encryption and decryption, timestamp, consensus mechanism and etc. to achieve decentralized point-to-point transactions. It has attracted increasing attention of more and more researchers in the field of education.

This paper discusses how to combine blockchain technology with the online learning systems in universities. Also it proposes to create an educaiton chain by connecting the private chains of various universities, share and protect teaching resources by using distributed ledger, traceability, and consensus mechanisms, establish an Ethereum-based token reward mechanism for participants, use immutability technology to track students' learning behavior, ensure the authenticity of digital certificates, and establish a fair and reasonable learning evaluation system.

The remainder of the paper is structured as follows. Section 2 discusses the related works of online learning system based on blockchain. Senction 3 describes the features of blockchain. Section 4 discusses the innovative design of blockchain-based online learning application in university. Finally, Sect. 5 concludes the paper.

2 Related Works

In 2008, Satoshi Nakamoto published the paper "Bitcoin: A Peer-To-Peer Electronic Cash System" [3]. The development of blockchained based application has experienced three main stages: Blockchain 1.0, 2.0, and 3.0. Blockchain 1.0 was used for crypocurrencies, while Blockchain 2.0 was used for smart contracts. Subsequently, in Blockchain 3.0, a lot of applications were developed in various sectors such as finance, health, government, education, arts, logistics [1]. The online learning systems that incorporate blockchain technology have been developed rapidly in universities.

Woolf University, founded by former Oxford University scholars in March 2018, was the first university to use blockchain technology for management. The school is similar to MOOC in form but different. The difference lies in the use of blockchain technology for management, using blockchain smart contracts to regulate contracts, tuition payments, salary payments, etc., and to record professor and student attendance, course progress, student performance, etc. Firstly, the university can manage the flow of information more efficiently. Secondly, learning transactions are managed automatically through smart contracts, thus reducing operational costs. Thirdly, as students' attendance and academic status are recorded on the chain, each student's academic experience can be guaranteed to be authentic and credible [4].

Blockchain application is very convenient in recording the learning process and practical activities of students. The "Learning as Earning" program proposed by the Institute For the Future (IFTF) and the US ACT Foundation (Gorbis, 2016) uses blockchain technology to store student learning records in a distributed ledger, including learning, training, activities, and school competitions, internship experience and etc., as their resumes for future job hunting.

Using blockchain can eliminate campus boundaries. In South Korea, Pohang University of Science and Technology (POSTECH) and Yonsei University cooperate to open courses, develop joint degree programs and research projects. POSTECH has launched a knowledge content sharing system "Engram" and a voting system "Voting" based on blockchain. In addition to sharing the knowledge and content produced by students, the "Engram" system can reward producers who produce high-quality content with "Neuron" virtual currency [5].

The traceability and immutability of blockchain play a very important role in the verification of academic certificates.With London based Gradbase's blockchain technology for instant verification of academic qualifications, University College London MSc Financial Risk Management graduates can display a verified Blockchain-based qualification on their CV through a Gradbase QR code which instantly provides tamperproof information about their qualifications [6]. Sony Global Education (GED) is a blockchain technology using Hyperledger Fabric. It can openly and securely share learning courses and record history data and certificates, without disclosing this information to the education management authority [7]. MIT started using Blockcerts to issue digital certificates for people in a community in 2015, which allows recipients to have more control over their certificates without relying on any third party [8]. Budhiraja et al. present the TUDocChain education platform to issue, validate and share academic certificates on public ledger in a reliable and sustainable format [9].

Moverover, blockchain helps establish incentive mechanisms and teaching evaluation systems. Taking Changzhou Open University as an example, Li proposed the application of blockchain technology to the encryption of student's personal digital files to realize the docking of different education platforms and use "credit coins" in the platform to motivate learners [10]. Shen combined big data, sentiment computing, blockchain and other technologies to explore the impact and role of big data on education evaluation [11].

3 Overview of Blockchain

The overview of blockchain is illustrated as below:

3.1 Concept of Blockchain

Blockchain is an open, public, distributed, and secure digital registry where information transactions are secured and have a clear origin, explicit pathways, and concrete value. [12]. It is a growing list of records, called blocks, that are linked together using cryptography [13].

The blocks are associated by a secure cryptographic hash that each block contains a cryptographic hash of the previous block. Thus, a timestamp that proves the transaction data existed is stored in the block and is recorded into hash. Then, blocks form a chain spreading over a peer to peer network. The blocks are represented as a Merkle tree also named hash tree, in which every leaf node is labelled with the crytographic hash of a data block and every non-leaf node is labelled with the cryptographic hash of the labels of its child nodes [14]. It is suitable to secure verification of the contents of large data structures.

3.2 Features of Blockchain

The following are the commonly known features of blockchain:

1) Decentralization
   Through distributed recording and storage of data, decentralization refers to no longer relying on third-party intermediaries and no longer subject to central control. The decentralized data is shared publicly through the nodes connected in the blockchain network, ensuring that program execution and data processing risk and liability are shifted from centralized systems to decentralized blockchain networks, where trust is built between network nodes through strong encryption and decryption techniques [15].
2) Traceability
   It means that all stored information is time-stamped and can be verified and traced at any time, promoting traceability of an event on the network.A block is connected with two adjacent blocks by the cryptographic hash function, so that every transaction is traceable by checking the block information linked by hash keys [16].
3) Transparency
   Transparency means that the stored information is open to public and anyone can access it. The entire information of the system is highly transparent. In other word, all participants in the blockchain are enable to monitor the transactions that are published. Those participants can detect and reject distrustful transactions and thus build a sense of openness, transparency and security [15].
4) Immutability
   Once the information is verified and added to the blockchain, it will be stored permanently. If someone attempt to make a modification on the node, the cryptographic hash key of adjacent blocks will be changed too and data tampering will be interrupted [17]. Unless more than 51% of the nodes in the system can be controlled at the same time, the modification of the database on a single node is invalid. It is not possible to alter or delete the authenticated transactions or the committed blocks. The logs of transactions are consistent in blockchain.
5) Smart contract
   It is a computer protocol proposed to digitally support, validate, or impose the specific conditions and criteria to be met before registering them in blockchain. Registration happens without the intervention of a third party, meaning that the transaction can be performed without a third party. Also, the transactions are traceable and permanent [1, 18].
6) Cryptocurrency
   To ensure the security of funds, transactions, and creation of new funds, cryptocurrency is a digital asset designed that electronic cash is able be exchanged by cryptography [19]. The cryptography means encryption and decryption.
7) Consensus mechanism

It is a mechanism of mutual consent (achieve agreement) amongst all nodes associated in the distributed P2P network to ensure security and provide integrity of the ledger. Thus, mediators are not required anymore. The mechanism are represented by Proof-of-work (POW), proof-of-stake (POS), delegated-proof-of-stake (DPOS) [18].

4 Innovative Design of Blockchain-Based Applications of Online Learning System in University

The development of online learning system relies on the development and sharing of online education resources and its copyright protection, tracking of students' learning behaviour and process, improvement of the learning evaluation system, and appropriate incentive mechanisms. Abundant online education resources, convenient learning experience, credible learning data and evaluation will all stimulate students' interest, and the increased interest will promote more people to invest in the development and production of online education resources.

4.1 Create a Community of Education Chain

At present, many universities have built websites of online courses. Those courses are usually open to students of the university, but rarely open to students of other universities. Blockchain has three types of chains: public chain, private chain, and consortium chain. Each university's online course website can be regarded as a private chain. The consortium chain is able to connect those private chains and can have a set of private chains, which forms the education chain.

On the education chain, online courses and other teaching resources can be shared across different universities. The education chain connected multiple private chains can change the status of Information Island of private chain and make information connected. Moreover, the non-tampering of data also protects the security of resources, which is conducive to the protection of intellectual property rights. The private chain can be authorized by the node of the education chain to obtain the access qualification, realizing the resource sharing between different universities.

Each university can be regarded as a node on the education chain, and nodes can share resources through the P2P network. The students have the opportunity to learn courses from different universities. It is beneficial for teachers and students from different universities to communicate, without involving the third parties. The decentralization of blockchain can save the expense of building central platform servers and their operating costs. Universities can reduce operating cost through resource sharing of infrastructure, academic programs, services and etc. Figure 1 is an example of online learning system connected with University A and B on the education chain.

In addition, university generally has a variety of information systems like teaching affair system, online learning system, etc. The data file formats of various systems are quite different. It is necessary to solve heterogeneous data sharing problem before the data are to be shared between different universities. In terms of knowledge co-construction and collaboration, relying on volunteers on the Internet to work together to generate new knowledge, we can see the example of Wiki University which became a separate project of the Wiki Media Foundation in August 2006.

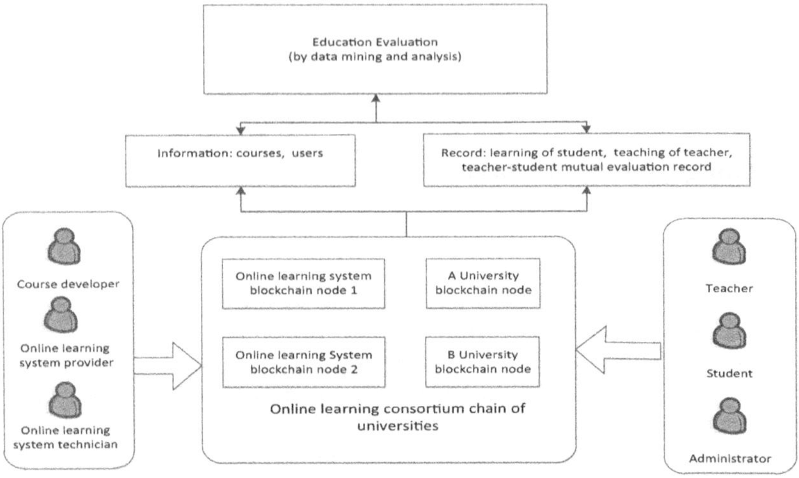

Fig. 1. The online learning system in the education chain

As a free and open learning environment and research community, Wiki University collects and creates learning resources for a variety of purposes and serves as an online community that integrates learning, teaching, and research activities, inviting a wide range of students, teachers and researchers to join [20]. In Wiki University, community members can post content they want to learn, and they can help collect or develop appropriate learning resources. If the platform incorporates virtual currency or token incentives to reward members for their contributions, it can facilitate knowledge collaboration.

4.2 Protecting the Sharing and Copyright of Online Education Resources

The encryption, decryption and timestamp technology of blockchain are highly credible and actionable in terms of copyright protection, serving as an umbrella for copyright. The rules of distributed ledger enable all data information to be stored on the nodes of the P2P network, and the data is non-tamperable and traceable. When the teachers upload resources to the education chain, their work information will be saved on the block and encrypted. Then those blocks will be recorded in the distributed ledger in chronological order. Each block has a timestamp. The proof of upload and download of any resource can be checked at any time and all copyright information can be traced.

Blockchain adopts asymmetric encryption technology to ensure data security by using public key and private key. For the safety of data transmission and acquisition, one key is used for encryption, and the other key is for decryption. On the education chain, the nodes record the access information of teaching resources to prevent teaching resources from being tampered with or stolen. During the process of data transmission, the access information of each node is judged, and the copyright information is broadcast to the entire network. Thus all users in the blockchain can participate in the supervision of copyright information, reducing the time and cost of copyright authentication.

Mine Labs, a company in New York, USA, has developed a metadata protocol based on blockchain technology, which enables resource creators to attach information to their works and store the data information in the block with a timestamp. The Digital Public Library of the United States and the Museum of Modern Art in New York have become the users of Mediachain (Li and Yang 2018). Figure 2 illustrates the resource created on the blockchain P2P network and authentication mechanism of the network.

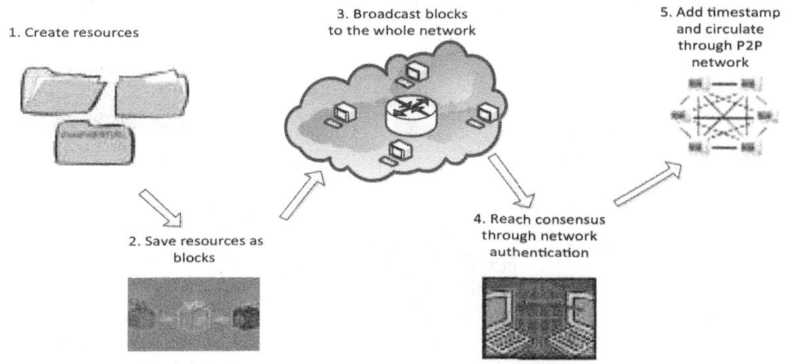

Fig. 2. Resource created on the P2P network and the authentication mechanism

4.3 Using Token Rewards as an Incentive Mechanism

The currency properties of blockchain have the potential to trigger many innovative applications for education because it can store a complete, trustworthy set of record of educational activities [21]. In order to improve the enthusiasm of online education of teachers and students, using smart contract technology, through the establishment of token circulation and incentives in the online learning platform, helps promote the teachers to produce high-quality teaching resources and makes the students more interested to take online courses. The reward mechanism can be fulfilled through smart contract. It means that the rules of reward are set in advance by the programming of smart contract. Once the contract is triggered, the system will automatically give tokens to reward the participants for their contributions.

For teachers, the online learning system will grant a certain amount of token rewards after they uploads the teaching resources such as courseware, videos, materials, exercises, and etc. When teachers answer students' questions, correct homework, or communicate with students online, the system will also give the teachers certain reward. After taking the online course, the students can give feedback on the content of course. According to the score level of students' feedback, the system will reward the author (teacher) with tokens. As all of the teaching process is saved on the blockchain, if a teacher's behaviour violates the regulation of the online learning system, his/her token will be deducted. The amount of tokens that the teacher gets in the system can be used for the evaluation of online teaching.

For students, the system will give token rewards for their learning behaviours like taking courses, answering questions, and completing exercises. When the tokens are accumulated to a certain number, the system will issue a virtual badge to encourage the student take more online courses. The student's learning behaviour is fully recorded and combined with the certificate of course completion, so that the university and the potential employer are able to understand the performance of the student. Figure 4 illustrates a blockchain-based online learning platform with the incentive mechanism. The platform has smart contract and it will issue token when the teachers upload learning resource to the online education platform and the students take courses from the platform.

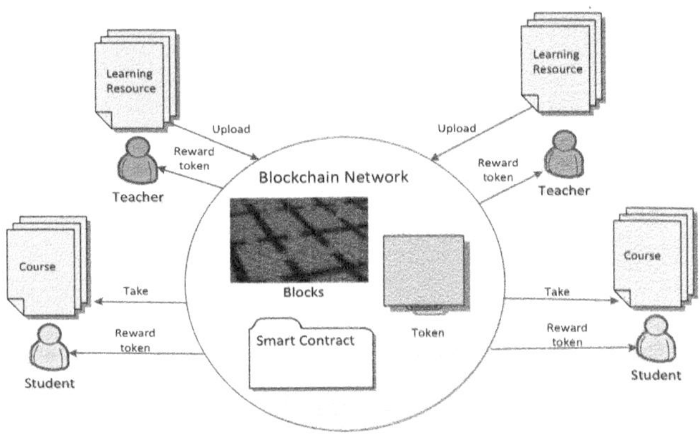

Fig. 3. A blockchain-based online learning platform with the incentive mechanism by rewarding token

Currently, there are a number of blockchain platforms that can pre-set tokens and issue tokens using e-wallets and smart contract, e.g. Ethereum, NEO, EOS and etc. Ethereum, as a decentralized platform, uses Solidity for programming smart contract. After building a smart contract, the contract will run without the possibility of downtime, censorship, fraud or third-party interference, and can be deployed to multiple blockchains. The Ethereum uses a tool named 'Truffle' to design, compile and deploy smart contract. Using the command ': > truffle create contract MD5SmartContract' will create a smart contract file 'MD5SmartContract.sol'. Figure 4 shows the structure of an online education system based on Ethereum and smart contracts. There is a browser used by the teachers and students as the front-end interface to process the data. The smart contract of Ethereum and EVM can be accessed through the interface of Nodejs and web3.js, with a NoSQL database or relational database running in the background.

4.4 Learner-Centered Recording on Learning Behavior and Process of Students

The immutability technology of blockchain enhances the credibility of online education. With this technology, the online education systems of universities can record the learning process of the students. The learning behaviours of the student will be precisely recorded chronologically and encrypted in blocks, facilitating the tracking and monitoring of the student's learning behaviour, and also fully guaranteeing the student's privacy. In 2016, the Open University in UK used blockchain technology to work with 143 UK and international organisations through Future Learn to combine credits earned by learners

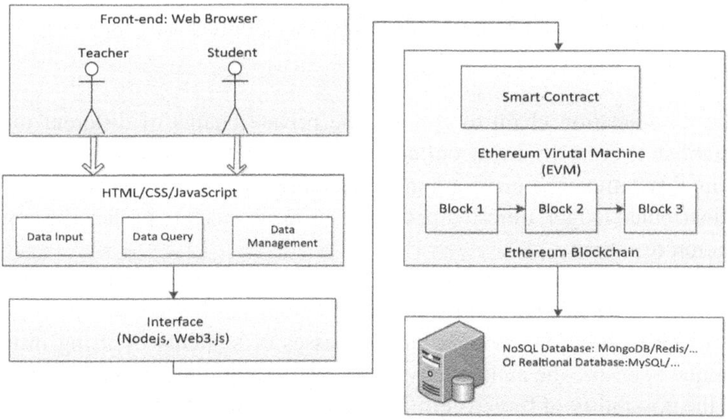

Fig. 4. The structure of an online education system based on Ethereum and smart contract

from different providers to develop "Micro-credentials", which allow applicants to obtain a combination of credits, a diploma and a digital CV [22].

4.5 Setting-Up a Fair and Reasonable Learning Evaluation System

A smart contract in a blockchain is a computer protocol that can be programmed to allow the exchange of something of value such as money and goods in a transparent, conflict-free manner without the involvement of an intermediary, and can be used to encrypt transactions in a blockchain. Using smart contracts, students receive a certificate of learning when they have completed the required online courses and passed the exam. The entire learning process, as well as the marks and certificates obtained by the students, are encrypted and cannot be tampered with, eliminating the possibility of forged certificates.

For potential employers, on the blockchain, a student's diploma is no longer the only proof of his or her learning experience, but a complete record of the student's learning process, making it easier for employers to understand the overall quality of the student and select the right person for the job. Furthermore, recruiting agencies could examine and evaluate the skill of student, or get involved in job-driven education to work with universities to develop the talent that the companies require [18].

Multiple subjects such as teachers, students and counsellors are involved to build a fair and reasonable evaluation system for university learning. Multiple private chains can be built within the university to evaluate participating subjects from various aspects such as learning, life and activities, integrating offline and online with each other. By writing and using smart contracts on the private chains, the index data of learning evaluation can also be integrated into the teaching quality evaluation of university, thus building a high-quality and efficient evaluation system [2].

5 Conclusion

The decentralisation, immutability and traceability of blockchain have given a new direction and impetus to the design of online learning applications. This paper explores blockchain technology adopted in online learning applications and proposes in the following aspects:

1) Create an education chain to connect the private chains of different universities to establish a consortium of online learning, which will promote the sharing of high-quality online resources among universities.
2) Use distributed ledger, timestamp, consensus mechanism to protect the copyright of education resources.
3) Establish an incentive mechanism based on token and smart contract to increase the enthusiasm of participation for teachers and students.
4) Record the learning behaviours and processes of students by using immutability technique to ensure the authenticity of the course or graduation certificate and eliminate the possibility of forged certificates, allowing university and employer to have a comprehensive understanding of the student's performance.
5) Build a fair and reasonable learning evaluation system that gives students the motivation to learn and give teachers the confidence.

The future research could involve enhancing the adaptability of blockchain to online education, improving and reforming the conventional online learning system by blockchain technology, and developing more novel applications for online learning to bring tangible benefits to teachers and students.

References

1. Alammary, A., et al.: Blockchain-based applications in education: a systematic review. Appl. Sci. **9**(12), 2400 (2019)
2. Yang, Y., Liu, Y., Wang, H.: Blockchain technology promotes the modernization of online education model development path. Sci. Technol. Econ. Guide **29**(09), 25–26 (2021)
3. Nakamoto, S.: Bitcoin: a peer-to-peer electronic cash system. Decent. Bus. Rev, 21260 (2008)
4. Zhang, S.: Former Oxford University Scholars Announced the Establishment of a Blockchain University-Woolf University (2018)
5. Wu, Y., et al.: Research situation, hotspots analysis and development thinking of "blockchain+education" at home and abroad. J. Dist. Educ. **38**(01), 38–49 (2020)
6. UCL: Bitcoin blockchain technology to verify qualifications on CVs (2018)
7. Sun, H., Wang, X., Wang, X.: Application of blockchain technology in online education. Int. J. Emerg. Technol. Learn. **13**(10) (2018)
8. Duy, P.T., et al.: A survey on opportunities and challenges of Blockchain technology adoption for revolutionary innovation. In: Proceedings of the Ninth International Symposium on Information and Communication Technology (2018)
9. Budhiraja, S., Rani, R.: TUDocChain-securing academic certificate digitally on blockchain. In: Smys, S., Bestak, R., Rocha, Á.: (eds.) Inventive Computation Technologies. ICICIT 2019. LNCS, vol. 98. Springer, Cham (2019). https://doi.org/10.1007/978-3-030-33846-6_17
10. Li, Q.: Analysis of the path of blockchain technology boosting the development of online education-concurrently discuss the practice thinking of Changzhou Open University. J. Xiamen City Vocat. College **21**(2), 84–89 (2019)
11. Shen, Z.: A probe into the education big data and educational evaluation from the perspective of new technology: also on the influence of block chain technology on the evaluation of online education. J. Dist. Educ. **35**(3), 31–39 (2017)

12. Funk, E., et al.: Blockchain technology: a data framework to improve validity, trust, and accountability of information exchange in health professions education. Acad. Med. **93**(12), 1791–1794 (2018)
13. Wikipedia: Blockchain (2021)
14. en.wikipedia.org: Merkle tree (2021)
15. Ramadhan, T., et al.: Analysis of the potential context of blockchain on the usability of gamification with game-based learning. Int. J. Cyber IT Serv. Manag. **1**(1), 84–100 (2021)
16. Chen, G., Xu, B., Lu, M., Chen, N.-S.: Exploring blockchain technology and its potential applications for education. Smart Learn. Environ **5**(1), 1 (2018). https://doi.org/10.1186/s40561-017-0050-x
17. Nyangaresi, V.O., Abeka, S.: Blockchain enabled e-learning delivery model for enhanced quality learning (2019)
18. Sharma, S., Batth, R.S.: Blockchain technology for higher education sytem: a mirror review. In: 2020 International Conference on Intelligent Engineering and Management (ICIEM). IEEE (2020)
19. Elrom, E.: The Blockchain Developer. Springer. New York (2019). https://doi.org/10.1007/978-1-4842-4847-8
20. Ye, J., Zhao, J.: The application prospect of blockchain in the construction of university network learning community. High. Educ. Forum **03**, 82–86 (2020)
21. Palanivel, K.: Blockchain architecture to higher education systems. Int. J. Late. Technol. Eng. Manag. Appl. Sci. (IJLTEMAS), **8,** 124–138 (2019)
22. Walsh, E.: A Digital System for the Authentication of Education Credentials (2020)

Experiential E-Learning: A Creative Prospect for Education in the Built Environment?

Karen Botes(✉) and Adriana J. M. Botha

Department of Architecture, Faculty of Engineering, Built Environment and Information Technology, University of Pretoria, Pretoria, South Africa
karen.botes@up.ac.za

Abstract. A novel e-learning initiative improved learning and cognitive understanding of learning outcomes in the Department of Architecture, within the Faculty of Engineering, Built Environment and Information Technology (EBIT) at the University of Pretoria, South Africa. This paper presents a typical case study of experiential e-learning through incorporating High Impact Teaching Practices (HIP) in the module Plant Sciences (PWT322), taught to third-year landscape architecture students. Learning was improved through self-paced interactive videos and videos of real-time projects, learning communities, group assignments, and constructive lecturer feedback. These activities were implemented within the Technological Pedagogical Content Knowledge (TPACK) framework. Results from a survey and focus group meeting revealed that online experiential learning, cross-disciplinary discussions, positive lecturer feedback and teamwork improve and enrich the learning experience and motivate students, although contact teaching and site visits are valued by students. Class averages for the integrated design module increased with 6% in the June examination and 2% in the December examination from 2019 to 2020.

Keywords: Experiential e-learning · High impact educational practices (HIP) · Implicit positive education pedagogy · Technological pedagogical content knowledge framework (TPACK)

1 The Context and Problem

1.1 Module Context

The Plant Sciences module (PWT322) is taught to the third-year landscape architecture students in the Department of Architecture within the Faculty of Engineering, Built Environment and Information Technology (EBIT) at the University of Pretoria, South Africa. This study was conducted in the context of three integrated modules, Design (ONT302), Plant Sciences (PWT322) and Construction (KON320), for fourteen weeks during the second semester of 2020, together with Plant Sciences (PWT312), taught in the first semester, as it forms the basis for PWT322. These are all year modules and build on outcomes of the first semester. PWT322 emphasizes plant community conservation based on ecological principles in the urban environment, including the technical

W. Zhou and Y. Mu (Eds.): ICWL 2021, LNCS 13103, pp. 102–114, 2021.
https://doi.org/10.1007/978-3-030-90785-3_9

aspects of planting in these complex environments. The goal is to prepare students to develop a design and working documentation to establish plants in the built environment. Design documentation refers to the design development for a construction project and entails a sketch plan, sections, elevations, and three-dimensional architecture or landscape architecture project proposals. Working documentation entails the construction and procurement documentation and includes construction drawings, specifications, and a schedule of quantities to enable the project's construction. The second semester focuses on plant community conservation in the urban environment and considering the technical aspects of planting in these complex environments, especially regarding finite soil volumes. Learning outcomes of PWT322 are set out in Table 1.

Table 1. PWT322: learning outcomes

No	Description of learning outcome
1	Evaluate complex urban environmental factors influencing plant material selection and apply them to design in urban conditions
2	Determine and design the detailed interaction between the built and natural environments to facilitate both plant habitats and human comfort
3	Apply planting design methodology, appraising social, technical, ecological and aesthetic factors
4	Identify considerations for specification of sound soil preparation, planting establishment and maintenance
5	Apply standards and conventions applicable to planting design communication and documentation for construction purpose

The module's structure firstly focuses on study precedents of urban agriculture projects enhancing ecosystem services, followed by the analysis and construction detailing different living wall systems, rooftop gardens and wetlands. The last part of the module provides research opportunities for students of different African Orphan crop species. Finally, students are required to apply what they have learnt through incorporating and detailing a living wall system, rooftop garden or constructed wetland in their final design.

1.2 Pedagogy

The nature of the lecture to student ratio in the Architecture Department at UP is relatively low, which has advantages for monitoring student well-being and learning success. For example, there were 13 students in 2019, 14 students in 2020 and 11 students in 2021 for PWT322. This ratio assists lecturers in the department to apply implicit positive education pedagogy, which involves creating a learning environment with greater emphasis on the overall well-being of students than on the content of learning outcomes [1, 2], amongst other pedagogical approaches, as well-being is vital in a creative learning or working environment. For PWT312 and PWT322, this was achieved through communication between the lecturer and all students via a WhatsApp group, emails and discussions during lectures.

Moreover, the lecturer developed an in-depth understanding of student knowledge gaps through communication, formative assessments and their application of all learning outcomes indicated in Table 1 in the design module. During the integrated Design module examinations in June and November 2019, the lecturer identified a gap in the understanding of the third-year students in their ability to apply learning outcomes 3, 4 and 5 of PWT322. Therefore, the pedagogical approach for the module Plant Sciences was adapted to address knowledge gaps in 2020 through student-centered, experiential learning. [3] (See Fig. 1).

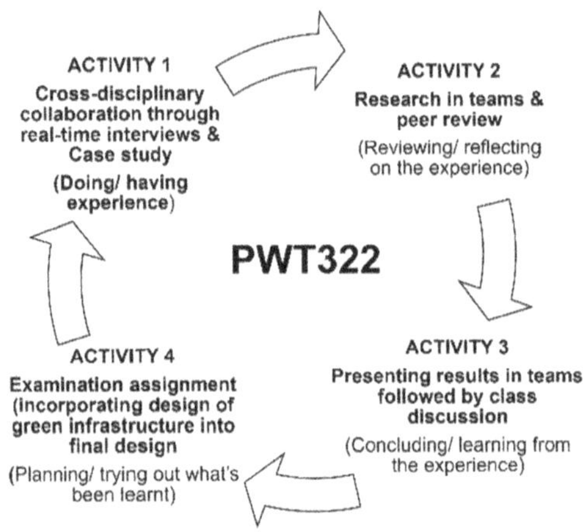

Fig. 1. Experiential learning cycle with activities applied to learning outcome 1 of the PWT322 module

The planned approach entailed active, physical participation and cross-disciplinary collaboration to assist students to gain a better understanding of module learning outcomes.

Kolb's learning theory [4] was applied for all five learning outcomes of the module. Activities were therefore introduced to assist students to experience the activity through real-time interviews with other disciplines, after which students did research to reflect on their experience and concluded what they learnt by presenting their findings in teams to other students in the class. The last activity entailed their module examination assignment and incorporating their learning outcomes in their design examination, which is the last activity of Kolb's learning cycle, namely, implementing what they have learnt.

The PWT322 module, which is the focus of this paper, was primarily offered online in 2020/21. The lecturer embraced the e-learning methodology and approach following the UP's hybrid teaching and learning model. E-learning can be defined as "using information and communication technologies in diverse education processes to support and enhance learning in higher education institutions, as a complement to traditional classrooms" [5].

The successful implementation and adoption of new learning technologies, such as the H5P (LTI) tool used in PWT322, requires a team approach between the lecturer, education consultant and instructional designer [6]. According to Neelen and Kirschner [6], teaching and learning can continuously improve, and a lecturer should seek opportunities to do so. They also emphasize that the learning experiences designed for learners should be effective, efficient, and enjoyable. They coined this as a 3-Star learning experience that requires the following for the facilitation and support of learning: the use of tools such as videos; techniques such as collaborative learning and feedback; and ingredients which include the domain knowledge to be mastered on the one hand, and assessment opportunities and tasks on the other [7].

Simply adding digital technology to e-learning practice does not guarantee meaningful and successful learning for learners. On the contrary, it requires lecturer competency to intentionally choose technologies best fit for supporting students to achieve the intended learning outcomes. The Technological Pedagogical and Content Knowledge Framework (TPACK) developed by Koehler and Mishra [8] is an effective guideline lecturers can utilize when considering integrating digital technologies to support e-learning and pedagogy of a specific subject area online environment. TPACK is thus the integration point where the lecturer uses and combines technology (e.g. computer, LMS, LTI tools, video's), pedagogy (e.g. Teaching methods and students' learning modalities), and extensive content knowledge (e.g. the specific subject).

The TPACK framework, [8, 9] steered the teaching of PWT322. This was achieved through combining 1) technological knowledge (TK) through additional Blackboard (LMS) functionalities over and above the standard teaching platforms, 2) content knowledge (CK) through the lecturer's extensive experience and content knowledge of the module she needs to teach and 3) pedagogical knowledge (PK) such as her teaching, assessment and evaluations methods and techniques used in PWT322. More specifically, the technological pedagogical knowledge (TPK) [8, 9] was achieved through interactive videos (H5P Blackboard LTI integration functionality), as a platform for online experiential learning, enhanced by a flipped-classroom approach, reflective discussions, cross-disciplinary discussions, collaborative assignments, group work, peer and lecturer interaction, and immediate feedback. Pedagogical content knowledge (PCK) [9] was gained through experiential learning aligned with the module outcomes. Finally, technological content knowledge (TCK) [9] was applied through teaching and assessment using the H5P Blackboard functionality, Blackboard Collaborate and peer review tools (iPeer and Qualtrics).

According to Peggi Maki, "course and educational experience design require identifying the pedagogies, academic practices, progressions, and contexts for learning, such as peer-to-peer learning online, that foster and engage all students' achievement of targeted outcomes" [10]. Therefore, High Impact Teaching Practices (HIP), as defined by George Kuh [11, 12], were implemented in the teaching of this module to ensure the engagement of all students. The features included everyday intellectual experiences through reflective discussions and self-paced interactive videos, learning communities (LCs) through dialogues and cross-disciplinary engagement, collaborative assignments and projects through teamwork, undergraduate research, diversity and global learning through peer and lecturer interaction, service-learning (through videos of real-time projects) [11–13].

In conclusion, the lecturer of PWT322 contributed to a learner-centered design [10] of her module to improve and advance a positive and enjoyable learner experience by implementing e-learning strategies and digital platforms that promote and supported her students to meet course expectations extend their knowledge and application beyond PWT322.

Scholarship of Teaching and Learning

In 2020 the lecturer received a Scholarship of Teaching and Learning (SoTL) grant for a project titled "African Food crops in living wall systems", which addresses the module Plant Sciences outcomes. The lecturer planned to expose students to two real-life projects where green principles were implemented to support ecosystem services. In addition, a real-time case study was also included to attune to the local context through the planting of African food crops on the Future Africa campus of the University of Pretoria in two different typologies of green wall systems.

The Covid-19 lockdown regulations, which were implemented in March 2020, impacted the module's planned teaching and learning methods. The lecturer had to reflect on the learning outcomes she wanted the students to achieve through an online environment, as contact teaching was no longer possible. Through this crisis, the opportunity arose to exchange ideas with the faculty Head Education Consultant, who provided a different perspective on approaching the online environment to achieve the required outcomes. This collaboration led to novel teaching and learning methods in the EBIT faculty. Throughout the teaching and learning initiative, the lecturer and Head Education consultant worked in close partnership. Weekly meetings added value to the result: the students' knowledge and learning experience and the lecturer's teaching journey.

The objective was to analyze and define student learning through virtually engaging with a real-life project and cross-disciplinary collaboration (landscape architecture, landscape technology and horticulture).

The purpose of the amended SoTL study was to assist students in the experiential learning process through participating virtually in the following activities:

- Evaluating the physiognomy of modular living wall infrastructure systems in South African urban environments, that show the most significant potential to provide suitable habitat conditions for cultivating African orphan crops for food production.
- Assessing plant species that are suitable for utilization for food production in South African urban environments.

The design approach for the SoTL project and engagement with students entailed:

- collaborative assignments through teamwork and cross-disciplinary discussions to understand diverse viewpoints,
- constructive feedback by the lecturer [14] following assignments, and
- self-paced learning through interactive videos, with in-video assessment and quizzes. The H5P platform, accessed through Blackboard, was utilized for this purpose.

1.3 The Problem

The hypothesis directing this study stated that; experiential e-learning in a higher education environment could improve learning for undergraduate students in the built environment.

The study aims to understand online experiential teaching and learning for undergraduate students in the built environment. The research questions are stated as follow:

- Does experiential e-learning in higher education improve learning for students in the built environment?
- Which practices enhance online experiential learning for landscape architecture and architecture students?

2 Methods

A qualitative exploratory typical case study research design was followed. The case study approach allowed for a more in-depth exploration and analysis of the module PWT322 and the experiential learning of the participating students in the module. Detailed information was obtained through data collection of numerous sources, after which a conclusion was reached by combining all the data [15].

Ethical clearance was obtained from the EBIT Faculty Research Ethics Committee at the University of Pretoria before feedback was requested from students. Student feedback was obtained through qualitative methods, with quantitative data obtained from marks.

Data was collected from three sources over 12 months to address the research questions. Firstly, students were requested to complete questionnaires regarding their experience and preferences related to the research at the end of the second semester in 2020. A total of 12 students completed the questionnaires. Secondly, a Qualtrics survey was conducted in December 2020 following the completion of the module. The survey comprised research-specific questions to reflect on the success of the interactive videos, cross-disciplinary discussions, teamwork and associated peer assessment and constructive feedback. Likert scale questions and open-ended question types were included in the survey.

Questionnaires were corroborated by comparing marks for the module Plant Sciences and Design for 2019, 2020 and 2021, as the second data source.

The third source was a focus group meeting, comprising 11 students, held in the first semester of 2021 to collate students' feedback of experiential learning and introduce different High Impact Practices (HIP's). In addition, open-ended questions were asked relating to the research questions. Finally, students reflected on the value of the teaching and learning experience during the first semester of the module Plant Sciences.

3 E-learning Tools and Platforms

Electronic learning, or e-learning, is "learning supported by digital electronic tools and media" as an alternative to contact learning [16]. Due to the changes required following the Covid lockdown regulations, tools and software for online teaching and assessment of module outcomes had to be considered an alternative for contact teaching. Tools and platforms utilized for instruction and assessment to support the pedagogy approach and TPACK and HIP principles are discussed in the sections below.

3.1 Tools and Platforms for Online Teaching

A 360-degree camera to record two and three-dimensional videos and images of the construction of projects was purchased with the SoTL funding. This enabled the recording of videos of the construction of projects, which showcased green infrastructure. Students, therefore, experienced the construction process of a living wall and completed projects with green infrastructure virtually to assist them to understand the module outcomes as an alternative to physical site visits.

The videos were imported into the Blackboard (Learning Management System) (BbLMS) LTI functionality H5P, a platform for interactive videos, to improve student learning. This functionality is part of clickUP, which is the in-house name for the BbLMS and official platform and communication mechanism of the UP between lecturers and students. ClickUp comprises a variety of functionalities for online teaching and assessment. During the lockdown period, lectures mainly took place through Collaborate, which entails synchronous or asynchronous communication with students. Interactive videos and the standard functionalities as a teaching platform were utilized to enrich the learning experience for students. Interactive videos included different activities such as explanations, additional images and questions. Questions in the videos were alternated to ensure various question types. They entailed true and false questions, multiple-choice questions, fill in the missing word questions, drag and drop questions, drag and drop text and images or diagrams to be uploaded. When submitting wrong answers, students were directed to the correct answers.

In addition to clickUP, students collaborated with the lecturer through a WhatsApp Group for the module. This platform allowed for more informal discussions between lecture times, which assisted the lecturer to develop a better understanding of the well-being of students.

3.2 Platforms for Grading of Online Assessment

Assignments for landscape architecture and architecture students at the University of Pretoria entail a design project for the main year module, Design 302, underpinned by and integrated with modules with fewer notional hours, such as PWT322. Design assignments are presented graphically and verbally. Assignments and examination assignments were uploaded on the clickUP platform and presented verbally through an online platform such as collaborate during online teaching in the Covid-19 lockdown period. The Semester 1 and 2 final design projects incorporated components of Plant Sciences. Therefore, their examination design projects provided insight into students' cognitive understanding of the outcomes of the module Plant Sciences, as students had to apply their outcomes in their designs.

An open-source web-based application, iPeer, which assists in peer evaluation by student groups completing a rubric to evaluate each group member's accountability

[17], was used to evaluate teamwork during the first assignment. Students evaluate individual contributions of other team members with this platform by completing a rubric that assesses criteria developed by the lecturer. Measures included the attendance of teamwork sessions, assistance with actions or advice, how the individual reacted to advice, listening and communication skills, and meeting deadlines. Unfortunately, it was found that some students rushed the completion of the rubric. Qualtrics, a web-based survey tool used by organizations to conduct surveys allowing respondents to remain anonymous [18], was used as a peer evaluation platform for the team assignment in the first semester of 2021.

4 Results

4.1 Module Marks

Following adjustments in the pedagogy approach in 2020, after knowledge gaps and concepts from the learning outcomes that students had difficulty with, were identified and observed in 2019, the class average increased with 6% between 2019 and 2020, and with 3% between 2020 and 2021 for the design examination in June, and with 2% for the final December examination. This improvement is illustrated in Table 2.

Table 2. Design (ONT302): comparison of average percentage marks of 2019, 2020 and 2021

Year	June examination (progress mark) class average (%)	December examination (final mark) class average (%)
2019	58	68
2020	64	70
2021	67	

Since 2019, where two students failed the Plant Sciences (PWT312) module, and one student failed the Design (ONT202) module, no failures were recorded for 2020 and 2021, and the class average increased by 2% between 2019 and 2020, and a further 5% between 2020 and 2021. Refer to Table 3 for a breakdown of the Plant Sciences module average marks.

The positive effect of the improved pedagogical approach for PWT322, and its cumulative impact on ONT302 is reflected below (Figs. 2 and 3). The figures illustrate the distribution of marks and the increase of marks above 60% for both modules. Looking at the throughput of ONT302, the percentage of distinctions, which doubled in 2020, is encouraging.

4.2 Student Feedback via Qualtrics Survey

Student feedback related to their experience of the pedagogy approach applied in 2020. Questions focused on the module Plant Sciences (PWT322) was obtained in December

Table 3. Plant sciences (PWT 312 and PWT322): comparison of average percentage marks of 2019, 2020 and 2021

Year	June examination (progress mark) class average (%)	December examination (final mark) class average (%)
2019	62	66
2020	64	67
2021	69	

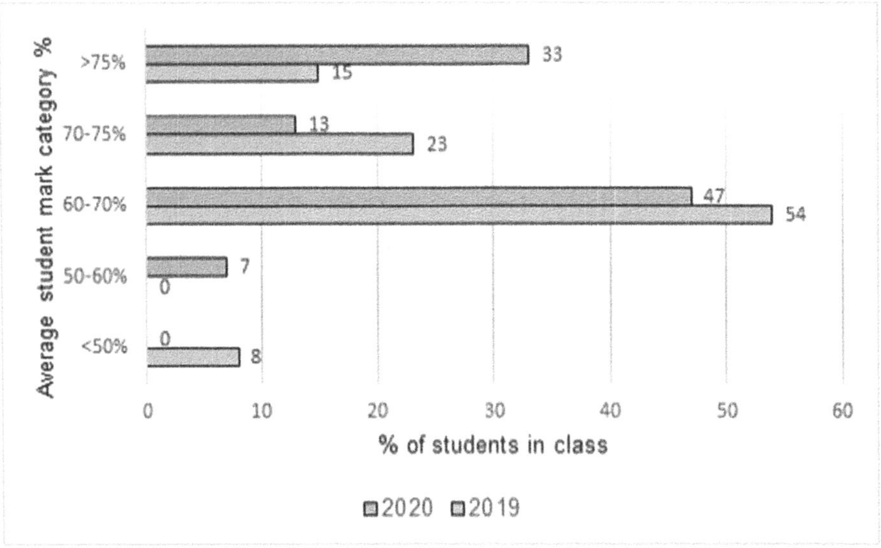

Fig. 2. Design (ONT302): comparison of 2019 and 2020 final year marks

2020. Students remained anonymous as part of the feedback process, and the questionnaires were submitted online to the Department for Education Innovation. Student responses are presented in this section. More than 90% of the students indicated that cross-disciplinary discussions enhanced learning, as illustrated in Fig. 4.

Although 81% of students found that experiential learning through interactive videos enhanced their learning (refer to Fig. 5), 58% of students indicated that they preferred combining interactive videos and synchronous teaching, with 42% of students selecting only synchronous teaching.

Students noted students' physical site visits and direct contact with peers and lecturers as crucial for future experiential learning (Refer to Fig. 6).

In order of preference, the most beneficial learning activities to students were 1) Constructive feedback by the lecturer and 2) experiential learning and teamwork (equal ratings), followed by team discussions. Students were divided on the advantages of peer evaluation, with 50% of students indicating that iPeer did not add value to their experience of teamwork. Students argued that the evaluation was time-consuming and

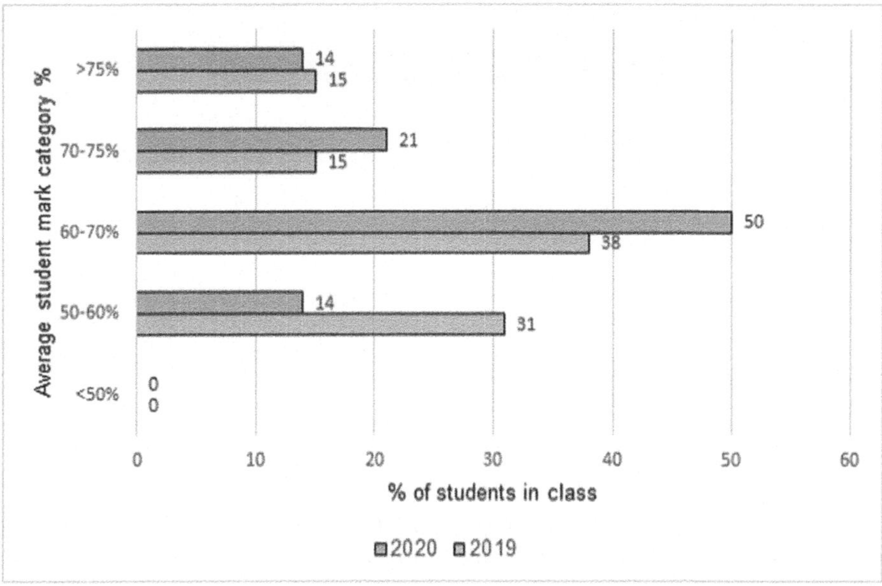

Fig. 3. Plant sciences (PWT322) comparison of 2019 and 2020 final year marks

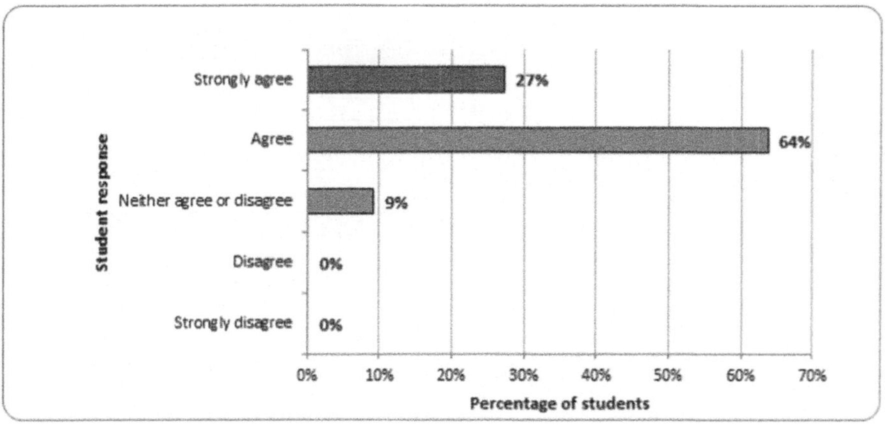

Fig. 4. Students' response to statement: Blackboard Collaborate sessions with guest from interdisciplinary network (Horticulture) regarding living wall systems enhanced my learning experience

therefore resulted in some students rushing off the evaluation process. Students also listed benefits, such as that their peers contributed better and put in a greater effort for team work to their performance being reviewed.

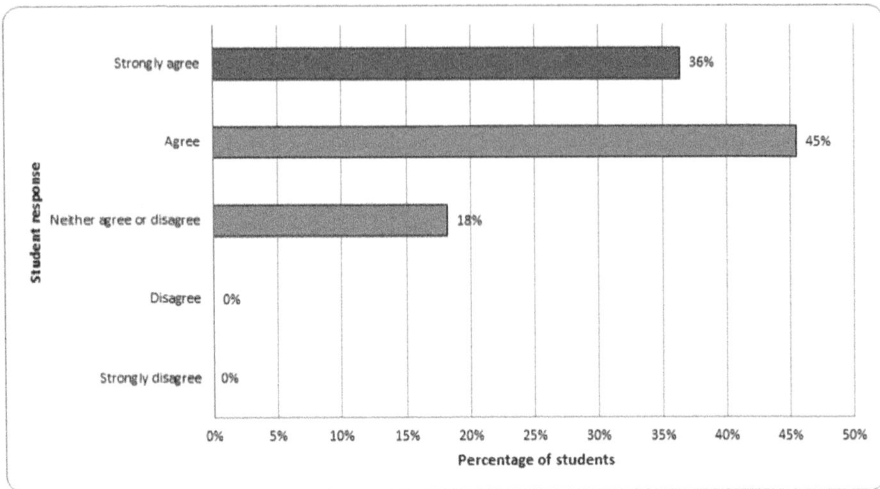

Fig. 5. Student feedback in response to statement: Experiential learning through self-paced interactive videos (H5P) enhanced my learning experience

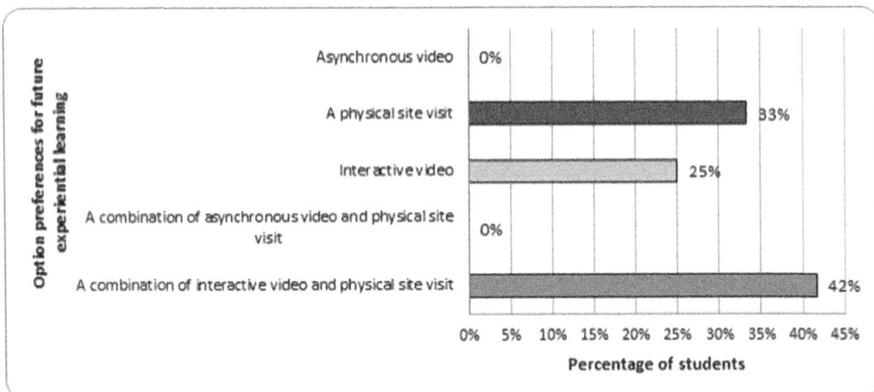

Fig. 6. Preferred options for future experiential learning

4.3 Student Feedback from Focus Group Discussion

A focus group meeting was held with the 2021 class for the module Plant Sciences. Similar questions were posed to students to determine the success of the pedagogy approach and student preferences.

Student preferences concurred with the priorities of the 2020 class, namely that cross-disciplinary discussions and constructive feedback were beneficial in terms of learning. They also indicated that they preferred physical site visits and that asynchronous videos would be beneficial in combination with site visits, but after the visit, to understand the full context.

5 Discussion

The findings of this study contribute to the understanding of experiential e-learning for undergraduate students in the built environment to inform future combined teaching and e-learning. From the annual improvement in the class average and distinctions in modules where learning outcomes are applied which doubled following experiential learning, it is evident that experiential e-learning succeeded in meaningful knowledge and a cognitive understanding of learning outcomes. This can be achieved through incorporating HIP practices, implemented within the TPACK framework. HIP practices which improved learning included reflective discussions, self-paced interactive videos, learning communities (LCs) through dialogues and cross-disciplinary engagement, collaborative assignments through teamwork, undergraduate research, diversity and global learning through peer and lecturer interaction and service-learning (through videos of real-time projects). These practices, except for peer and lecturer interaction, are independent of the scale of student groups due to the electronic platforms.

Although students indicated that self-paced interactive videos contributed to their learning, it was clear from their preference of constructive feedback and a combination of a physical site visit and an interactive/asynchronous video that contact with peers, other disciplines and the lecturer was important. Learning communities through dialogues and cross-disciplinary engagement were also valued by students. This underpins the implicit positive education pedagogy, with the well-being of students being pivotal to their learning and motivation.

Peer evaluation through the iPeer and Qualtrics platforms assisted in showing how behavior and accountability in teamwork can be improved, although further research is required to ensure that feedback adds value to teamwork in alignment with the program outcomes.

6 Conclusions

The authors conclude that experiential e-learning in a higher education environment can improve learning and cognitive understanding of learning outcomes for undergraduate students in the built environment. Moreover, the incorporation of HIP practices, implemented within the TPACK framework can enhance student engagement and create meaningful learning. These entail self-paced interactive videos and videos of real-time projects, learning communities, group assignments, and constructive lecturer feedback. In combination with e-learning through HIP practices, cross-disciplinary discussions, contact teaching and site visits are valued by students. With the support of the HOD, this initiative has been noticed and supported by the Department of Architecture for introduction in other modules comprising larger groups. Longitudinal research will therefore be conducted on bigger sample groups to assess the success of combined contact teaching and e-learning. In addition, this research will further assist in improving benefits of peer assessment for teamwork.

References

1. Kern, M.L., Wehmeyer, M.L. (eds.): The Palgrave Handbook of Positive Education. Springer, Cham (2021). https://doi.org/10.1007/978-3-030-64537-3

2. Waters, L.: Positive education pedagogy: shifting teacher mindsets, practice, and language to make wellbeing visible in classrooms. In: Kern, M.L., Wehmeyer, M.L. (eds.) The Palgrave Handbook of Positive Education, pp. 137–164. Springer, Cham (2021). https://doi.org/10.1007/978-3-030-64537-3_6
3. Kolb, A.Y., Kolb, D.A.: Enhancing experiential learning in higher education. Acad. Manag. Learn. Educ. **4**(2), 193–212 (2015)
4. Institute for Experiential Learning. What Is Experiential Learning? - Institute for Experiential Learning. https://experientiallearninginstitute.org/resources/what-is-experiential-learning. Accessed 31July 2021
5. Arkorful, V., Abaidoo, N.: The role of e-learning, the advantages and disadvantages of its adoption in higher education. Int. J. Educ. Res. **2**(12), 397–410 (2014)
6. Leek, D., Olson, M., Shea, P.: A guide for successful integration and support of learning technologies. In: Transforming Digital Learning and Assessment – A Guide to Available and Emerging Practices and Building Institutional Consensus. Stylus. Sterling, Virginia (2021)
7. Neelen, M., Kirschner, P.: Evidence-Informed Learning Design. Kogan Page Limited. Great Britain (2020)
8. Koehler, M., Mishra, P.: What is technological pedagogical content knowledge (TPACK)? Contemp. Iss. Technol. Teach. Educ. **9**(1), 99–110 (2009)
9. Kurt, S.: TPACK: technological pedagogical content knowledge framework - educational technology. Educational Technology. https://educationaltechnology.net/technological-pedagogical-content-knowledge-tpack-framework. Accessed 31July 2021
10. Maki, P.: Real-time Student Assessment. Meeting the Imperative for Improved Time to Degree, Closing the Opportunity Gap, and Assuring Student Competencies for 21st Century Needs. Stylus Publishing. Sterling (2017)
11. Kuh, G.D.: What we're learning about student engagement from NSSE: benchmarks for effective educational practices. Change Mag. Higher Learn. **35**(2), 24–32 (2010)
12. Kuh, G.D., Schneider, C.G., Association of American Colleges and Universities: High-impact Educational Practices - What They Are, Who Has Access to Them, and Why They Matter. Association of American Colleges and Universities, Washington (2008)
13. Linder, K.E., Mattison, H.C.: High-Impact Practices in Online Education. Research and Best Practices. Stylus Publishing. Sterling. http://search.ebscohost.com.uplib.idm.oclc.org/login.aspx?direct=true&db=nlebk&AN=1918610&site=ehost-live&scope=site. Accessed 21 July 2021
14. Rodriguez, R.J., Koubek, E.: Unpacking high-impact instructional practices and student engagement in a teacher preparation program. Int. J. Scholar. Teach. Learn. **13**(3). https://doi.org/10.20429/ijsotl.2019.130311, Accessed (2019)
15. Kumar, B.S., Wotto, M., Bélanger, P.: E-Learning, M-Learning and D-Learning: conceptual definition and comparative analysis. E-Learn. Digit. Media **15**(4), 191–216 (2018)
16. Lthub.ubc.ca: iPeer Instructor Guide|Teaching with Technology. https://lthub.ubc.ca/guides/ipeer-instructor-guide. Accessed 31 July 2021
17. Csulb.libguides.com: Research Guides: Qualtrics: What is Qualtrics? https://csulb.libguides.com/qualtrics/about. Accessed 31 July 2021
18. Creswell, J.: Research Design: Qualitative, Quantitative, And Mixed Methods Approaches. Sage publications, Thousand Oaks (2013)

Strengths and Limitations of Using e-Learning for Chinese Learners on Creative Engagement

Bernard C. S. Tan[1], Hio Man Lei[2(✉)], Erdan Ma[3], and Victor Chan[2]

[1] Honlam Education and Research Association, Macao, China
[2] Macao Polytechnic Institute, Macao, China
{hmlei,vkychan}@ipm.edu.mo
[3] Yunnan University of Finance and Economics, Kunming, China

Abstract. This research is linked to important questions currently being asked by educationists in China. For example, what can 21st century cutting-edge technology contribute to a relatively undeveloped education system in China? To what extent can innovative instructional design improve education in China? What are the strengths and limitations of using e-learning in such set-tings? This paper reports on a longitudinal study by the Pearl River Delta Network of Science Learning Centers in China, examining how affordance of electronic-learning framework might enhance learners' creativity and innovativeness. This becomes increasingly challenging at a time when most progressive institutions around the world are promoting creative learning that orient around thinking and reflection, experience and activity, conversation and interaction. The paper investigates the strategic potential of a conceptual model and discusses its implications for technology integration, alignment and convergence on Chinese learners' creativity and engagement in the Knowledge Age.

Keywords: e-Learning · Competence-based education · Creativity · Higher order thinking skills · New learning strategies · China

1 Introduction

Educational reforms in the People's Republic of China in recent years have led to constructive and innovative changes in the use of Information and Communications Technologies (ICT) in education settings in China. The purpose of this paper is to examine critically the social and political factors, both beneficial and limiting, affecting the use of e-learning in China, and propose a conceptual model for technology integration, alignment and convergence to facilitate learners' creativity and engagement. As a way for setting the stage for discussion of supports to e-learning process, China's education system, its background and present situation -such as its (i) central control of schools; (ii) large class sizes; (iii) passive students; and (iv) heavy testing focused curriculum -will first be examined. The paper will then attempt to advance the case for e-learning in China by exploring the conceptual and substantive factors that could promote and influence the success of e-learning mode in China. Learning characteristics of the net generations and

W. Zhou and Y. Mu (Eds.): ICWL 2021, LNCS 13103, pp. 115–126, 2021.
https://doi.org/10.1007/978-3-030-90785-3_10

issues such as the use of education technology to develop students' competency, creativity and critical thinking through problem-based learning and constructivist approaches will be discussed. Throughout, this paper will explore the relationships between the various factors contributing to students' learning in general, and the development of students' higher order thinking skills in particular. The specific question posed to guide the study was: what combination of instructional strategies and delivery media will best produce the desired learning outcome for students? Or more specifically, what combination of content, pedagogy and technology will best develop students' higher-order thinking skills, i.e. synthesis, analysis and creativity. This research is in line with China's current education policy of developing 'key skills' of all its students. Next, let us examine in greater detail how this study will contribute to our understanding of the development of education in China.

1.1 A New Era in China's Education

China's education is presently undergoing an unprecedented period of change. Symbolically, the 4th May 1919 is seen generally as marking the start of modernization in China, characterized by the slogan, Science and Democracy. In 2009, China celebrated the 90th Anniversary of the Educational Reform Movement, and in 2011, the centennial of the founding of the People's Republic of China. There is currently a strong recognition of the need to train the next and future generations to meet the transitional needs of Science, Technology and Society, both in China and globally. Specifically, these needs were addressed in the proposal, Vision for Scientific Excellence, by China's Premier Wen who officially instituted the country's national strategy to counter the global financial crisis – education. It is possible to examine this briefly and consider its implications, which had led to constructive and innovative change in educational practices by permitting schools to develop their ICT capabilities. Specifically, the 12-year Vision for Scientific Excellence places education as the cornerstone of national development and challenges education policymakers to shatter old mindsets and structures and be daring in exploring reforms in school management, pedagogy and assessment (Zhung 2009). China's decision to leverage educational technology carries huge implications for teaching and learning. In Beijing, capital of China, March 6, 2021, at the fourth session of the 13th National Committee of the Chinese People's Political Consultative Conference (CPPCC), President Xi Jinping on Saturday stressed giving "strategic priority" to safeguarding people's health and building a high-quality and balanced basic public education service system. On education, Xi said China must strive to build a high-quality and balanced basic public education service system. To build a high-quality education system, the reform of the evaluation system should be in the lead, so as to push forward reforms in other aspects of education. Given the scope of these recent policies, the following gives an overview of the present situation of schools in China:

1. Central control of school. Schools in China are run by state official, not educators;
2. Large class sizes. Traditional learning of chalk and talk is common. Although according to de Arriba (2017) many teachers are able to man-age these large groups successfully in ways that challenge students' high-level thinking abilities through training and careful listening, and keep the majority involved;

3. Students often passive in classrooms, accepting the burden of heavy homework, limited liking for learning, highly marks-focused (The Program of International Student Assessment 2003);
4. Heavy testing focus, as a control mechanism, not necessarily a learner tool (Melo 2020) In the following reviews of literature, first the seemingly benefits and limitations of e-learning in China is unpacked using varied perspectives. Next, the paper synthesizes current research regarding harnessing e-learning to promote students' creativity and foster engagement in the context of science education. Finally, it identifies the knowledge gap in current research. **Sample Heading (Third Level).** Only two levels of headings should be numbered. Lower level headings remain unnumbered; they are formatted as run-in headings.

2 Literature Review

2.1 Benefits and Limitations of e-Learning

As a way for setting the stage for discussion of supports to e-learning process in China, let us consider issues that promote or hinder its implementations. A substantial body of research has revealed that quality of on-line learning varies greatly. Riis (2017) argues that ordinarily students do not maximize their learning, whereas Alfina and Irfan (2020) suggests that the implementation of learning technology could be counter-productive, as studies have revealed students feeling overwhelmed and alienated by the intimidating learning interfaces. His view is further supported by Srilekshmi (2017) who warned of high drop-out rates among students enrolled in online courses. Cuban reasons that unless that is second order change, i.e. the relationship between learners and teachers – attitudes to people, approaches to knowledge, love/passion for specific subject; the change is only superficial: Innovations have to be absorbed into the systems of practice. (Chen 2021) In relation to educational technology, this predicament has been well-recognized and clearly documented. Too often, in the present author's own view, talk of new teaching techniques and curriculum upgrading fails to have the desired impact because of the lack of a common language and experience needed to understand the concepts, especially when viewed through the cultural lens of traditional Chinese schooling. Teachers schooled and trained in a traditional Chinese system may be more comfortable with learning situations where students prefer (i) to work alone rather than in groups, (ii) not be asked, or ask questions, (iii) to present no over challenges to authority, and (iv) hold the belief that there is not much value in peer discussion (Chang 2021).

On an individual level, Fincheira (2020) lists three major themes that can limit the uptake of an innovation such as the SI/SSE process, by an individual teacher:

1. Teachers work on their own with what they have usually used and focus on the present moment;
2. When change is imposed, it is confusing and threatening;
3. Teachers react to change by actively changing as little as possible (Magen-Nagar 2019).

A Becta report highlighted the importance to build on more interpretative and critical learning strategies, to extend and empower learning by focusing on the following learning strategies:

1. Pictorial representation
2. Note taking/annotation strategies to support higher order cognitive activity
3. Transforming or re-representing information
4. Collaborative and supported learning
5. Probing expertise
6. Self and peer assessment

(Sharif 2018) He argues that to facilitate the success of e-learning, it may be necessary to capitalize on the learners' learning styles. Furdyk high-lighted the following learning characteristics most Net Generations possess, including kids in China:

1. kids engaged in frequent, continuous and increasingly multiprocessing and multi-tasking activities;
2. kids are multi-media literate and highly I.T. savvy;
3. kids preferred discovery-based learning and liked to be challenged by their teachers to create their own products; and
4. kids displayed a bias towards action, to demonstrate their own learning, and to create real world impact.

It is the heart of problem or competence-based education: dynamic, engaging, self-directed, and reflexive, within an open environment, for both teachers and students.

2.2 e-Learning to Develop Students' Higher Order Thinking

The Harnessing Technology Strategy Review indicates: the possibilities ICT offers for teaching and learning are not fully exploited, particularly for creative and collaborative learning opportunities and for personalized, flexible learning (Cinquin 2020). The challenge is to design effective e-learning models that could promote creative and collaborative learning through interaction and interactive activities that are problem and competence-based. At its simplest, e-learning framework can provide an open, interactive, and collaborative environment where learning can be approached in a spirit of discovery and experimentation among students and teachers. After all, developing students' higher order thinking skills, such as creativity, through science education, are imperative in educating students in the Knowledge Age.

As an effective learning framework, e-learning, i.e. learning through the use of computer technology; seems most promising within China's social and political contexts. Laurillard defines instructional strategy as a technique that may be use to capture attention, increase motivation and provide cue to facilitate learning (Sampaio 2016). Therefore by exploring the critical factors that contribute to successful conceptualization and implementation of the use of such instructional strategy and weighing them against the China situation, the proposed model could be adapted to create a more conducive learning environment that cultivates collaboration and interaction among students in China. Biggs defines education technology as harnessing technology namely IT, for more effective teaching (2018). Until quite recently, the use of education technology and instructional strategy is still relatively new inmost educational settings in China. This paper aims to examine the western concept of e-learning as it could be applied in the China setting and context. As e-learning is considered an innovation for the majority of Mainland teachers, there is a possibility that the findings from this study could assist them in their efforts to introduce e-learning approaches, first through understanding the benefits and limitations of e-learning approaches, and their role as facilitators to ensure success. This paper can contribute to the field of e-learning in China.

2.3 Research Gap

In recent years, an emphasis on education technology has become the new requirement for success in teaching and learning. Traditionally, effective teaching has always been dependent on content (curriculum), pedagogy (teaching methods) and assessment (procedures). However, with the ubiquity and availability of educational technology in classrooms the recent years, implications for teaching and learning as a research focus have aroused significant interest. The growing body of literature clearly points to a need to optimize new tools to develop learners' multi-faceted needs, especially increasingly important soft skills such, a screative thinking, innovation and inventiveness. On the other hand, there is a strong evidence that current educational technology research are inadequate as there is apparently a problematic link aligning the use of ICT with curriculum, pedagogy and assessment (Newhouse 2017). Bell et al. argues: Too many researchers have tried to assess the impact of technology on student learning separate from the teacher and the instructional method – or even the content – as if the tool itself could somehow bring about increases in learning. Of the existing studies on educational technology that examines learning outcomes, few specify all three dimensions – pedagogy, content, and technology affordance (Wangyal 2019).

3 Study Context

This longitudinal study focused on high school students (n = 588), consists of two key stages: namely, Stage One and Two. Stage One (2010–2014) was undertaken in urban China, and its follow-up research, Stage Two (2014–2018) to be under taken in rural China. This paper only discussed the preliminary outcomes of the study of Stage One. The e-learning module is developed for high school students (aged 12–16) in urban China, in the learning of science. Blended learning was employed as a supplement to face-to-face teaching. The instructors were dedicated teachers as well those with experience in designing e-learning interfaces, yet given the big class sizes, and heavy testing focus curriculum, faced a greater challenge of inspiring students to be genuine passionate about science.

4 Discussion

4.1 Benefits e-Learning in China

This study explores the relationship between the various factors contributing to students' learning in light of the proposed e-learning approach: that of introducing e-learning in China, as a support to solve problems of large class sizes, students' passivity and heavy testing focus of the curriculum. As this would be a new, school-wide, pioneering effort, it could help Chinese teachers improve their day-to-day teaching; however the most immediate impact is on the student, in term of better understanding of content, increased self-esteem and confidence (Gambhir 2017).The paper argues that the applicability of, and arguments for, the introduction of e-learning in China have been beneficial in six significant ways:

a) Timeliness. With the large class sizes, it seems that the problem could be addressed through the introduction of e-learning modules in schools in China. It is common to find the teacher to student ratio in classrooms in most parts of Mainland China to be from a manageable 1:50, to an unimaginable 1:500, or more. Given this reality, it is only logical for Chinese educationists to leverage Information Communication Technology (ICT). Especially for highly theoretical subjects like science, the need for instructional support is immediate and growing. Whelan (2012) agree with this idea when discussing the use of education technology and their effects on teachers.
b) Appropriateness. E-learning represents an example of the future ways in which teachers will be expected to fulfil their roles as educators, both on personal and institutional basis, using skills as consultation, cooperation and collaboration. The growing acceptance of practices of collegiality through cooperation, collaboration and peer support is changing the traditional view of teaching as a private, individual profession (Banik 2016). Teachers' professional development has been shaped by this trend, where teachers are encouraged to take greater personal and financial responsibility for their own learning, alongside collaborative approaches via team teaching, paired work, observation and reflection (Department of Education and Training Melbourne 2017).

   Such new ways of communicating could prove a challenge to China's teachers, yet could lead to the development of educational technology. Evans and Nations agrees with this when discussing of the continuing significance of educational institutions as a place for helping students to learn and grow intellectually, creating a climate within which scholars can create and test knowledge, and reaching out to enlighten a civilized community (Leicht et al. 2018).
c) Accessibility and Adaptability. Along with a focus on teaching that is flexible, with a less formal approach, e-learning allows for easy ac-cess by all users. A technician could be responsible for managing the e-learning modules, leaving teachers free to avail themselves for face-to-face interactions, genuine interaction between teachers and students could be fostered. Further, the extension of e-learning to a virtual component is possible in China with the rise of internet usage.
d) Usefulness. Once teachers overcome any reluctance to be involved with e-learning environments, they may have the opportunity to experience professional empowerment that results from meeting different learner's needs. However, the effective

use of educational technology is very dependent on the teachers' ability to create meaningful teaching-learning activities and experiences (Zaytseva 2019).

e) Collaborative Learning. Laurillard defines collaborative learning as "'learning in groups where students work together to achieve shared goals" (Sukstrienwong 2017). Another term commonly used is cooperative learning which is "learning in small groups where students work together to achieve shared goals" (Lajoie 2015). Traditional Chinese instruction places emphasis on the lecturer and deep learning through memorization (Lei 2015). On the other hand, collaborative learning benefit teachers as it facilitates groups of teachers to pool together their resources and expertise. It is a question of synergy or building better solutions to problems through professional collaboration. The benefits of increased self-esteem, knowledge and motivation can lead to more effective learners and consequently to results improvement (Dusadee 2020).
f) Facilitator. A 10-year research focused on Joseph Schwab's 'the practical', argues that China's new curriculum reform since 1999 have significantly "transformed the roles (of teachers) from being book-knowledge transmitters to curriculum developers (Cui 2014). To facilitate the success of e-learning in China, it may be necessary for the teacher to be a facilitator rather than an instructor. Unlike traditional structured learning, e-learning puts the onus on the learner to first, acquire independent learning and thinking skills, and subsequently, to apply the acquired skills, knowledge and understanding through purposeful learning outcomes. Besides facilitating an effective learning environment, the teacher should leverage educational technology to enhance learner's creativity and problem-solving skills. Hence, student-centered learning that characterize e-learning can develop in ways that actively engages students, promotes independent enquiry and self-directed learning (Al 2019).

4.2 Technology Alignment, Integration and Convergence

As mentioned, current educational technology research are inadequate as there is apparently a problematic link aligning the use of ICT with content and pedagogy. The seminal paper,

"Technological Pedagogical Content Know-ledge (TPACK): A Framework for Teachers Knowledge, by Mishra and Koehler, de-scribes "the complex role of, and the interplay among the three main components of learning environment: content, pedagogy, and tech-nology" (Kurt 2019), in great depth, and is graphically simplified in Fig. 1 and 2.

What are the implications? Firstly, e-learning resources need to be carefully designed to maximize learning. Instructional designers need to be knowledgeable about issues of curriculum and pedagogies; aligning technology with both content and pedagogy, as shown graphically in Fig. 3 and (Fig. 4).

Secondly, e-learning resources should leverage technology's multimedia features. The aim is to subsequently achieve technological convergence, as shown graphically in Fig. 5.

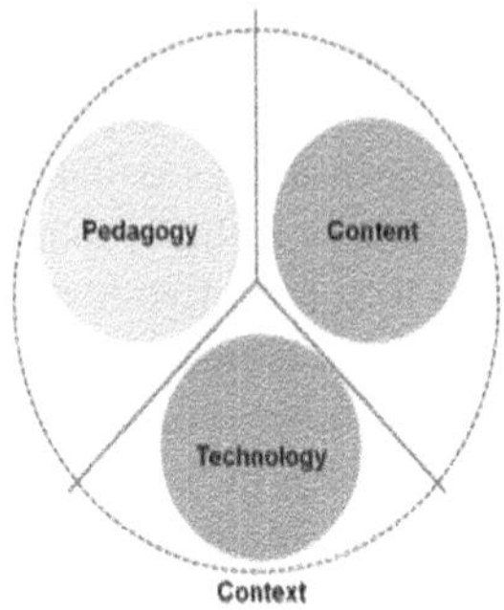

Fig. 1. What doesn't work

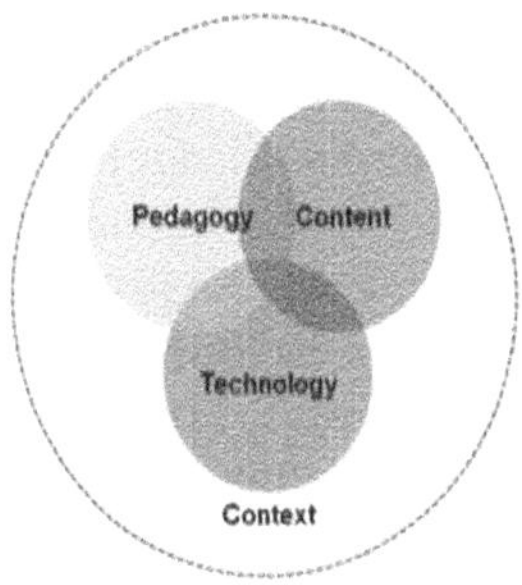

Fig. 2. What works

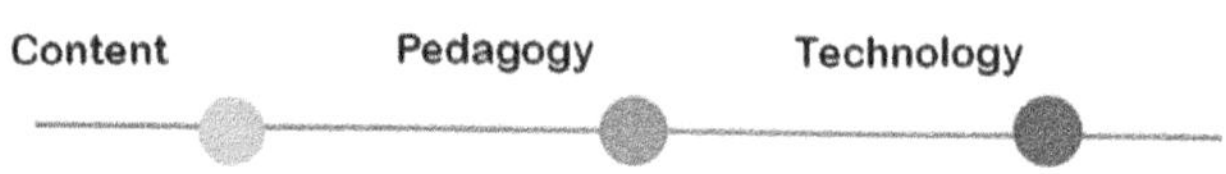

Fig. 3. Technology alignment (Tan 2011)

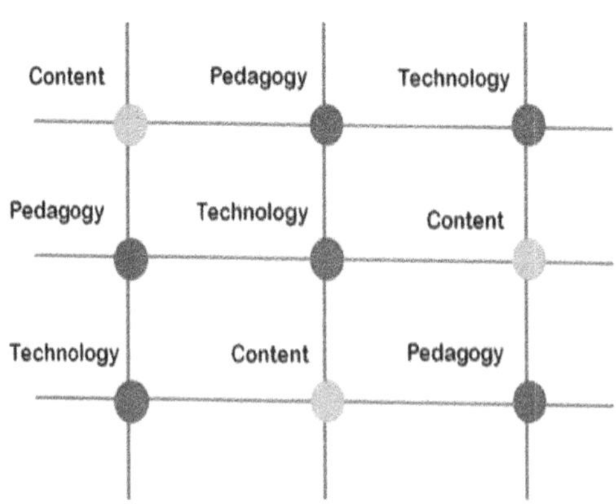

Fig. 4. Technology integration (Tan 2011)

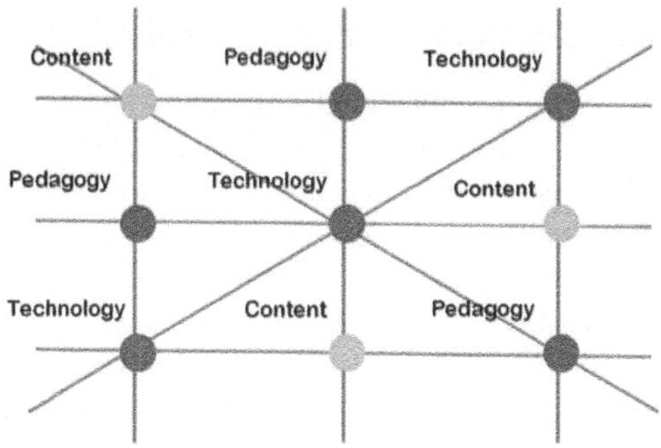

Fig. 5. Technology convergence (Tan 2011)

Thirdly, the study so far reveals the real challenge for any instructional designer is to design learning resources that are easy to experience, sensible, and design around the user. Perhaps the most important lesson is the challenge offered to instructional designers to design learning interfaces that develops students' higher-order thinking skills: synthesis, analysis, flexibility, adaptability and creativity.

Next, what else can be achieved in China as compared to what has already been done? There are basically three areas. The first is to set up a strong education infrastructure throughout China. Concretely, the state's Education Bureau has encouraged IT use by equipping staffrooms with computers, and many students are connected with the internet in China, thus, it is conceivable to offer e-learning through a virtual component. Salar (2021) suggest simple ways to add this, such as interactive lesson plan templates, multimedia databases, podcasts, web-conferencing, chat-rooms, and e-mail to enhance ongoing professional collaboration. These services can be amalgamated through such programs as Moodle. The advantage of such systems is that they can be extended to teacher networks around the world, thus offering teachers and students a much wider and more innovative learning base than is traditionally available (Fig. 6).

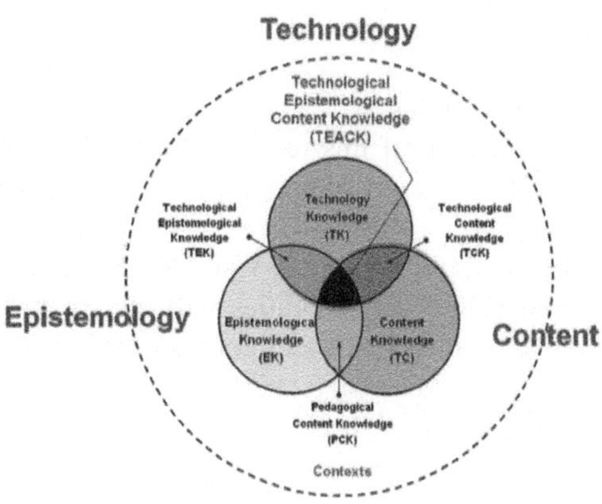

Fig. 6. Technology epistemological content knowledge (TEACK) – a framework for students' knowledge (Tan 2011)

4.3 TECK – A Framework for Student's Knowledge

Finally, the paper proposes a conceptual model of an 'epistemic learning innovation' – a framework for learners knowledge. Building on Shulman's Pedagogical Content Knowledge (PACK) which focuses on "what teachers should know and be able to do", and Mishra and Koehler's Technological Pedagogical Content Knowledge (TPACK) which focuses, among others, on the dynamics of technology integration, as well as the complex role of teachers to ensure high quality instruction through online teaching. The concept of Technological Epistemological Content Knowledge (TEACK) focuses on the end-user of any online instruction, i.e. the learner. What the learner should know and be able to do is crucial, if not, the raison d'être for any good teaching. In examining how learners should be prepared to learn in online environments in the Knowledge Age, TEACK addresses the three domain areas needed to ensure deep and strategic learning approaches to achieve positive learning outcomes. This lens offers a way to examine students' knowledge about their understanding of their own learning, specifically: personal conceptions of learning, epistemological beliefs (Frisque 2017), and intrinsic learning orientations. In a nutshell, TEACK is the integration of the development of learners' beliefs and attitudes with the use of educational technology and how they impact the learning content. The proposed framework probably needs further study to understand whether, and to what extent, student varied knowledge, i.e. 'Technological Epistemological Content Knowledge (TEACK)', are impacted by the interplay among the three main components of learning environment: content, pedagogy, and technology. It definitely warrants further investigation to fully understand what factors truly makes students 'TEACK'?

4.4 Limitations of the Study

There are several limitations to this preliminary study:

The longitudinal study consists of two key stages: namely, Stage One and Two. This paper only discussed the preliminary outcomes of Stage One.

As mentioned, the e-learning module is developed for first-year high school students (aged 12–13) in urban China. It is unsure if the results can be generalized to similar aged students in rural China.

There are important implications:

A major practical implication of this research to this field of enquiry will be to highlight the potential of e-learning environments to the teaching and learning of science in schools in China.

The implications of China's recent policy, Vision for Scientific Excellence, encouraging schools to develop their ICT capabilities will require further research – both qualitative and quantitative -as it represents a significant top-down innovative education policy in China.

5 Conclusion

The paper has explored critical social and political factors, both beneficial and limiting, affecting the use of e-learning in China, and to solve China's education system problems, such as its (i) central control of schools; (ii) large class sizes; (iii) passive students; and (iv) heavy testing focused curriculum among others. The proposed conceptual framework.

'Technological Epistemological Content Knowledge (TEACK) could potentially meet the needs of developing Chinese National Science Curriculum. To an extent, this study has shown the potential of e-learning as a sustainable learning strategy in China. The use and design of e-learning science resources represents a paradigm shift for China teachers and students. To a substantial degree, this exploratory study has provided new insights into the ways in which the use of ICT can bring about improvements in Chinese schools.

References

Alfina, Irfan, R.: Analysis of E-learning implementation using human organization technology approach (HOT) fit models. In: Journal of Physics: Conference Series, vol. 1456, p. 012058, 10 p. (2020)

Leicht, A., Heiss, J., Byun, W.J.: Issues and Trends in Education for Sustainable Development, pp. 18–23 (2018)

Banik, G.: Strategies and techniques for new tenure-track faculty to become successful in Academia (2016). Reference no. 12

Chang, Q.: A survey of attitudes toward mediation among Chinese EFL teachers and their classroom constraints. In: MSCI 2018 – Proceedings of the 12th International Multi-Conference on Society, Cybernetics and Informatics, vol. 2018, no. 2, pp. 135–139 (2021)

Chen, Q.: Exploiting digitalization for the coordination of required changes to improve engineer-to-order materials flow management. Constr. Innov. (2021). Reference no. 58

Cinquin, P.A.: Designing accessible MOOCs to expand educational opportunities for persons with cognitive impairments. Behav. Inf. Technol. **40**(11), 1101–1119 (2020). Article no. 20201308334526

De Arriba, R.: Participation and collaborative learning in large class sizes: wiki, can you help me? Innov. Educ. Teach. Int. **54**(4), 364–373 (2017)

Dusadee, N., Piriyasurawong, P., Nilsook, P., Wannapiroon, P.: Professional learning community training model through cloud technology to enhance competence learning management teacher. In: Auer, M.E., Hortsch, H., Sethakul, P. (eds.) ICL 2019. AISC, vol. 1135, pp. 764–777. Springer, Cham (2019). https://doi.org/10.1007/978-3-030-40271-6_75

Frisque, B.: Conducting a social constructivist epistemology for students of computing disciplines. In: 2017 IEEE Frontiers in Education Conference (FIE) (2017). Reference no. YXB7-1903-445

Fincheira, P.: Current applications of nanotechnology to develop plant growth inducer agents as an innovation strategy. Crit. Rev. Biotechnol. **40**(1), 15–30 (2020)

Department of Education and Training Melbourne: High Impact Teaching Strategies: Excellence in Teaching and Learning, pp. 5–18 (2017)

The University of Hong Kong Press, p. 24 (2007)

Gambhir, V.K.: Social Return on Investment (SROI) for Hindustan Unilever's (HUL) CSR initiative on livelihoods (Prabhat). Procedia Comput. Sci. **122**, 556–563 (2017)

Harrison, C.: e-learning technology: convergence with the mainstream. In: Weert, T.J., Munro, R.K. (eds.) Informatics and the Digital Society. ITIFIP, vol. 116, pp. 37–50. Springer, Boston, MA (2003). https://doi.org/10.1007/978-0-387-35663-1_4

Lajoie, S.P.: The role of regulation in medical student learning in small groups: regulating oneself and others' learning and emotions. Comput. Hum. Behav. **52**, 601–616 (2015)

Tian Lei, X., Liu, L.W., Chen, T., Wang, Y., Xiong, L., Wei, S.: The impact of natural utilization of traditional Chinese cultural elements on the user experience in mobile interaction design. In: Patrick Rau, P.L. (ed.) CCD 2015. LNCS, vol. 9181, pp. 46–56. Springer, Cham (2015). https://doi.org/10.1007/978-3-319-20934-0_5

Abuqadumah, M.M.A.: Deep transfer learning for human identification based on footprint: a comparative study. Periodicals Eng. Nat. Sci. **7**(3), 1300–1307 (2019)

Nagar, N.: Changing the learning environment: teachers and students' collaboration in creating digital games. J. Inf. Technol. Educ. Innov. Pract. **18**, 61–85 (2019)

Melo, S.M.: Testing education: a survey on a global scale. In: Proceedings of the 34th Brazilian Symposium on Software Engineering, pp. 554–563 (2020)

Newhouse, C.P.: Stem the boredom: engage students in the Australian curriculum using ICT with problem-based learning and assessment. J. Sci. Educ. Technol. **26**, 44–57 (2017). https://doi.org/10.1007/s10956-016-9650-4

Riis, J.O.: Dealing with complex and ill-structured problems: results of a Plan-Do-Check-Act experiment in a business engineering semester. Eur. J. Eng. Educ. **42**(4), 396–412 (2017)

Salar, H.C.: Online (virtual) exhibitions application in education. DESIDOC J. Libr. Inf. Technol. **33**(3), 176–182 (2021)

Sampaio, D.: Pedagogical strategies for the integration of augmented reality in ICT teaching and learning processes. Procedia Comput. Sci. **100**, 894–899 (2016)

Kurt, S.: TPACK: technological pedagogical content knowledge framework, pp. 1–6. Educational Technology (2019)

Nauman, S.: Metadata features evaluation for Twitter based e-learning recommendation. In: Proceedings of the 34th Information Systems Education Conference, ISECON 2018, pp. 109–116 (2018)

Al, S.S.: Problem based learning: a student-centered approach. Engl. Lang. Teach. **12**(5), 73–78 (2019)

Srilekshmi, M.: Learning analytics to identify students at-risk in MOOCs. In: Proceedings of the IEEE 8th International Conference on Technology for Education, T4E 2016, pp 194–199, 11 January 2017

Sukstrienwong, A.: A genetic-algorithm approach for balancing learning styles and academic attributes in heterogeneous grouping of students. Int. J. Emerg. Technol. Learn. **12**(3), 4–25 (2017)

Tan, C.S.: An innovative nexus – bridging technological pedagogical content knowledge (TPACK) with technological spistemological content knowledge (TEACK): a learners' framework. Paper Submitted to Ubiquitous Learning: A International Conference, California, United States, 11–14 September 2011 (2011)

Wangyal, T.: An affordance based design framework for technology-enabled learning spaces, pp. 598–602 (2019)

Whelan, E.: Changing the introductory is course to improve future enrollments: an irish perspective. J. Inf. Syst. Educ. **23**(4), 395–406 (2012)

Cui, Y.: Curriculum reforms in China: history and the present day. In: International Review of Sèvres Education Symposium: Education in Asia in 2014: What are the Challenges Global?, pp. 1–6 (2014)

Zaytseva, T.: Computer modelling of educational process as the way to modern learning technologies. In: ICTERI 2019 - Proceedings of the 15th International Conference on ICT in Education, Research and Industrial Applications. Integration, Harmonization and Knowledge Transfer. Volume II: Workshops, pp. 849–863 (2019)

Online Learning Privacy Issues and Special Tools

Security and Privacy in E-learning

Weigong Feng[1,2](✉), Wennan Wang[1], and Fengling Wang[1,3]

[1] Institute of Data Science, City University of Macau, Macao 999078, China
[2] Beijing Institute of Technology, Zhuhai 519000, China
[3] Hezhou University, Hezhou, Guangxi 542899, China

Abstract. E-learning has the advantages of flexible and diverse learning methods, and the high-quality teaching resources can be shared without limitation by time and space, it has been developed rapidly. Especially after the outbreak of the COVID-19, World began to widely replace traditional classroom teaching with E-learning methods, it leading to an explosive growth. During the use of E-learning, many security problems and privacy leakages have occurred. In This paper, we have analyzed the four main security threats faced by E-learning, summarized the current main research results and gave corresponding countermeasures and suggestions, which have certain positive significance for improving the security and privacy in E-learning.

Keywords: E-learning system · Data security · Communication safety · Virus prevention · Intrusion defense

1 Introduction

E-learning refers to the use of computers or other smart devices and Internet technology to use certain methods to teach in a virtual space online. E-learning systems have the advantages of flexible learning forms, diverse learning methods, and high-quality teaching resources that can be widely disseminated. In the past two years, especially in the context of the global COVID-19 pandemic, there is a great demand for E-learning and online meetings, leading to an explosive growth. E-learning platforms include ZOOM, MOOC, Tencent Class, NetEase Cloud Class, Litchi Micro Class, etc. Although they have corresponding privacy protection protocols and measures, they still have security issues and the privacy leakage risks in the application process. So the research on the security and privacy protection of E-learning is of great practical significance.

2 Main Threats Facing E-learning

E-learning are faced with the risk of man-made, natural or external intrusions, which are specifically reflected in:

W. Zhou and Y. Mu (Eds.): ICWL 2021, LNCS 13103, pp. 129–133, 2021.
https://doi.org/10.1007/978-3-030-90785-3_11

2.1 Computer Virus Attacks

Computer viruses will cause different degrees of damages to the computer or network, including disrupting normal operations, deleting data, occupying system resources, stealing privacy, automatically restarting the computer, crashing, and freezing, etc. In the large-scale E-learning carried out since 2020, virus infections have often occurred, Therefore, virus attacks are one of the main threats to the security of E-learning platforms.

2.2 Data Leakage of E-learning Platforms

E-learning platforms hold huge amounts of data which are related to personal privacy. If these data or part of the data are leaked, attackers can obtain a large amount of personal private information through data analysis and mining. If this information is used to infringe upon others, it will inevitably have a serious impact on the people involved. Recently, there have been many incidents of data leakage from online teaching platforms. Therefore, it is very necessary to take corresponding measures to protect the data of E-learning platforms.

2.3 Risks of Online Communication

E-learning is a way of classroom teaching and knowledge dissemination through PC, mobile phone, PAD, Internet, wireless network and so on. Due to the openness and complexity of the system, it inevitably has some defects and vulnerabilities, such as protocol vulnerabilities, hardware vulnerabilities, and system vulnerabilities. Therefore, the network communication security in E-learning is also one of the key topics of research.

2.4 Illegal Invasion

Illegal intrusion is leading to the destruction of the availability, confidentiality and integrity of the system or network. From the beginning of E-learning practice, it can be seen that illegal intrusions have occurred from time to time, and there are diversified ways of intrusions. Therefore, in the face of the new complex environment, traditional intrusion detection is not suitable for direct deployment, and a new solution should be designed to deal with illegal intrusions.

3 Countermeasures

3.1 Virus Detection and Removal

Computer virus detection technologies are mainly divided into two types, one is to establish virus detection based on the feature classification. The other is a detection technology that does not target the viruses themselves. Antivirus software can detect the existence of computer viruses, prevent infection and damage caused by the viruses, and repair programs infected by viruses. At present, the mainstream domestic antivirus software includes Rising Antivirus, 360 Antivirus, Norton Internet Security Guardian, etc. Anti-virus software is mainly used to prevent the harms caused by viruses, and firewall software can be used to prevent hacker attacks. In order to prevent illegal platform data access and maintain the security of the system, E-learning systems should install anti-virus software in the terminals, and set up firewall software between the system and the Internet. Regular maintenance and upgrades are also necessary.

3.2 Solutions of E-learning Data Security

One of the security technologies can be used in E-learning data security is data encryption. Since the teaching platform terminals include devices with limited computing capacity and storage space, lightweight cryptography can be used to provide security protection. The method of digital signature can provide security performance which is difficult to achieve by other methods. The elliptic curve digital signature algorithm has the characteristics of high computational efficiency, so it is widely accepted in many applications with short key lengths. Such typical lightweight password protection technologies be adopted for the data or part of the data in E-learning platforms.

In terms of copyright protection, data authorization management is one of the main strategies to reduce the copyright risk of E-learning. In terms of student privacy and trust. Deraw [1] proposed solutions to the security vulnerabilities of Moodle, an open-source E-learning platform. Amor AB et al. [2] proposed a security fog E-learning solution, achieve the effects of data confidentiality, fine-grained access control, anti-collusion in exams, high efficiency and low encryption cost. Banerjee et al. [3] proposed an E-learning system security model based on the Unified Modeling Language (UML) to ensure the trust and security among participants in the E-learning system.

In terms of data statistics and release, a differential privacy mechanism can be used, it can ensure that the statistical characteristics of the data set remain unchanged, while protecting the privacy of the users. In terms of data identification in the process of E-learning, blockchain technology can be adopted. Combining blockchain technology with E-learning platforms will be the future trend.

3.3 Communication Security Protocol of E-learning

IP security (IPsec) is an open standard of IP network security. It provides a security strategy for each IP data packet transmitted from the source to the destination, and provides a security performance in the communication on LAN, WAN, and Internet. Another security encryption protocol is the Transport Layer Security (TLS), which can provide a complete set of digital certificate-based identity authentication and data encryption solutions. Hyper Text Transfer Protocol over Secure Socket Layer (HTTPS) provides methods of identity verification and encrypted communication, and is widely applied in security-sensitive communications on the World Wide Web. Secure Shell (SSH) can effectively prevent information leakage in the process of remote management. The security of E-learning platforms may also involve the security of the wireless network. The main threats faced by wireless transmission are eavesdropping, modification of messages, insertion of messages, and damages. The security countermeasures against eavesdropping are signal hiding technology and encryption; the standard methods for dealing with attacks of modification or inserting are encryption and authentication protocols;

the technologies against DOS attacks include prevention, detection, filtering, tracking, and identification.

3.4 Intrusion Prevention Technologies

Intrusion detection technology is currently one of the core technologies for network security defense It is an active defense technology that can effectively prevent unknown attacks. It is a necessary supplement to the firewall, and the two together constitute a complete solution of network security. H Ibrahim [4] put forward the idea of using firewall, biometric authentication, data encryption and digital rights management to build an E-learning database management system to cope with network security challenges.

Intrusion detection technology can detect attacks, send alarms, and form logs, while intrusion prevention system (IPS) can conduct real-time active detection, prevent intrusions and attacks from occurring. IPS integrates firewall technology and intrusion detection technology. IPS can be divided into host-based intrusion prevention system (HIPS) and network-based intrusion prevention system (NIPS). HIPS can monitor file operation and registry modification in the host, and make requests for permission. It represents a trend in the development of system security, which can prevent information tampering, Trojan horse backdoor attacks, process termination, etc. But HIPS cannot prevent other computers on the network from attacking the host; NIPS can provide various functions of attack detection and defense, accurately identify network traffic, reduce the rate of false reports and under-reports, and can meet high-performance requirements, guarantee the quality of normal network communication. Nowadays, in the context of increasing threats of viruses, worms, Trojan horses, spyware, DDOS, and hacker attacks, E-learning platforms should deploy intrusion prevention systems in a timely manner based on their actual conditions.

4 Suggestions

E-learning security is a systemic issue, and only a robust security mechanism can ensure the safe operation of the teaching system. For different risks of the E-learning, different protection methods can be adopted. The traditional method of password login has high security risks; Therefore, third-party authentication, dynamic password authentication, or face recognition should be used to improve security. At the same time, platforms must have mechanisms to defend against viruses, Trojan horses, and various types of attacks, and constantly improve their defense capabilities.

Platform developers should regard security and privacy protection as part of system development, continuously enhance the security performance of the system. In the process of platform development and use, they should do a good job in the security maintenance of the platform, and conduct timely inspections and updates. Relevant administrative authorities should establish and improve relevant legal systems and establish a complete legislation system of network safety. Users of E-learning platforms should do a good job in the safety management of the terminal equipment, deal with the security incidents of the terminal equipment in a timely manner, use the E-learning platform in a reasonable and normative manner, thus jointly creating a safe and stable teaching and learning environment.

References

1. Derawi, M.: Securing e-learning platforms. In: International Conference on Web and Open Access to Learning, IEEE (2015)
2. Amor, A.B., Abid, M., Meddeb, A.: Secure Fog-Based E-Learning Scheme. IEEE Access **8**, 31920–31933 (2020)
3. Banerjee, S.: Designing a secure model of an e-learning system—a UML-based approach. IEEE Potentials **29**(5), 22–27 (2010)
4. Ibrahim, H., Karabatak, S., Abdullahi, A.: A study on cybersecurity challenges in e-learning and database management system. In: 2020 8th International Symposium on Digital Forensics and Security (ISDFS), IEEE (2020)

Digitalization of Firm's Innovation Process - A Bibliometric Analysis

Zornitsa Yordanova(✉)

University of National and World Economy, Sofia, Bulgaria
zornitsayordanova@unwe.bg

Abstract. Innovation process is a critical business process in any organization. Being a horizontal process impacting the whole organization, its standardization, automation, and further digitalization is reckoning a serious challenge for innovative organizations. In this research, we are conducting a bibliometric analysis in order to reveal the current understanding and application of digitalization as a concept within the firm's innovation process. The research is based on 81 high-quality publications indexed in the Scopus database. Several bibliometric analyses have taken place to disclose the current state of the art and to reveal the knowledge gap in the field of digitalization of the firm's innovation process. The results contribute to the digital transformation and innovation management theories as well as to scholars and practitioners working on optimizing the innovation performance on firm's level.

Keywords: Digitalization · Innovation process · Digital transformation · Innovation management · Bibliometric analysis

1 Introduction and Motivation

What the potentials of digitalizing the innovation process are is on focus in this study. Digitalization has already proven its values in business process management [1]. Still, many companies do not have a clear plan on how to approach it [2]. Innovation process is amongst the most cardinal business process in an enterprise impacting all others. This is mainly backed by the crucial role of innovation for any kind of organizations since it has been accepted as a strong means of leadership, competitiveness and profit. From another hand, digitalization would also provide much more data which could be analysed and involved within the process for decision making and innovation sustainability. This data could also improve the performance of assessments of innovation which has been identified in the literature as a knowledge gap from many scholars [3].

The increasing number of publications examining digitalization [4] reflects on out motivation to examine the possibilities of digitalization of one of the most critical for the success of a business organization process – the innovation process. As it has been largely discussed in the literature, organizations would innovate more rapidly if they incrementally improve their innovation processes [5]. This is what we strive to contribute to with this research - to extend the vision for innovation process improvement with the

W. Zhou and Y. Mu (Eds.): ICWL 2021, LNCS 13103, pp. 134–141, 2021.
https://doi.org/10.1007/978-3-030-90785-3_12

means of digitalization. For doing so, we conduct a bibliometric analysis in order to reveal the currently application of the concept of digitalization and digital transformation in innovation process.

2 Theoretical Background

2.1 Firm's Innovation Process

The firm's innovation process is a complex coordination of activities, organization of resources, pursuing goals and strive for leadership and competitiveness [6]. It can also be considered as an organized and controlled sequence of activities in which inputs in form of innovation ideas or problem statement are transformed into outputs in form of innovations [7]. From strategical and managerial perspective, the innovation process is amongst the essential business process in organizations which directly influence to firm's profits [8]. A common definition of the firm's innovation process is missing in the literature, as it is quite complex, as well as specific to the firm's sector and approach of application [9].

Amongst the most important features of the firm's innovation process is identified to be the need of gathering information from and transmit information to several internal and external information areas within and out of the organization [10]. Digitalization provides promising automations and tools to support and improve these process [11].

2.2 Digitalization of Business Processes and Innovation Process

Digital technologies have become an increasingly important particle of several functional areas of firms and in most of the cases – a goal for an organizational transformation and project releases. The wide use of digital technologies allows extensive collaboration between the participants in the firm's innovation process, provides a tool for managing team efforts, assists competitive advantages, optimizes the use and organization of resources, and also enhances coordination and communication [12].

In most organizations, digitalization of innovation process is still in its begging – at the first stage of innovation: idea management. Being able to accumulate and put into action external ideas would boost innovation processes and its digitalization [13].

3 Research Methods

3.1 Data Extraction and Scope Definition

The scope of this research was set by a Boolean search in the Scopus database for extracting high-quality publications [14] on the matters of digitalization and innovation process in the same time. The formula used was the following:

TITLE-ABS-KEY ("innovation process" AND "digitalization" OR "digitalisation") AND (LIMIT-TO (LANGUAGE, "English")).

We did not apply any limitation since the search aimed at focusing on clear targeted research on both innovation process and its digitalization. The search resulted in 84 publications in English from 2005 until 2021. Three (3) publications were removed because they were not research-based but conference reviews and a book. The scope was established on 81 publications from 64 sources. The conference papers were not removed on purpose since many of the newly developed and experimental research as well as case studies were published specifically in such type of publications. These are basic details about the publications in scope (Table 1).

Table 1. Publication types in scope

Document types	Amount of publications
Article	39
Book chapter	7
Conference paper	35

These are the sources that publish the most on the topic: E3S WEB OF CONFERENCES – 3; EUROPEAN JOURNAL OF INNOVATION MANAGEMENT – 3; IFIP ADVANCES IN INFORMATION AND COMMUNICATION TECHNOLOGY – 3; LECTURE NOTES IN NETWORKS AND SYSTEMS – 3; ACM INTERNATIONAL CONFERENCE PROCEEDING SERIES – 2; ADVANCES IN INTELLIGENT SYSTEMS AND COMPUTING – 2; AMCIS 2017 – AMERICA'S CONFERENCE ON INFORMATION SYSTEMS: A TRADITION OF INNOVATION – 2; DIRECCION Y ORGANIZACION – 2; INTERNATIONAL JOURNAL OF ADVANCED SCIENCE AND TECHNOLOGY – 2; JOURNAL OF OPEN INNOVATION: TECHNOLOGY MARKET AND COMPLEXITY – 2; JOURNAL OF PHYSICS: CONFERENCE SERIES – 2; JOURNAL OF SMALL BUSINESS AND ENTREPRENEURSHIP – 2; SUSTAINABILITY – 2.

Countries which are most active in research digitalization of the innovation process (based on authors) are: Germany (3100, Italy (11), Finland (9), Ukraine (8), Spain (7), Australia (5) and Denmark (5). The next figure reveals the hugely increasing trend of publication in this area (the dataset was set on April 2021, which explains the decrease in the last year but if it is calculated on an annual base, it would also prove the trend).

3.2 Bibliometric Analysis

Bibliometric analysis was introduced as a systematically proven type of research by Pritchard [15] and is currently considered one of the most effective scientific methods for understanding the research field from a historical, holistic and interdisciplinary perspective [16]. Bibliometric analysis facilitates the mapping of current research done as well as identifies knowledge gaps, streams of research already done, authors information, and recognizes further research agenda [17]. This method is widely used in the domain of digitalization and innovation [18]. Bibliometric analysis is an effective method to explore the emergence of a research domain [19] and has the power to monitor the research status of a particular domain and forecasting future research trends [20].

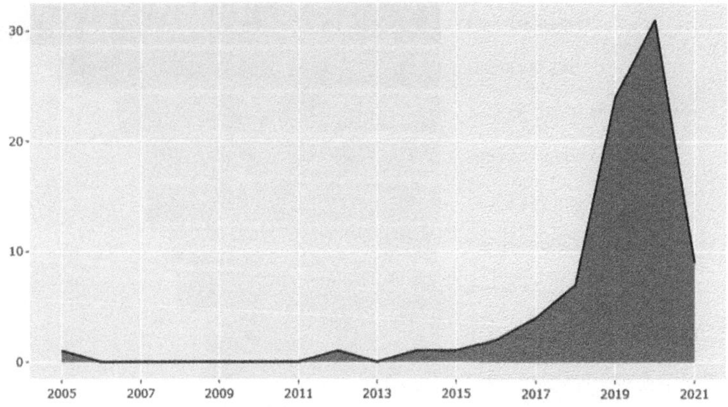

Fig. 1. Publications trend on digitalization of innovation process

In this study, we applied the following bibliometric analysis to address the core topic of digitalization of the firm's innovation process:

- Wave analysis – three-plot (countries, sources, keywords, journal labelling)
- Citation analysis
- Keywords analysis
- Top-tier Journals
- Country of research analysis

For the purpose of bibliometric analysis, R software has been used and its package biblioshiny in particular.

4 Research and Discussion

Digital transformation as a central motor for digitalizing business processes, has been a focus of a research of digitalization of business model innovation in innovation labs in European banks [21]. This research contributes to the theory with implications for how managers could design innovation process to support organizations to engage effectively their employees, ideas, communications channels and interactions within processes.

The most cited sources in the area of digitalization of innovation process are amongst the primary sources in the field of Technology and Innovation Management (a SJR search proved the statement). These are presented on Fig. 1.

The country publication production (based on authors of research) is presented on Fig. 2 and pinpoints Germany (31), Italy (11), Finland (9) on top 3 on the matters. Since Germany and Italy (along with Denmark, Finland which are in the first 10 in this criterion) are amongst the most innovative countries in Europe, searching digitalization of the innovative process specifically from these two countries directs the research agenda for all other innovation-following countries (Fig. 3).

On the next figure, we are presenting a three-fields plot on sources of publication, keywords and countries of the publication origin (Fig. 4).

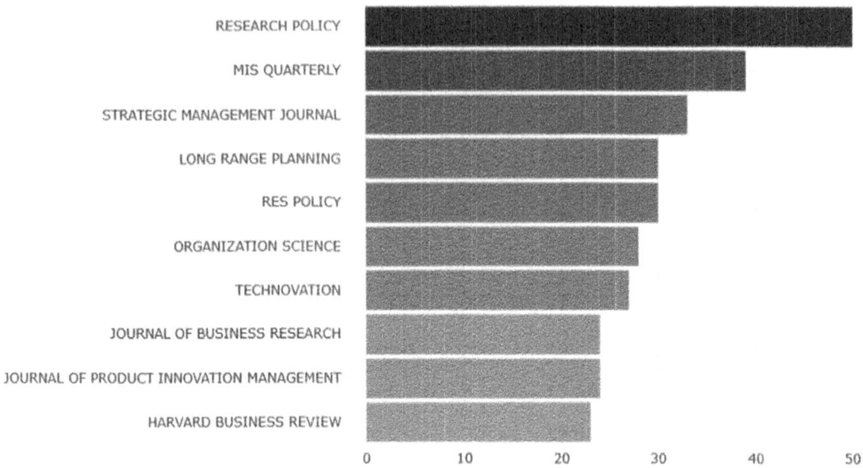

Fig. 2. Most cited sources in publications dealing with Digitalization of firm's innovation process

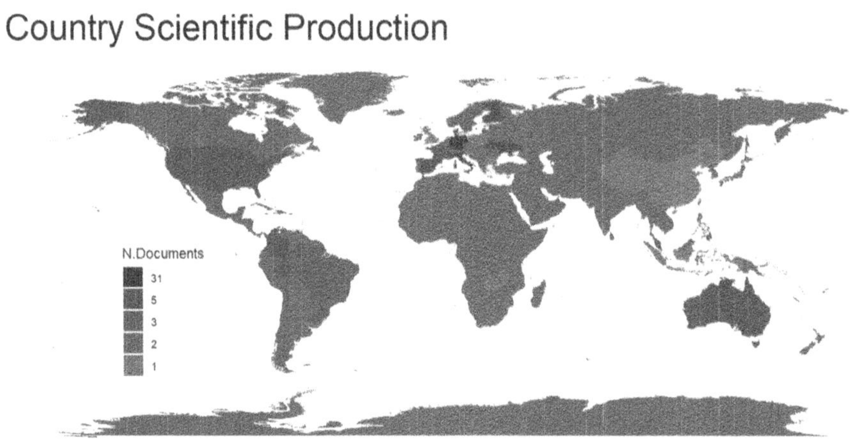

Fig. 3. Country of origin of publications on digitalization of firm's innovation process

The results show that the largest amount of research was done on digitalization as a core keyword which word was a centre of research of all countries producing the most publications on the matters. 40% of digitalization research on the line of innovation process was done by German scientists and 40% of them dealing with the theme were directly engaged to digitalization (other research allocates on innovation technology, open innovation, digital transformation and Industry 4.0).

A most frequently used words' analysis is presented on Table 2.

From the keyword analysis, based on the described data set focusing on both digitalization and innovation process, we can conclude that innovation process is still a focus

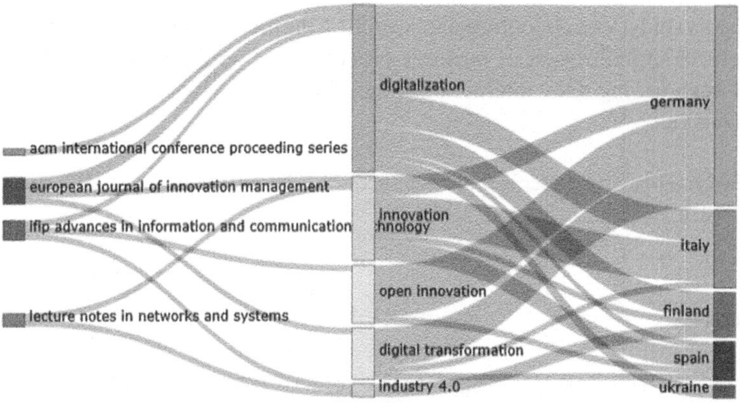

Fig. 4. Three-fields plot: sources of publication, keywords and countries of the publication origin

Table 2. Keywords analysis

Author keywords	Frequency
Innovation process	14
Digitalization	10
Information systems	6
Innovation	6
Digital transformation	5
Business models	4
Competition	4
Digitization	4

of research in digitalization and not the contrary. Still, other keywords (out of innovation and digitalization) reveal niches for further research such as: business models and competition.

5 Conclusion

In conclusion, this study provides contribution to the field of digital transformation and digitalization of innovation process in specific. Main research streams, authors, sources and countries performing research are identified. These are Germany, Italy, Finland and Spain. Most frequent keywords used, out of the centrally scoped digitalization and innovation process are 'business models' and 'competition'. The core topic of this research is surely a hot one since most of the research citations come from top-tier journals in the field of Technology and Innovation Management such as Research Policy, MIS quarterly, Technovation, Journal of product innovation research, etc.

With this study, we call for further research on the themes concerning different knowledge areas of digitalization of business processes being impacted by emerging technologies such as: big data, internet of things, business analytics, artificial intelligence, blockchain, etc.

Acknowledgments. The paper is supported by UNWE NI-NID 09/2021 and BG NSF Grant No KP-06 OPR01/3-2018.

References

1. Baiyere, A., Salmela, H., Tapanainen, T.: Digital transformation and the new logics of business process management. Eur. J. Inf. Syst. **29**(3), 238–259 (2020). https://doi.org/10.1080/0960085X.2020.1718007
2. Fischer, M., Imgrund, F., Janiesch, C., Winkelmann, A.: Strategy archetypes for digital transformation: defining meta objectives using business process management. Inf. Manag. **57**(5), 103262 (2020). https://doi.org/10.1016/j.im.2019.103262
3. Dewangan, V., Godse, M.: Towards a holistic enterprise innovation performance measurement system. Technovation **34**(9), 536–545 (2014)
4. Hausberg, J.P., Liere-Netheler, K., Packmohr, S., Pakura, S., Vogelsang, K.: Research streams on digital transformation from a holistic business perspective: a systematic literature review and citation network analysis. J. Bus. Econ. **89**(8–9), 931–963 (2019). https://doi.org/10.1007/s11573-019-00956-z
5. Benner, M., Tushman, M.: Process management and technological innovation: a lon-gitudinal study of the photography and paint industries. Sci. Q. **47**, 676–706 (2002)
6. Teece, D.J.: Competition, cooperation, and innovation: organizational arrangements for regimes of rapid technological progress. J. Econ. Behav. Organ. **18**(1), 1–25 (1992). https://doi.org/10.1016/0167-2681(92)90050-L
7. Lendel, V., Hittmár, Š., Siantová, E.: Management of innovation processes in company. Procedia Econ. Fin. **23**, 861–866 (2015). https://doi.org/10.1016/S2212-5671(15)00382-2
8. Galanakis, K.: Innovation process make sense using systems thinking. Technovation **26**(11), 1222–1232 (2006). https://doi.org/10.1016/j.technovation.2005.07.002
9. Becheikh, N., Landry, R., Amara, N.: Lessons from innovation empirical studies in the manufacturing sector: A systematic review of the literature from 1993–2003. Technovation **26**(5–6), 644–664 (2006). https://doi.org/10.1016/j.technovation.2005.06.016
10. Tushman, M.L.: Special boundary roles in the innovation process. Adm. Sci. Q. **22**(4), 587 (1977). https://doi.org/10.2307/2392402
11. Chirumalla, K.: Building digitally-enabled process innovation in the process industries: a dynamic capabilities approach. Technovation 102256 (2021). https://doi.org/10.1016/j.technovation.2021.102256
12. Bykovskaya, E.N., Kharchilava, G.P., Kafiyatullina, Yu.N.: Modern trends of digitalization of innovation process. Upravlenie. 2018;6(1):38–43. (In Russ.) https://doi.org/10.26425/2309-3633-2018-1-38-43
13. Apostolov, M., Coco, N.: Digitalization-based innovation — a case study framework. J. Int. J. Innov. Technol. Manag. **18**, 2050025 (2021). https://doi.org/10.1142/S021987702050025X
14. Meho, L.I., Rogers, Y.: Citation counting, citation ranking, andh-index of human-computer interaction researchers: a comparison of Scopus and Web of Science. J. Am. Soc. Inform. Sci. Technol. **59**(11), 1711–1726 (2008). https://doi.org/10.1002/asi.20874
15. Pritchard, A.: Statistical bibliography or bibliometrics. J. Document. **25**, 348–349 (1969)

16. Caviggioli, F., Ughetto, E.: A bibliometric analysis of the research dealing with the impact of additive manufacturing on industry, business and society. Int. J. Prod. Econ. **208**, 254–268 (2019). https://doi.org/10.1016/j.ijpe.2018.11.022
17. Donthu, N., Kumar, S., Pattnaik, D.: Forty-five years of journal of business research: a bibliometric analysis. J. Bus. Res. **109**, 1–14 (2020). https://doi.org/10.1016/j.jbusres.2019.10.039
18. Zhang, X., et al.: A bibliometric analysis of digital innovation from 1998 to 2016. J. Manag. Sci. Eng. **2**(2), 95–115 (2017). https://doi.org/10.3724/SP.J.1383.202005
19. Ellegaard, O., Wallin, J.A.: The bibliometric analysis of scholarly production: how great is the impact? Scientometrics **105**(3), 1809–1831 (2015). https://doi.org/10.1007/s11192-015-1645-z
20. Tseng, Y.H., Lin, Y.I., Lee, Y.Y., Hung, W.C., Lee, C.H.: A comparison of methods for detecting hot topics. Scientometrics **81**(1), 73–90 (2009). https://doi.org/10.1007/s11192-009-1885-x
21. Sund, K.J., Bogers, M.L.A.M., Sahramaa, M.: Managing business model exploration in incumbent firms: a case study of innovation labs in European banks. J. Bus. Res. **128**, 11–19 (2021). https://doi.org/10.1016/j.jbusres.2021.01.059

Entrepreneurship Education and E-Learning in the Greater Bay Area of China

Yiyun Wang[1(✉)], Linkai Zhu[2,3(✉)], Guang LI[2], and Weigong Feng[2]

[1] Department of Applied Psychology, Beijing Normal University-Hong Kong Baptist University United International College (UIC), Zhuhai, China
evayywang@uic.edu.cn

[2] Institute of Data Science, City University of Macau, Macau, China
linkai@iscas.ac.cn

[3] Institute of Software, Chinese Academy of Science, Beijing, China

Abstract. China's new economy calls for innovation-driven development and entrepreneurship-focused strategies. As China's new corporate formation rate is rising, plenty of educators and policymakers are looking forward to building a better context to support entrepreneurship. It is worth noting that the development and fusion of the Greater Bay Area highly depend on joint and cross-regional entrepreneurship. While the system, law, language, and cultural differences hinder this progress. E-learning is a great way that could break the barriers and boost the effectiveness of entrepreneurship education in the Greater Bay Area.

Keywords: Entrepreneurship education · E-learning · The greater bay area

1 Introduction

In just 30 years, China has developed into the world's second-largest economy, and entrepreneurship was considered to be a key driver of China's rapid growth. China plans to develop its Greater Bay Area to be an international innovation and technology center. Innovation and entrepreneurship resources are shared in the area to provide more opportunities for the Mainland of China, Hong Kong, and Macau's entrepreneurs. Currently, the Greater Bay Area blueprints some policies for future direction, including many innovation and financial hubs. Meanwhile, it provides more incentives for youth and opens many related courses and incubation base opportunities [1].

However, many youths begin their entrepreneurship with little or even no business-related knowledge. Moreover, the system, law, and culture disparities in the Greater Bay Area make them have a wait-and-see approach for joint entrepreneurship and cross-regional development [2]. Compare to traditional teaching and learning methods, e-learning has some irreplaceable advantages, especially in transregional and cross-culture contexts [3, 4].

W. Zhou and Y. Mu (Eds.): ICWL 2021, LNCS 13103, pp. 142–147, 2021.
https://doi.org/10.1007/978-3-030-90785-3_13

2 Entrepreneurship in China

The Global Entrepreneurship Monitor survey has shown that there was a consistently high rate of entrepreneurship in China over the past few years [5], and most Chinese adults perceived that there were good opportunities to start their own business [6]. Ever since Premier Li Keqiang proposed mass entrepreneurship and innovation in the 2014 Summer Davos forum in Tianjin, "mass entrepreneurship and innovation" had been regarded as the new power of China's economic growth. Premier Li said, "Mass entrepreneurship and innovation has been an effective driver for both economic growth and the consistent transition between traditional and new growth engines. It has also significantly contributed to the creation of new jobs and the increase in incomes" [7].

3 The Greater Bay Area Context

Hong Kong, Macau, and Guangdong had become a global regional metropolis. Meanwhile, a new and closer integration has started since July 1, 2017. President Xi Jinping signed the framework of building the Guangdong-Hong Kong-Macau Greater Bay Area. The Greater Bay Area is a huge and densely populated geographic space in the south of China and it includes Guangdong Province's nine cities, Hong Kong and Macau. This blueprint not only would boost the development in the Greater Bay Area and it plays a key role in the Belt and Road Initiative of China [8]. Deep integration has numerous advantages, which could increase the ability to attract Foreign Direct Investment and become increasingly diverse and commercialized [9]. Hong Kong and Shenzhen had merged into one block in many fields. In addition, it is a similar interconnection as Macau and Zhuhai. While the Hong Kong Basic Law limits the fusion between Hong Kong and Shenzhen on some level until 2047 [10].

The majorities of Hong Kong and Macau were migrants from the mainland of China. Cantonese-speaking Chinese culture is the dominant cultural concept in these areas and may bring social harmony to the Greater Bay [11]. While we should face the reality that Hong Kong and Macau separated from mainland China more than one hundred years. They had governed under British and Portuguese rules respectively and developed their unique socioeconomic system and local culture. The two special administrative regions of China have some extraordinary characters, such as an efficient financial system, free market, and western organizational culture. Meanwhile, living under both colonial and post-colonial periods, the residents have their unique memories, loyalties, and values, which may differ from people in the mainland of China [12]. These differences may lead to some barriers and obstacles for entrepreneurship knowledge spreading and start an undertaking together [10].

The population in the Greater Bay Area needs to be more united. A survey including 1033 interviewees showed that less than 8% of Hongkongeses work in the mainland and only 54% visited Guangdong Province. 42% of Hongkongeses were afraid of losing their special benefits from the Hong Kong government if they move to the mainland of China [10]. Meanwhile, youths are the future of this area, the administrator of the Greater Bay Area should motivate and convince youth residents to leave their comfort zone and become more open to the future united. Both Carrie Lam and Ho Iat Seng, who are Hong Kong and Macau chief executives, said the future of their youth residents is in the mainland of China [13].

4 Entrepreneurship Education

It is obvious that entrepreneurship brings immense benefit for the Greater Bay Area so that there is considerable attention for how to raise future successful entrepreneurs [2]. An entrepreneur, as be defined by Henry et al., is "someone who has the ability to see and evaluate business opportunities; gather the necessary resources to take advantage of them, and initiate appropriate action to secure success" [14]. Entrepreneurship education provided students with information and inspiration in establishing their own company, which indirectly increases their willingness to become entrepreneurs [14]. In a survey, that investigated more than 1500 young entrepreneurs in G20 countries, most of the participants agreed that entrepreneurial skills should be trained and taught [15].

The study of characteristics of entrepreneurs began to emerge in the middle of the 20th century, unifying the domains of economics, psychology, sociology, and business management to attempt to shed light on this issue [16]. However, China's entrepreneurship education started late and did not fully meet the needs of Chinese students [17]. In China, entrepreneurship education usually is delivered by an innovative system, which is beyond the regular curriculum [18]. The "Enterprising and entrepreneurial education" policy was announced in 2015 since then entrepreneurial education and training had developed and spread tremendously in university context [19].

Many kinds of researches of entrepreneurs have been carried out by scholars with economic or management backgrounds, and they have a less deep understanding of the educational philosophy, especially e-learning [20]. Some researchers identify that entrepreneurial education should include learning mathematics, economics, and behavioral sciences. The format of teaching could include scenarios, role-playing, and real business experiences, real project teaching by business people [21, 22]. Cope and Watts emphasis the importance of learning by doing, the real experience could build students' problem-solving skills, in further improve their self-efficacy by continuing reflect on their progress [23]. However, the scholars have underlined the delivery methods' impact on effectiveness.

5 E-Learning

The e-learning method starts to change the nature of study for all students, which is be defined as the use of the Internet and digital technologies to educate people. It usually used the network to generate communities and systems that facilitate the knowledge spreading and offer remote students a friendlier environment to learn [24].

6 How E-Learning Techniques Contribute to the Joint Entrepreneurship Education in the Greater Bay Area

There are some barriers to joint teaching among mainland China, Hong Kong, and Macau students. That may include the distance, and culture, law, and system differences.

Meanwhile, entrepreneurs usually are thoughtful practitioners who not only learn things but also have a goal to achieve and could work to rapid changes and developments after learning, so entrepreneurs are their own agencies for their learning process [14]. One report showed that entrepreneurs are more likely to learn from a task-oriented approach compare to the conventional teaching method [14]. Entrepreneurship education is to help those entrepreneurs or future entrepreneurs to adapt to their own context that caused the entrepreneurship education content to be highly diversified and flourishing [25]. Those features for entrepreneur education in the Greater Bay Area are unable to be fulfilled by the traditional teaching methods. The advantages of e-learning stand out in this situation.

6.1 Remote Learning

The e-learning techniques provide geographically dispersed students to study from experienced entrepreneurs. The developed technology-based systems or platforms could enable remote access for both students and teachers. The youth entrepreneurs were not asked to do a full-time study, so they could practice what they learned in their own business at the same time [20]. Apart from the official e-learning platform, the Connectivist theory brought the idea that people are in a networked environment in this digital age. Andrews said that people could use e-community, such as social networking sites, virtual meetings, and emails or chats, to support their learning whenever and wherever possible [26].

6.2 Continue and Shared Learning

Learning is a circle, and it is an unending process that people continuously interact with the environment [20]. As to entrepreneurship education, e-learning could use cloud computing to storage and share the recording of lectures with different communities [27]. That is a valuable method for knowledge management in a big region. In this way, qualified students could access the platform in an unlimited time. They could reflect on their needs and restudy the previous lectures.

6.3 Adaptive Learning

A report showed that e-learning was very dependent on students' abilities to be self-directed and internally motivated which is the same as entrepreneurship [28]. The people with the power and mode of communication usually decide the content of teaching. The student could gain a lot from the real business cases, while the diversified nature of entrepreneurship makes the teaching resource is hard to be concentrated just in a typical course. For e-learning, students could set their own standard for exclusions and inclusions the content they need to learn [29]. So that teaching could be adaptive and customized to all students.

6.4 Cross-Language Learning

People living in the Greater Bay area use at least four different languages, which are Mandarin, Cantonese, English, and Portuguese [11]. The variety of languages cause many troubles in commutation and knowledge delivery. E-learning platforms could combine with artificial intelligence systems, for example, the synchronous translation system, to resolve this difficulty [30].

7 Conclusion

Today, researchers have a huge interest to investigate entrepreneurship, and youth could access more curriculums that delivering entrepreneurship-related knowledge. A better understanding of the combination of entrepreneurship education and e-learning is highly valuable. Youth is essential for the Greater Bay Area's future. The delivery method for entrepreneurship education should enable people from different backgrounds and locations to enhance their capabilities for innovation and entrepreneurship. Overall, E-learning techniques could boost joint entrepreneurship education in the Greater Bay area.

References

1. Xinhua. Xinhua Headlines: China's Greater Bay Area busy laying foundation for innovation. Xinhua news (2015)
2. Zhu, Q.: Exploring how to build innovation and entrepreneurship education ecosystems in universities in Guangdong against the backdrop of the Guangdong-Hong Kong-Macau Greater Bay Area. E3S Web Conf. **165**, 02005 (2020)
3. Hunter, P.: The virtual university: digital tools for e-learning and remote learning are becoming an increasingly important tool for teaching at universities. EMBO Rep. **16**, 146–148 (2015)
4. Edmundson, A.L.: The cross-cultural dimensions of globalized E-learning. Int. J. Inf. Commun. Technol. Educ. **1**, 47–61 (2005)
5. Yang, K.: Entrepreneurship in China. Routledge, London (2000). https://doi.org/10.4324/9781315579924
6. Bosma, N., et al.: Global Entrepreneurship Monitor 2019/2020 Global Report. Global Entrepreneurship Research Association (2020)
7. The State Council of the People's Republic of China. Mass entrepreneurship and innovation as new growth engine.
8. Xinhua. Guangzhou incubator gives HK, Macau businesses a leg-up. Xinhua news (2019)
9. Xinhua. Spotlight: China's Greater Bay Area, model of development, driver for world. Xinhua news (2019)
10. Berlie, J.A., Hung, S.: The Greater Bay Area and the Role of Hong Kong and Macau SARs in the Belt and Road Initiative. In: Berlie, J.A. (ed.) China's Globalization and the Belt and Road Initiative. PDCC, pp. 77–100. Springer, Cham (2020). https://doi.org/10.1007/978-3-030-22289-5_5
11. Yu, H.: The Guangdong-Hong Kong-Macau Greater Bay Area in the making: development plan and challenges. Cambridge Rev. Int. Aff. (2019). https://doi.org/10.1080/09557571.2019.1679719
12. Wong, H.C.J., Fung, S.L.: Cultural contestations and social integration: what Guangdong-Hong Kong-Macao Greater Bay Area can learn from the experiences of Malaysia and Singapore? In: Islam, M.N. (ed.) Silk Road to Belt Road, pp. 159–174. Springer, Singapore (2019). https://doi.org/10.1007/978-981-13-2998-2_10
13. Cui, F.: 21 years after returning to motherland, Macao sets example for neighboring HK. Global Times (2020)

14. Henry, C., Hill, F., Leitch, C.: Entrepreneurship education and training: can entrepreneurship be taught? Part I. Educ. Train. **47**, 98–111 (2005)
15. Ernst and Young: Avoiding a Lost Generation: Young Entrepreneurs Identify Five Imperatives for Action (2012)
16. Stephan, U., Drencheva, A.: the person in social entrepreneurship: a systematic review of research on the social entrepreneurial personality (2017)
17. Tang, M., Chen, X., Li, Q., Lu, Y.: Does Chinese university entrepreneurship education fit students' needs? J. Entrep. Emerg. Econ. **6**, 163–178 (2014)
18. Liu, T., Walley, K., Pugh, G., Adkins, P.: Entrepreneurship education in China. J. Entrep. Emerg. Econ. **12**, 305–326 (2020)
19. Mei, W., Symaco, L.: University-wide entrepreneurship education in China's higher education institutions: issues and challenges. Stud. High. Educ. 1–17 (2020). https://doi.org/10.1080/03075079.2020.1735330
20. Sudarwati, N., Rukminingsih, R.: Evaluating e-learning as a learning media a case of entrepreneurship e-learning using schoology as media. Int. J. Emerg. Technol. Learn. **13**, 269–279 (2018)
21. Corbett, A.C.: Experiential learning within the process of opportunity identification and exploitation. Entrep. theory Pract. **29**, 473–491 (2005)
22. Heinonen, J., Poikkijoki, S.-A.: An entrepreneurial-directed approach to entrepreneurship education: mission impossible? J. Manag. Dev. **25**, 80–94 (2006)
23. Cope, J., Watts, G.: Learning by doing - an exploration of experience, critical incidents and reflection in entrepreneurial learning. Int. J. Entrep. Behav. Res. **6**, 104–124 (2000)
24. Bodea, C.-N., Mogos, R.I., Dascalu, M.-I., Purnus, A., Ciobotar, N.G.: Simulation-based e-learning framework for entrepreneurship education and training. Amfiteatru Econ. **17**, 10–24 (2015)
25. Gentile, T.A.R., Reina, R., De Nito, E., Bizjak, D., Canonico, P.: E-learning design and entrepreneurship in three European universities. Int. J. Entrep. Behav. Res. **26**, 1547–1566 (2020)
26. Haythornthwaite, C.A., Andrews, R., Fransman, J., Meyers, E.M.: The SAGE Handbook of E-Learning Research, SAGE Publications, Los Angeles (2016)
27. Masud, A., Huang, X.: Architecture based on cloud computing. World Acad. Sci. Eng. Technol. **62**, 74–78 (2012)
28. Schott, M., Chernish, W., Dooley, K., Lindner, J.: Innovations in distance learning program development and delivery. Online J. Dist. Learn. Adm. VI **6** (2003)
29. Pitsoe, V., Letseka, M.: Foucault's discourse and power: implications for instructionist classroom management. Open J. Philos. **3**, 6 (2013)
30. Gomaa, Y.A., AbuRaya, R., Omar, A.: The effects of information technology and E-learning systems on translation pedagogy and productivity of EFL learners. In: 2019 International Conference on Innovation and Intelligence for Informatics, Computing, and Technologies, pp. 1–6. IEEE (2019). https://doi.org/10.1109/3ICT.2019.8910326

Design and Implementation of Learning System Based on T-LSTM

Yongjun Ma[1] and Wei Lu[2(✉)]

[1] City University of Macau, Macau, China
[2] Zhuhai College of Science and Technology, Zhuhai, China
luwei@jluzh.edu.cn

Abstract. One-to-one teaching is an ideal way to realize personalized and adaptive learning, but limited to teachers, it can't be applied on a large scale. Now artificial intelligence has been widely used, so we can design a learning system to assist teaching, so as to realize part of the personalized and adaptive learning. In this paper, a learning system based on T-LSTM's recurrent neural network is proposed to help achieve this goal. On the one hand, it can balance subjects, on the other hand, it can avoid the exercise too difficult to affect learning confidence or too simple to affect learning efficiency.

Keywords: Deep learning · RNN · Adaptive learning

1 Introduction

The class teaching system commonly used in today's education was born in the 16th century. Usually, a certain number of students are divided into different groups according to their age, and all students are taught uniformly by teachers at a fixed time and place. In 1632, the Czech educator Comenius systematically expounded the basic theory of class teaching system in his works [1]. The class teaching system can improve the teaching efficiency. However, the consideration of each student's basic knowledge, cognitive structure and ability level is limited.

Now artificial intelligence has been widely used, and it is a hot topic how to apply artificial intelligence technology to the field of education, so as to realize the personalized and adaptive learning. This paper mainly involves the design and implementation of learning system.

2 Related Theories and Research

The models in personalized and adaptive learning mainly include knowledge model, student model and teaching model [2]. This paper mainly discusses the student model, which is the core and foundation of personalized and adaptive learning. The model can reflect the individual differences in the relationship between learners themselves and their behavior, and predict different learning behavior [3].

W. Zhou and Y. Mu (Eds.): ICWL 2021, LNCS 13103, pp. 148–153, 2021.
https://doi.org/10.1007/978-3-030-90785-3_14

The traditional methods of student model mainly include item response theory (IRT), Bayesian knowledge tracing (BKT), deterministic inputs, noise and gate (Dina), performance factor analysis (PFA), learning factor analysis (LFA) [4, 5]. IRT method is the earliest method of student model, and it was established and developed by Danish statistician Rasch and American psychologist Lord in the 1960s. IRT method believes that whether learners can answer the questions correctly is related to themselves and the questions. The BKT method is proposed by Corbett and Anderson, and it is actually a hidden Markov model (HMM) [6].

Today in the field of artificial intelligence deep learning is booming, and has outstanding performance in image processing, speech recognition and other applications. Similarly, the artificial intelligence assisted learning also benefits from the development of deep learning.

The model in deep learning is relatively complex, the data from input to output flows through multiple linear and nonlinear components, and each component processes information and will affect other components. Therefore, the final output result is not clear about the contribution of each component. This problem is called credit assignment problem (CAP) [7]. The best model that can solve the CAP is the artificial neural network (ANN). The artificial neural networks include convolutional neural networks (CNN), recurrent neural network (RNN), generative adversarial network (GAN), etc. [8–11].

Recurrent neural network can spread information between neurons in time line, that is, the output of neuron at one time can be put into the neuron as a parameter in the next time. It is especially suitable for seq2seq. The basic model was proposed by Jordan and Elman in 1986 and 1990 respectively [10].

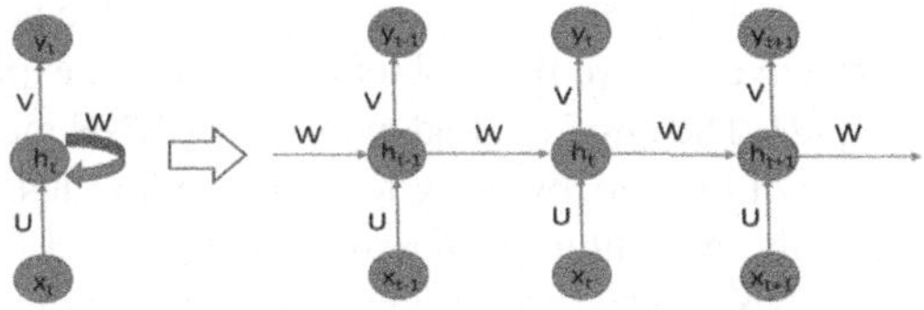

Fig. 1. Recurrent neural network.

In Fig. 1, although the RNN seems to have only one hidden layer, if it is expanded from the time dimension, a deep learning network model along the w direction is formed. It can be seen that the output of the current time of RNN is related not only to the input of the current time, but also to the output of the previous time. RNN uses backpropagation through time (BPTT) to train model parameters, and it is like the BP algorithm. With the deepening of the basic RNN, as CNN, the gradient will become larger or smaller, resulting in input-output mismatch, precision degradation and other problems.

Hochreiter and Schmidhuber introduced gate unit to save historical information in RNN, and it can effectively solve the problems of gradient explosion and gradient disappearance in RNN [12]. The model is often called LSTM.

In Fig. 2, the straight line at the top from Ct−1 to Ct is similar to the conveyor belt, and it can send the most information of the previous unit to the next unit, that is, the information will basically be transmitted on it.

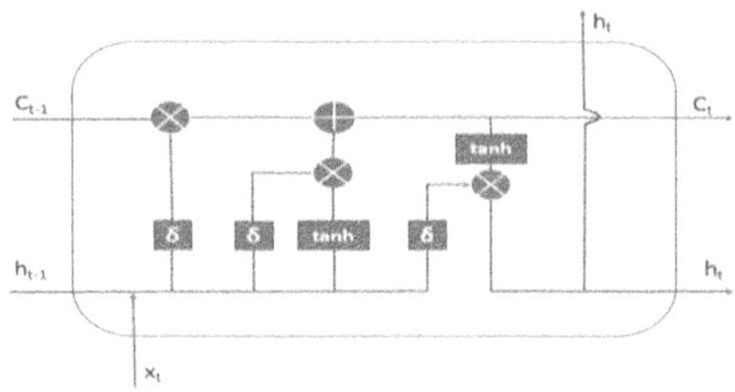

Fig. 2. LSTM unit structure diagram.

Piech Chris from Stanford University proposed the deep knowledge tracing (DKT) method in 2015, which based on RNN belong to the deep learning family. This method can be modeled based on the historical data of learners' answer, and tracks the learners' knowledge proficiency over time through RNN [13]. Its input is the data that the learner has answered the question, and its output is the probability of correctly answering all the questions. With the increase of the amount of data, the effect of the deep learning model will improve. Yeung in his paper added the regular term and regular function to enhance the model [14]. Minn in his paper proposed a clustering method based on students' abilities and added it to the DKT method [15].

3 Design of T-LSTM

LSTM model has strong feature learning ability and self-adaptive ability, and it considers the influence of time series. The larger the amount of data is, the better the effect is. In addition, LSTM can effectively solve the problems of gradient explosion and gradient disappearance in RNN [12]. The DKT method, which uses RNN model, can predict the knowledge mastery status of learners by using learners' answer history as input [13].

In the framework of the algorithm proposed in this paper, LSTM model is used to replace the ordinary RNN model. The framework is divided into two steps, and it uses DKT method twice. The model was implemented by pytorch and verified on the assistments2009 data set to prove the effectiveness and accuracy of the model.

ASSISTments (https://new.assistments.org/) is a free open online education project jointly funded by the U.S. Department of education and the U.S. National Foundation and hosted by the Worcester Polytechnic Institute (WPI), which allows researchers to use platform data for experiments and research. ASSISTmentsData (https://sites.google.com/site/assistmentsdata/home) is the data set published by Professor Heffernan's team, and it is the largest data set in the field of knowledge tracking [13]. The assistments2009 data set contains 525535 pieces of data, including 4217 students' submission records. Each record is divided into three lines, which respectively represent the count of answers, the number of questions to be answered and whether the question is answered correctly (1 means correct and 0 means wrong), for example:

40
79,79,79,79,55,37,79,55,45,45,55,37,55,81,81,82,82,82,82,82,82,82,
96,82,82,82,82,82,82,82,82,82,18,27,82,82,82,82,38,38

0,1,1,1,0,0,1,1,1,1,1,1,1,1,1,0,0,0,0,0,0,0,0,0,0,0,0,0,0,0,0,0,0,0,0,0,0,0,0,0

It means that the student has answered 40 questions, wrong answer of question no. 79, correct answer of question no. 79, correct answer of question no. 79…

The experiment in this paper selects 3237 records as the training set and 810 records as the test set. In the model, the initial learning rate is set to 0.01, the number of hidden layers is set to 1, the number of hidden layer nodes is set to 200, the number of training rounds is set to 30, and the neuron activation function is set to sigmoid function. The output format of the model is.

[−4.1701e−01, 1.6980e−01, 3.3340e−01, 1.9446e−01, 2.1524e−01 …

The value indicates the possibility of correct answer of question.

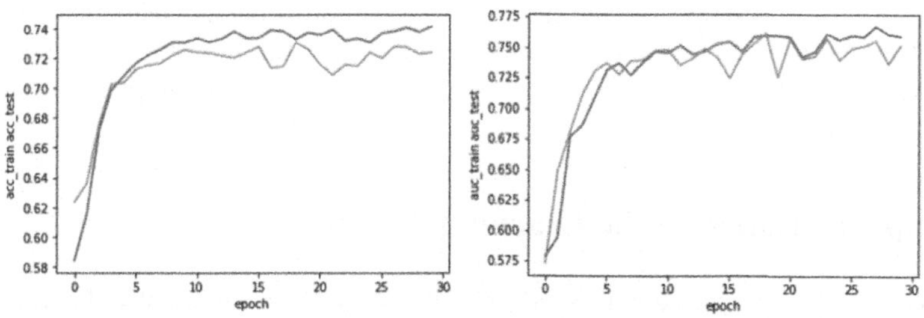

Fig. 3. Iterative convergence diagram of ACC and AUC by epoch. (Color figure online)

Figure 3 shows the trend of ACC and AUC in the model under different iteration times (blue line from train set, and orange line from test set). After the model iterates to a certain number of times, as shown in Fig. 3, the model basically converges and stabilizes within a certain value. Continue training will not learn useful knowledge, or even over fitting.

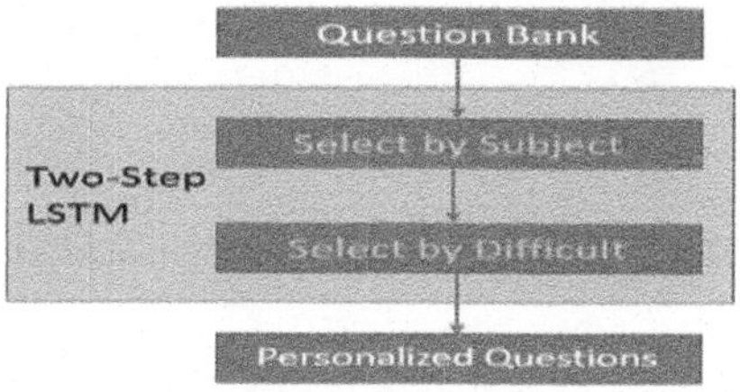

Fig. 4. Two-step LSTM.

The framework of the algorithm which named T-LSTM proposed in this paper is shown in Fig. 4, and it is divided into two steps with LSTM model. The system with algorithm tracks the historical answers of learners, and predicts the knowledge mastery status of learners. The system knows what knowledge learners have mastered and what knowledge the learners have not mastered, and then dynamically adjusts the questions to push to the learners, so it can help learners to achieve the purpose of personalized and adaptive learning.

Firstly, all the questions in the question bank are divided into different categories and labeled according to the subject. According to the historical answers of learners, the DKT method is used to predict the error rate of the questions in different subjects in the question bank, and the questions in different subjects are recommended according to the proportion of error rate in different subjects. Questions in subjects with high error rate are recommended more, and questions in subjects with low error rate are recommended less. The purpose of this step is to balance subjects or to strengthen the weak subjects. Then the questions in the same subject, and recommend the questions with the suitable difficult level to learner according DKT method. If the recommended questions are too difficult, it is easy to cause learners to fear difficulties, reduce their learning motivation and make them give up. If the recommended questions are too simple, it is easy to cause learners to waste too much time and can't ensure the improvement of learners' knowledge level. The purpose of this step is to find the questions with the suitable difficult level according DKT method, so as to bring the best learning effect and improve the learning experience.

4 Implementation of the Learning System

After completing the core algorithm design, the software of personalized and adaptive learning system is completed with JavaEE. The learning system uses browser-server (BS) architecture, and it uses MySQL as its database. the learning system is developed on the framework of springboot and mybatis (Fig. 5).

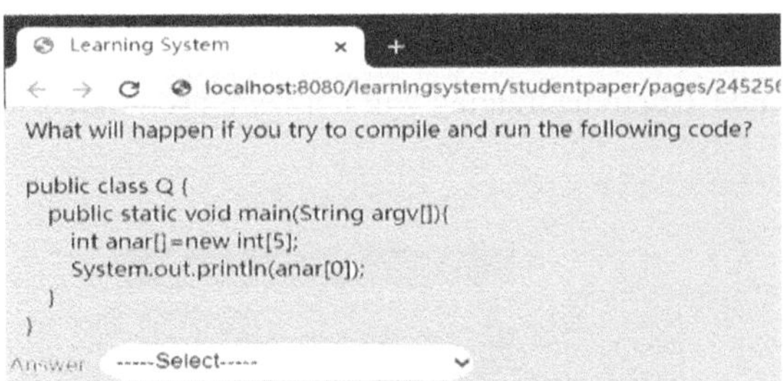

Fig. 5. Learning system operation interface.

The system includes administrator module and user module. The administrator module includes user management, learning resource management, subject information management. The user module includes registration and login, subject setting, personal information setting and learning resource.

5 Conclusion and Prospect

From the research, it can be seen that with big data, deep learning has shown its advantages. Deep learning can carry out feature learning, so as to make the model more optimized. The DKT method based on LSTM model can track learners' learning status, and with this method it is feasible to realize personalized and adaptive learning system. The two-step LSTM scheme proposed in this paper is used in the learning system, on the one hand, it can balance subjects or strengthen the weak subjects, on the other hand, it can avoid the exercise too difficult to affect learning confidence or too simple to affect learning efficiency.

With the application of artificial intelligence technology, all aspects of human society are being changed. The problems of personalized and adaptive learning are gradually solved with the help of artificial intelligence.

References

1. Keatinge, M.W.: Great Didactic of Comenius. Kessinger Publishing LLC, Montana (1992)
2. Normadhi, N.B.A., Shuib, L., Nasir, H.N.M.: Identification of personal traits in adaptive learning environment: systematic literature review. Comput. Educ. **130**, 168–190 (2019)
3. Jiang, Q., Zhao, W., Li, S.: Research on personalized adaptive learning – a new normal form of digital learning in big data era. China Educ. Technol. **2**, 25–32 (2016)
4. Aderson, J.R., Boyle, C.F., Reiser, B.J.: Intelligent tutoring system. Science (Washington) **228**(4698), 456–463 (1985)
5. Murray, T.: Authoring intelligent tutoring systems: an analysis of the state of the art. Int. J Artif. Intell. Educ. (IJAIED) **10**, 98–129 (1999)
6. Corbett, A.T., Anderson, J.R.: Knowledge tracing: modeling the acquisition of procedural knowledge. User Model. User Adapt. Interact. **4**(4), 253–278 (1994)
7. Minsky, M.: Steps toward artificial intelligence. Proc. IRE **49**(1), 8–30 (1961)
8. LeCun, Y., Bengio, Y.: Convolutional networks for images, speech, and time series. In: The Handbook of Brain Theory and Neural Networks, vol. 10, p. 3361. MIT Press, Cambridge (1995)
9. Krizhevsky, A., Sutskever, I., Hinton, G.E.: ImageNet classification with deep convolutional neural networks. Adv. Neural. Inf. Process. Syst. **25**(2), 1097–1105 (2012)
10. Lipton, Z.C., Berkowitz, J., Elkan, C.: A critical review of recurrent neural networks for sequence learning. Computer Science (2015)
11. Goodfellow, I.J., Pouget-Abadie, J., Mirza, M.: Generative adversarial networks. Adv. Neural. Inf. Process. Syst. **3**, 2672–2680 (2014)
12. Hochreiter, S.: Schmidhuber, J.: Long short-term memory. Neural Comput. **9**, 1735–1780 (1997)
13. Piech, C., Bassen, J., Huang, J.: Deep knowledge tracing. In: Proceedings of the 28th International Conference on Neural Information Processing Systems, pp. 505–513.MIT Press, Montreal, Quebec (2015)
14. Yeung, C.K., Yeung, D.Y: Addressing two problems in deep knowledge tracing via prediction-consistent regularization. arXiv preprint arXiv:1806.02180 (2018)
15. Minn, S., Yu, Y., Desmarais, M.C.: Deep knowledge tracing and dynamic student classification for knowledge tracing. In: IEEE International Conference on Data Mining (ICDM), pp. 1182–1187. IEEE (2018)

Situational Awareness of E-learning System Based on Cyber-Attack and Vulnerability

Linkai Zhu[1,2](✉), Wennan Wang[2], Ruijie Luo[2], Zhiming Cai[2](✉), Sheng Peng[2,4], and Zeyu Zhang[3]

[1] Institute of Software Chinese Academy of Sciences, Beijing, China
linkai@iscas.ac.cn
[2] Institute of Data Science, City University of Macau, Macau, China
caizhiming@cityu.mo
[3] School of Applied Sciences, Macao Polytechnic Institute, Macau, China
[4] Zhuhai Yingying Technology Co., Ltd., Zhuhai, China

Abstract. As technology changes and advances, E-learning has come a long way, providing a personal and interactive wealth of content. However, unethical behavior and the severity of network security attacks have received limited attention. While E-learning systems have been embraced for training and virtual team collaboration, little is known about the motivations of these systems for cybersecurity attacks. E-Learning network security situation assessment technology can synthesize various network attack data and combine them with security elements to reflect the network security status of E-Learning systems. This paper is based on the analysis of the existing network security situation assessment methods and technologies, so it proposes a situational awareness framework based on an E-learning system and implements an E-learning situation monitoring and warning system prototype system. Finally, we tested the real system in seven days to calculate the network security situation value. The proposed evaluation model, quantitative evaluation algorithm, and prediction algorithm are verified.

Keywords: Cybersecurity · Cyber-attack · E-learning systems security · Situational awareness · Vulnerability

1 Introduction

The main source of network hidden danger is that the system platform and some important service programs have found significant security loopholes, especially since several serious vulnerabilities were disclosed in the Windows' system in successive months, followed by the widespread prevalence and outbreak of worm programs using the vulnerabilities [1]. There are security loopholes in many E-learning network applications. The threat of network attacks is increasingly rampant. The risk of network security is increasingly complex, which has caused great economic losses to the education system and individuals [2]. Meet the security requirements of e-learning systems is a complicated problem since it is not only the content, services, and personal data that must be secured,

W. Zhou and Y. Mu (Eds.): ICWL 2021, LNCS 13103, pp. 154–159, 2021.
https://doi.org/10.1007/978-3-030-90785-3_15

but the E-learning system manager or staff [3]. E-learning course resources face security threats, since E-learning data is distributed, shared, open, and based on teamwork, so it is critical to protect confidentiality and integrity from any security issues. The purpose of the paper is to synthesize different cyber-attacks that will affect the E-learning system. And against these cyber threats, we propose a network security situational awareness system for detection, prediction, and protection by analyzing the internal relationship between the data and the network events, it can help network administrators to predict the possible network security problems in the next period, to prevent and respond in time based on E-learning system.

2 Background

2.1 E-learning

Traditional distance education is referred to teach by correspondence commonly. Educational information is mainly disseminated through the printed word. It is characterized by low cost, easy to organize and implement. But the drawbacks are also obvious, less information, difficulty in learning, lack of communication between teachers and students, the long learning cycle, and the low learning efficiency. E-learning is a new educational pattern with the rapid development of network technology and multimedia technology [4]. Compared with traditional education, it is not limited by the time and space of education. E-learning is a new educational pattern with the rapid development of network technology and multimedia technology. People cannot be limited by time and space and complete interactive teaching and learning activities anytime and anywhere. They do not have to be at the designated place and time.

2.2 Situational Awareness

Before situational awareness, the main idea of the security event statistical analysis method is to obtain the network security situation by using the influence of the intrusion detection system or other detection systems. The generated alarm logs are statistically analyzed to obtain network security event information to analyze the network attack.

Tim Bass [5] proposed to use distributed multi-sensor data fusion method of the intrusion detection system to evaluate the security situation of computer networks and to evaluate the security of computer networks through data fusion and data mining method. The intrusion detection data fusion framework is shown in Fig. 1. The security situation assessment results are obtained through steps such as data extraction, object extraction, situation extraction, threat assessment, and resource management.

Situational awareness is an environment-based, dynamic, and comprehensive insight into security risks. It is based on security big data to improve the ability to detect, identify, understand, analyze, and respond to security threats from a global perspective [6]. It is to predict the future development trend of the network for decision-making and action. Situational assessment first appeared in the field of aviation and military, and then gradually spread to various technical fields, including traffic management, production control, logistics management, medical research, and ergonomics. In recent years, situation assessment techniques have been applied to computer networks. The cyberspace situational awareness process [7] can be divided into three stages.

2.3 Cyber Security and E-learning

The security of an e-learning system includes steps to limit the danger and threat of network assaults, such as the deployment of security management (security rules, procedures, and processes), enhanced verification tools and control of access; Users with varying levels of permission based on their status; Backup software that runs automatically; Encrypt critical or sensitive data; Firewall, antivirus, and anti-spam software [3]. Most of the E-learning security research is focused on four areas: vulnerabilities, security threats, cyber-attacks and privacy.

Ramim and Levy (Ramim & Levy, 2006) advocate for academic institutions to develop proactive security measures for e-learning systems. Zuev [1] suggests using cybersecurity metrics as a tool that can also help assess the level of risk in not performing a particular action, and in that way provide direction in prioritizing corrective action. Rjaibi et al. [8] discuss that security techniques for quantifying security threats in E-learning are like those used in other E-services. Anghel and Pereteanu [10] stated that E-learning devices can be vulnerable, hacked, and when connected to networks, they can cause cybersecurity breaches and influence data that are vulnerable to protection and privacy. Hage [11] E-learning systems can collect information about learners, which has implications for their privacy, and people are concerned about protecting the privacy of learners.

3 Methodology

Raw data are classified into asset data, threat data, and vulnerability data. The security event data set is obtained through comprehensive analysis by correlating asset threat and vulnerability. After obtaining the threat information, it is necessary to carry out intrusion detection on the E-learning system. By collecting and analyzing network behavior, security logs, audit data, other information available on the network, and information of some key points in the E-learning system, it checks whether there is behavior violating security policy or signs of an attack in the network or system.

3.1 E-learning Situation Monitoring and Warning System

Based on the network attack database to form a multi-dimensional knowledge map of the event components, and based on the algorithms, tools, and knowledge models of relational reasoning, network terrorist attack events can be excavated and analyzed in the space-time dimension. The situation analysis of the cyber-attack event "4W1H" (who, when, where, what, how) is realized in the department of electronics.

The security situation assessment value of the whole network can be written as:

$$A = \sum_{i=1}^{n} (V_i, T_i, S_i) * (s_{iv}, s_{iT}, s_{iw})$$

Where Vi represents the vulnerability state value of node i, Ti represents the threat state value of node i, and Si represents the operating state value of node I. S_{iV} represents

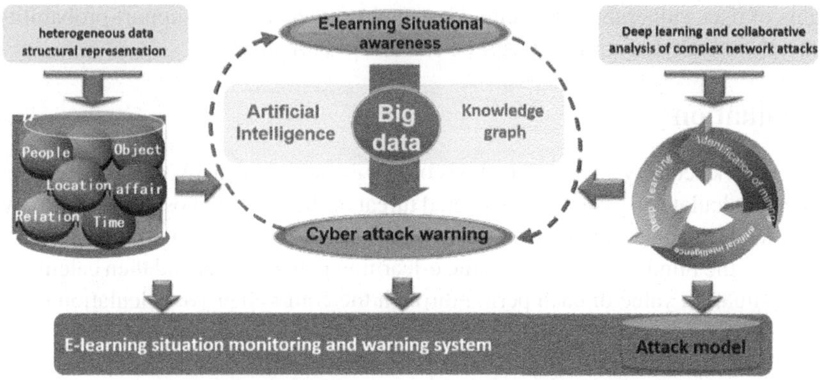

Fig. 1. E-learning situation monitoring and warning system

the vulnerability weight of node i, S_{iT} represents the threat weight of node i, and SIS represents the health status weight of node i. The value weight of each situation can be based on the topology structure of different nodes in the network and the importance of the cluster.

Algorithm 1 E-learning cyber-attack detection rate

Input: Enter E-learning system information, Vulnerability of user, cyber-attack infomation;
Output: Attack detection rate

HashMap ElearningInfo(key:userVulnerability, value:List[Cyber-attackInfo])
HashMap
DetectElearningAttack(userVulnerability,cyber-attackInfo, ElearningInfo)
function MatchVulnerability(userVulnerability,cyber-attackInfo)
$att_i == Hashmap(vul_i)$
return vul_i
end function
let *Attack detection rate* = *0*
for attack type att_0, att_1, ..., att_n **do**
    $Elearning\_Defence = detect\_vul(vul_i, UserInfo)$
end for
if then(Elearning_Defence == 1)
    $Attack\_detection\_rate += weight_i$
    Where weight is the weight vul_i
else
    return 0;
end if
return *Attack_detection_rate*

As shown in Algorithm 1, the E-learning system vulnerability information contains all the necessary vulnerabilities store in a HashMap. The vulnerabilities match the cyber-attack, for example, DDoS, that exploit the type of E-learning system vulnerability to attack. If the E-learning defensive successful rate is 1, then it will return the add up the weights of user vulnerabilities included, namely, attack success support probability Si. Finally, the attack detection rate will be calculated correctly.

4 Evaluation

In the network security situation analysis of this example, the network security situation is directly calculated by using the expected threat of the network host node. The network security situation quantitative assessment algorithm uses the information fusion method to calculate the number of attacks on the e-learning network host and then calculates the security situation value of each period through the comprehensive calculation method.

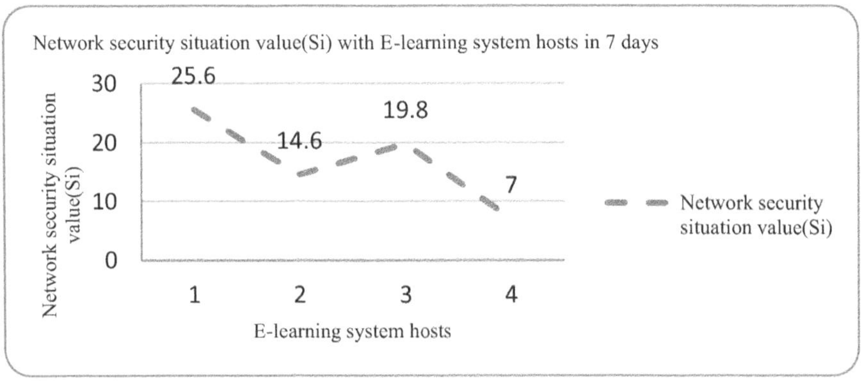

Fig. 2. Network security situation value with E-learning system hosts in 7 days

According to the calculation results of the actual e-learning system experiment, the graph of the network security situation is obtained, as shown in Fig. 2. Then, when the weight of the No.1 Host is relatively large, the system will be subjected to a relatively large value of network security situation.

5 Conclusion

This paper proposes three functional requirements, namely situational awareness scheme to access E-learning system, emergency disposal decision support and intelligent optimization of network security system, analyzes the E-learning system network security situation value and corresponding technical requirements of the network security vulnerability data platform, and designs the technical architecture of the platform accordingly. The system adopts a layered modular architecture with high scalability. Combined with operational modules such as work order distribution and one-click processing, the system can run a detection algorithm of network attack rate based on an E-learning system. The application layer of the E-learning situational awareness system platform can cover the network security domain, from the whole chain of attack detection, threat awareness, event processing, knowledge base construction, and sustainable feedback improvement, to realize a more comprehensive, timely, and intelligent network security comprehensive defense and protection.

Acknowledgment. This research is supported by the: 1. project funded by Zhuhai Industry-University-Research Cooperation Project: Research on Key Technologies of Cross-domain Data Compliance and Mutual Trust Computing in Zhuhai and Macau (No. ZH22017002200011PWC) 2. Research on knowledge-oriented probabilistic graphical model theory based on multi-source data (FDCT- NSFC Projects: 0066/2019/AFJ) 3. Research and Application of Cooperative Multi-Agent Platform for Zhuhai-Macao Manufacturing Service (0058/2019/AMJ).

References

1. Zuev, V.I.: E-Learning security models. Manag. Inf. Syst. **7**, 24–28 (2012)
2. Mohd Alwi, N.H., Fan, I.S.: Information security threats analysis for e-learning. In: Lytras, M.D., et al. (eds.) Technology Enhanced Learning. Quality of Teaching and Educational Reform. TECH-EDUCATION 2010. Communications in Computer and Information Science, vol. 73, pp. 285–291 Springer, Berlin (2010)
3. Costinela-Luminita, C.D., Nicoleta-Magdalena, C.I.: E-learning security vulnerabilities. Proc. Soc. Behav. Sci. **46**, 2297–2301 (2012)
4. Lam, T. Y., Dongol, B.: A blockchain-enabled e-learning platform. Interact. Learn. Environ. 1–23 (2020)
5. Bass, T.: Intrusion detection systems and multisensor data fusion. Commun. ACM **43**, 99–105 (2000)
6. Li, Y., Huang, G., Wang, C.Z., Li, Y.C.: Analysis framework of network security situational awareness and comparison of implementation methods. Eurasip J. Wirel. Commun. Netw. **2019**(1), 1–32 (2019)
7. Vicentel, K.J., Rasmussen, J.: Proceedings of the human factors society 32nd annual meeting 1988, pp. 254–258 (1974)
8. Rjaibi, N., Rabai, L., Aissa, A., Louadi, M.: Cyber security measurement in depth for E-learning systems. Int. J. Adv. Res. Comput. Sci. Softw. Eng. **2**, 1–15 (2012)
9. Ramim, M., Levy, Y.: Securing e-learning systems: a case of insider cyber attacks and novice IT management in a small university. J. Cases Inf. Technol. **8**, 24–34 (2006)
10. Anghel, M., Pereteanu, G.C.: Cyber Security Approaches in E-Learning. INTED2020 Proceedings, vol. 1, pp. 4820–4825 (2020)
11. Hage, H.: Web2.0, Knowledge Sharing and Privacy in E-learning. vol. NR74910 (2010)
12. Aïmeur, E., Hage, H., Onana, F.S.: M. Anonymous credentials for privacy-preserving E-learning. In: Proceedings 2008 International MCETECH Conference e-Technologies, MCETECH 2008, pp. 70–80 (2008). https://doi.org/10.1109/MCETECH.2008.26

Research on Cross-Project Software Defect Prediction Based on Machine Learning

Baoping Wang[1,3], Wennan Wang[1], Linkai Zhu[1,2], and Wenjian Liu[1(✉)]

[1] Faculty of Data Science, City University of Macau, Macau, China
wwwennan@zcst.edu.cn, andylau@cityu.mo
[2] Institute of Software, Chinese Academy of Sciences, Beijing, China
linkai@iscas.ac.cn
[3] Beijing Huayuexun Technology Co., Ltd., Beijing, China
D19092105076@cityu.mo

Abstract. In recent years, machine learning technology has developed vigorously. The research on software defect prediction in the field of software engineering is increasingly adopting various algorithms of machine learning. This article has carried out a systematic literature review on the field of defect prediction. First, this article studies the development process of defect prediction, from correlation to prediction model. then this article studies the development process of cross-project defect prediction based on machine learning algorithms (naive Bayes, decision tree, random forest, neural network, etc.). Finally, this paper looks forward to the research difficulties and future directions of software defect prediction, such as imbalance in classification, cost of data labeling, and cross-project data distribution.

Keywords: Machine learning · Software defect prediction model · Metric

1 Introduction

With the breakthrough development of various technologies and the increasing software requirement, the functions of software products are becoming more and more powerful, but the system is also becoming more and more complex. Due to the complexity of the software itself, technical architecture, team capabilities, and use environment, there are various defects in software products. Software defects can cause serious accidents and even great economic losses and casualties. 2018 In October and March 2019, two Boeing 737MAX planes belonging to Lion Air Singapore and Ethiopian Airlines crashed one after another, causing a total of 346 people to die. The 737MAX series were subsequently grounded globally, and Boeing's reputation was also severely damaged. The follow-up air crash report pointed out that the accident was caused by Boeing engineers' wrong technical assumptions, the lack of transparency in Boeing's management, and the serious inadequacy of FAA supervision; in November 2020, a software failure in Michigan, the United States, erroneously 6,000 votes Vote for Biden, as many as 47 counties have been affected, causing the US general election process to be questioned.

W. Zhou and Y. Mu (Eds.): ICWL 2021, LNCS 13103, pp. 160–165, 2021.
https://doi.org/10.1007/978-3-030-90785-3_16

The defect prediction model is established by software measurement data and historical labeling data. Through the collected software historical data, Use various algorithms of machine learning to obtain a predictive model, and predict subsequent software defects on this basis, so as to reduce the cost of defect repair and improve software quality. ensuring the availability and reliability of software, have important scientific value and social significance.

2 Software Defect Prediction Research

Since the 1970s, research on software defects has begun, and software defects have been studied more through correlation and causality. Since 2000, with the popularity of configuration management tools, the software development process and software measurement data have become more and more abundant. At the same time, the performance of computer hardware has continued to improve, and machine learning algorithms have been more applied to software defect prediction research. Software defect Prediction methodologies are shown in the table below (Table 1).

Table 1. Software defect Prediction methodology

Number	Category	Methodology
[S1]	Metrics	The relationship between software defects and code lines (Akiyama 1971)
[S2]	Control flow	Cyclomatic complexity (McCab 1976)
[S3]	Error-prone modules	Metrics related to the amount of data and the structural complexity (DE) of programs (Shen et al. 1985)
[S4]	Software complexity metrics	The relationship between program complexity measures and program faults (Munson and Khoshgoftaar 1992)
[S5]	Object-oriented methods	A new suite of metrics for OO design (Chidamber and Kemerer 1994)
[S6]	Relative code churn	Relative code churn metrics (Nagappan and Ball 2005)
[S7]	Metrics—performance measures	Network analysis on these dependency graphs (Zimmermann and Nagappan 2008)
[S8]	Network measures	Logistic regression (Ma et al. 2011)
[S9]	Complex network	Sampled K-fold cross-validation method (Yang et al. 2018)

The defect prediction model is established by software measurement data and tagged defect data collected from historical data. Through the collected historical data, the machine learning method is used to construct a software defect prediction model, and then to predict the subsequent software, provide support for decision-making and improve the quality of the software, and ensure the availability and reliability of the software as an infrastructure. The software defect prediction process based on machine learning algorithms is shown in the figure below (Fig. 1).

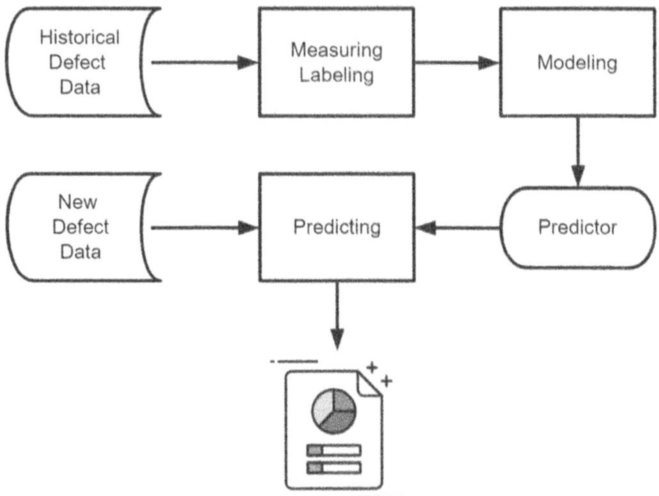

Fig. 1. Defect prediction process

In the 1970s, (Akiyama 1971) based on the hypothesis that complex source code may cause defects, and clearly gave the relationship between software defects and code lines: $D = 4.86 + 0.018L$. (McCabe 1976) and (Halstead 1977) respectively proposed cyclomatic complexity metric and Halstead complexity metric. During this period, the research was not on predictive models, but only on fitting models with the correlation between the number of defects and the measurement.

From the 1980s to the 1990s, (Shen et al. 1985) established a linear regression model and tested it on a new software module. (Munson and Khoshgoftaar 1992) proposed a modular classification model that is divided into high-risk and low-risk categories. (Chidamber and Kemerer 1994) proposed several object-oriented metrics, namely CK metrics, (Basili et al. 1994) used CK metrics to predict defects in object-oriented systems.

Since 2000, because of the popularization of configuration management tools, there have been more and more measurement data in the software development process, and the application of measurement data in defect prediction has become more and more extensive. (Nagappan and Ball 2005) proposed relative code change churn indicators, (Zimmermann and Nagappan 2008) proposed dependency graph indicators. (Yang et al. 2018) established an object-oriented software network based on the relationship between software elements and their evolutionary relationship. (Tian 2020) proposed a software defect prediction model based on program slicing.

3 Cross-Project Defect Prediction Research

Cross-Project Defect Prediction (CPDP) refers to the use of predictive models trained from software metrics of other projects to identify software modules that are prone to defects in software projects.

(Zimmermann et al. 2009) collect data from open-source software and commercial software, and build defect prediction models based on logistic regression algorithms. They considered the recall rate, precision and accuracy values of performance indicators, and assumed success when all indicators were equal to or greater than 0.75. Studies have shown that only 3.4% meet this standard.

(Ma et al. 2011) proposed the "naive Bayesian transfer" method, which uses the naive Bayes method to weight the training data in the training set. The NASA MDP and SOFTLAB data sets are used. Studies have proved that, compared with the nearest neighbor sample selection and the traditional naive Bayes method, the prediction model produces better recall and PF results without any further processing.

(Pan 2013) proposed a transfer defect learning method that uses the existing method to transfer component analysis (TCA), and then performs TCA+by extending TCA. They studied different data normalization techniques. TCA+applies automatic selection for the best standardization strategy. The research concluded that z-score normalization provides better results than no normalization.

(Goel et al. 2018) This article takes the multi-class/polynomial classification of cross-item defect prediction as an example. Use set-based statistical models-gradient enhancement and random forest for classification. To determine the performance of polynomial classification for cross-project defect prediction, an empirical study was conducted. According to the number of defects, the class level information can be divided into one of three defined multi-class class 0, class 1 and class 2. The conclusion is: multiple/multi-category classification is applicable to cross-project data, and the results are comparable to project defect data.

(Li et al. 2019) First, a new domain adaptation method based on subspace alignment (SA) is introduced in CPDP, which can reduce the difference in data allocation between the source item and the target item. Then, a discriminant SA (DSA) method is proposed for CPDP, which can make full use of the class label information of the source item. The experimental results of five public projects in the NASA data set show that DSA is superior to related competitive methods.

(Gong et al. 2020) A new class imbalance learning method is proposed for the problem of class imbalance within and across projects. The conclusion of the study is that this method has better area under the curve (AUC), recall rate and F measurement. (Zhu et al. 2020) proposed an improved Transfer Naive Bayes (ITNB) based on Naive Bayes. The conclusion of the study is that in WPDP and CPDP defect prediction, the accuracy and accuracy of the ITNB model have achieved better results. (Wang 2020) This article focuses on the comparative study of oversampling and ensemble learning methods in software defect prediction. Aiming at the treatment of category imbalance in software defect prediction, it is studied how to effectively combine the imbalance processing method at the data level and the imbalance processing method at the algorithm level to obtain better defect prediction performance. Aiming at the problem of category imbalance in defect prediction, a hybrid sampling technique HS SKM based on S MODE and X-mode s clustering is proposed, and this technique is combined with the traditional random forest algorithm to obtain a Hybrid sampling random forest algorithm HSRF. Aiming at the problem of feature selection in defect prediction, a feature selection algorithm based on conditional information entropy and random subspace, FSC ERS, is proposed, and an integrated learning algorithm combining this algorithm with Bootstrap sampling.

4 Conclusion

From the above research status at home and abroad, it can be seen that in recent years, many studies have been carried out on cross-project software defect prediction, and according to the characteristics of cross-project software data, various algorithm improvements have been used to improve the accuracy of defect prediction. Several key issues of the existing cross-project software defect prediction technology have not been effectively resolved, and can be used as a direction for future research considerations.

1. The problem of imbalanced training data classification
   Classification imbalance is the main factor that affects the quality of the data set. The defective data set contains defective modules and non-defective modules. Among them, defective modules often belong to a minority category, while non-defective modules belong to a majority category. Traditional classification models often aim to maximize the overall classification accuracy, but reduce the classification accuracy of minority classes, which will affect the performance of the defect prediction model to a certain extent.
2. The problem of labeling cost of unlabeled training data
   Marking defective modules is costly. How to select samples that can build a better predictive model for marking without marking samples, avoid marking the entire software project module, thereby reducing the high cost of marking samples.
3. Data distribution of source and target projects in cross-project defect prediction
   For the defect data of different projects, due to the different programming styles of the developers of different projects, the different development platform environments, and the different functions and complexity of the projects, the distribution of the defect data of different projects will be very different. In order to construct an effective defect prediction model, reducing the difference in the distribution of defect data of different projects is the key.

Acknowledgement. The work was supported by Macau Foundation, Project number: MF2012.

References

Akiyama, F.: An example of software system debugging. In: Freiman, C.V., Griffith, J.E., Rosenfeld, J.L. (eds.) IFIP Congress, no. 1, pp. 353–359. North-Holland (1971). ISBN: 0-7204-2063-6

Basili, R., Marziali, A., Pazienza, M.T.: Modelling syntactic uncertainty in lexical acquisition from texts. J. Quant. Linguist. **1**(1), 62–81 (1994). https://doi.org/10.1080/09296179408590000

Chidamber, S.R., Kemerer, C.F.: A metrics suite for object oriented design. IEEE Trans. Softw. Eng. **20**(6), 476–493 (1994). https://doi.org/10.1109/32.295895

Goel, L., Sharma, M., Khatri, S., Damodaran, D.: Prediction of cross project defects using ensemble based multinomial classifier. ICST Trans. Scalable Inf. Syst. 159974 (2018). https://doi.org/10.4108/eai.13-7-2018.159974

Gong, L., Jiang, S., Bo, L., Jiang, L., Qian, J.: A novel class-imbalance learning approach for both within-project and cross-project defect prediction. IEEE Trans. Reliab. **69**(1), 40–54 (2020). https://doi.org/10.1109/TR.2019.2895462

Halstead, M. H.: Elements of Software Science, Operating, and Programming Systems Series. Elsevier Science, 7 (1977)

Li, Z., Qi, C., Zhang, L., Ren, J.: Discriminant subspace alignment for cross-project defect prediction. In: Proceedings of the 2019 IEEE SmartWorld, Ubiquitous Intelligence and Computing, Advanced and Trusted Computing, Scalable Computing and Communications, Internet of People and Smart City Innovation, SmartWorld/UIC/ATC/SCALCOM/IOP/SCI 2019, pp. 1728–1733 (2019). https://doi.org/10.1109/SmartWorld-UIC-ATC-SCALCOM-IOP-SCI.2019.00308

Ma, Y., Luo, G., Li, J., Chen, A.: Software defect prediction using transfer method. In: 2011 International Conference on Computational Problem-Solving, ICCP 2011 (2011). https://doi.org/10.1109/ICCPS.2011.6092261

Mccabe, T. J.: A Complexity Measure. IEEE Trans. Softw. Eng. **SE-2**(4) (1976). https://doi.org/10.1109/TSE.1976.233837

Munson, J.C., Khoshgoftaar, T.M.: The detection of fault-prone programs. IEEE Trans. Softw. Eng. **18**(5), 423–433 (1992). https://doi.org/10.1109/32.135775

Nagappan, N., Ball, T.: Use of relative code churn measures to predict system defect density. In: Proceedings of the 27th International Conference on Software Engineering, ICSE 2005 (2005). https://doi.org/10.1145/1062455.1062514

Nagappan, N., Murphy, B., Basili, V.R.: The influence of organizational structure on software quality: an empirical case study. In: Proceedings of the International Conference on Software Engineering (2008). https://doi.org/10.1145/1368088.1368160

Pan, S.J.: Transfer defect learning. In: Proceedings of the International Conference on Software Engineering, pp. 382–391, 22 May 2013

Shen, V.Y., Yu, T.J., Thebaut, S.M., Paulsen, L.R.: Identifying error-prone software—an empirical study. IEEE Trans. Softw. Eng. **SE-11**(4), 317–324 (1985). https://doi.org/10.1109/TSE.1985.232222

Tian, Y.: Research on software defect prediction based on program slice (2020)

Wang, H.: Research on software defect predication based on ensemble learning (2020)

Yang, Y., Ai, J., Wang, F.: Defect prediction based on the characteristics of multilayer structure of software network. In: Proceedings of the 2018 IEEE 18th International Conference on Software Quality, Reliability, and Security Companion, QRS-C 2018 (2018). https://doi.org/10.1109/QRS-C.2018.00019

Zhu, K., Zhang, N., Ying, S., Wang, X.: Within-project and cross-project software defect prediction based on improved transfer Naive Bayes algorithm. Comput. Mater. Contin. **63**(2), 891–910 (2020). https://doi.org/10.32604/cmc.2020.08096

Zimmermann, T., Nagappan, N.: Predicting defects using network analysis on dependency graphs. In: Proceedings of the International Conference on Software Engineering (2008). https://doi.org/10.1145/1368088.1368161

Zimmermann, T., Nagappan, N., Gall, H., Giger, E., Murphy, B.: Cross-project defect prediction: a large scale experiment on data vs. domain vs. process. In: ESEC-FSE 2009 - Proceedings of the Joint 12th European Software Engineering Conference and 17th ACM SIGSOFT Symposium on the Foundations of Software Engineering (2009). https://doi.org/10.1145/1595696.1595713

Research on Teaching Reform of Digital Media Technology Under the Background of New Engineering Course Construction

Dan Lin[1](✉) and Liang Xue[2,3]

[1] Guangzhou Nanfang College, Faculty of Innovation and Design, City University of Macau, Macau, China
[2] Institute of Data Science, City University of Macau, Macau, China
[3] Guangdong University of Education, Guangzhou, China

Abstract. To meet the needs of the development of the times and to promote the industrial transformation and upgrading and the conversion of new and old kinetic energy, this paper analyzes the requirements for the training of digital media technology professionals under the background of new engineering, and proposes the integration of new media technology professional courses with other engineering courses, in order to strengthen the cultivation of innovation ability and practical ability, and conduct research on teaching reform. The new media technology professionals can adapt to the new economic characteristics, such as new technologies, new industries, new formats, and new models, and think about the construction of professional education from the development perspectives of strategic, innovative, systematic and openness. It can provide a reference for the practice reform of digital media technology professional under the background of the new engineering.

Keywords: New engineering · Digital media technology · Teaching reform · Pedagogical issues · Practice

1 Introduction

The new scientific and technological revolution and industrial transformation are an all-around transformation that will have a profound impact on the mode of production, way of life and values of mankind. China has implemented major strategies such as "Innovation-driven Development", "Made in China 2025", "Internet Plus" and "Artificial Intelligence" and promoted the "One Belt And One Road" cooperation initiative. The new economy, featuring "new technologies, new forms of business and new industries", is developing rapidly. This rapid development has an urgent need to support new engineering talents with higher innovation and entrepreneurship ability and cross-border integration ability [1].

In 2019, General Secretary Xi Jinping sent a congratulatory letter to the Sixth World Internet Conference: "At present, a new round of scientific and technological revolution and industrial transformation are accelerating, and new technologies, new applications

W. Zhou and Y. Mu (Eds.): ICWL 2021, LNCS 13103, pp. 166–172, 2021.
https://doi.org/10.1007/978-3-030-90785-3_17

and new business formats such as artificial intelligence, big data and the Internet of Things, are in the ascendency." Among them, digital media technology is the process of studying "human", guiding technology and forming human-machine common behavior. In this process, it satisfies and creates human natural feelings and realizes natural information exchange. In order to adapt to the development of the communication industry and promote the transformation of traditional media, we should consider the construction of professional courses for the specialty of digital media technology under the background of new engineering, so as to meet the demand for talents of digital media technology during the transformation of national industry.

2 Content and Development of Digital Media Technology

Digital media technology is based on virtual reality, augmented reality, holographic image, film and television artistic effects, 3D animation, games, big data, artificial intelligence and other digital technologies, supported by digital, intelligent and networked technologies; With interdisciplinary knowledge in the humanities, arts and sciences. These innovative forces directly promote the development of a number of industries, which is not only reflected in the digital publishing industry, film and television media industry, game entertainment industry, animation industry and other core industries, but also driven the AR/VR industry, online education, interactive entertainment and other emerging industries. And intelligent product design, intelligent living environment design, intelligent home product manufacturing, tourism and cultural industry, leisure and health industry and other cross-border fields [2]. Digital media represents the direction of China's new round of scientific and technological revolution and industrial change, and it is also a key field to gain competitive advantage in the future.

3 The Necessity of Training Digital Media Professionals Under the Background of New Engineering

Facing the rapid development of the information age, digital media graduates should not only be operators engaged in related majors, but also designers who are proficient in information communication theory and have strong innovative and creative capabilities. To carry out the combination of technology and art courses is advantageous to the digital media graduate for their related work designed and manufactured to provide more innovative thinking and creative ideas, becoming an interdisciplinary and compound talent with strong innovative design ability and practical application ability, break the barriers of technology and art disciplines, for more complete knowledge system, and more scientific thinking pattern.

4 New Requirements for Talents Training of Digital Media Technology Majors Under the Background of New Engineering

The new engineering majors are mainly based on the Internet, as well as the emerging majors with artificial intelligence as the core. Digital media technology majors fall into this category. For China's higher education sector, it is the main responsibility to adapt to the market demand as soon as possible and train digital media professionals to make up for the huge talent gap in the current industry. The development of the future society requires high-quality talents with stronger practical, innovative and competitive ability, but the traditional engineering major can no longer meet this need. This requires new engineering talents not only to have a deep research in a single subject, but also to have a broader knowledge, to meet the characteristics of interdisciplinary integration [6]. Under the background of new engineering, the cultivation of talents majoring in new media technology should focus on the following four core qualities, as shown in Fig. 1.

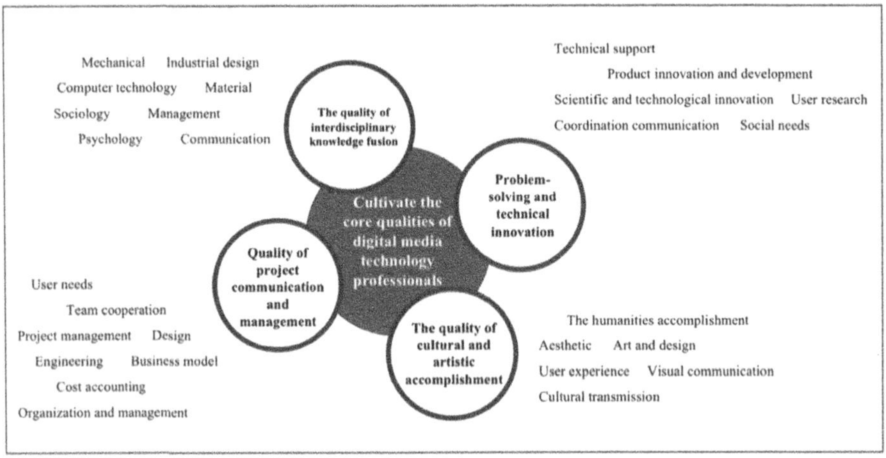

Fig. 1. The quality requirements for the training of digital media technology professionals under the background of new engineering

The first, quality of interdisciplinary knowledge integration. The second, improve the ability to solve problems and the comprehensive quality of technological innovation. The third, quality of project communication management. The fourth, the quality of humanities and arts accomplishment. Strengthening art education and humanistic literacy is an indispensable need for self-development [3]. Combining technology and art, communicating with users through visual presentation, will play a leading role in the follow-up development of future technology and related industries.

The above-mentioned talent training requires students to be able to contact the actual projects of the enterprise and the rapidly developing industry knowledge. The teaching of new media technology under the background of new engineering needs to combine the perspective of advanced technology and artificial intelligence to carry out the project practice of innovative thinking and establish the practical teaching platform under the background of new engineering [11].

5 Teaching Reform Framework of Digital Media Technology Major Under the Background of New Engineering

In 2018, MIT believes that the current engineering education has entered a period of acceleration and fundamental change [4]. Digital media discipline is a systematic discipline, and every media project is a systematic engineering. Participants should not only have rich cultural background and broad thinking, but also need the guarantee of artistic design ability and technical support during the implementation. It mainly includes courses such as graphic design, 2D and 3D animation, film and television editing, game design, program design, website construction, APP product design and so on.

The practical teaching framework of digital media technology under the background of new engineering should focus on the characteristics and objectives of the new engineering. Combined with the new technology, new system and new mode, through the comprehensive discussion of the core, representation and extension of digital media technology, characterized by harmony in humanities, technology, and business [5]. Adhere to application-oriented and practice-oriented talent training, closely combine with local enterprises, integrate multi-source and interdisciplinary scientific and technological new knowledge and innovative ideas, and establish a practical teaching system framework coordinated by diversified platforms [10]. The diversified platform under the new engineering background is mainly composed of professional knowledge teaching, outside the classroom, course contests, professional training bases, mentor workshops, holiday practice platforms and staff [13].

The construction of the teaching reform framework of digital media technology major is the necessary guarantee to realize the seamless connection between colleges and universities and the requirements of the industry and the needs of enterprises, and it is also an important mode to improve the comprehensive quality of students majoring in digital media technology.

6 Discussion on the Teaching Reform of Digital Media Technology Specialty Under the Background of New Engineering

Under the background of new technology, the digital media need to closely around the new professional teaching system of engineering, the characteristics of professionalism and core ability training to students as the center, play the advantages of multiplatform teaching, let the traditional teaching model of 'teacher as the instructor' be transformed into a practical teaching model in which the 'teacher is the guide', where students explore and learn while playing their subjective initiative. At the same time, students should be more exposed to the society and understand the needs of enterprises, so as to promote industry-university-research cooperation in the context of new engineering, bring technology to the market, and change products with demand [12].

6.1 Discussion on Professional Knowledge Teaching

Professional knowledge of new media technology is a core part of the teaching system. Because each school for the course design and credit ratio will be different. The main core courses of Digital Media Technology are as follows: Introduction to digital media technology, interactive multimedia website development, 2D dynamic media design and production, Web new media design and production, virtual interaction implementation, IOS mobile platform theory and design specifications, After Effect interactive animation and production, UI design, APP product front-end design training, etc.

6.2 Outside the Classroom Practice Discussion

Extracurricular classrooms are an important platform for the development of professional extracurricular practice projects [7]. Teaching activities such as after-class expert lectures, design project sharing sessions, hot spot discussions, special topics, and alumni sharing sessions are all open, regardless of grade level.

6.3 The Discussion of Course Contests

Course contests can expand students' scope of knowledge, cultivate students' thinking innovation and practical ability. Students are actively encouraged to participate in academic competitions to enhance their advantages in employment competition.

6.4 Discussion on Professional Training Bases

Establish a professional training base, emphasizing students' practical ability and practical ability [8]. To promote the construction of new disciplines, we should adhere to the principle of "coming from industry, going to industry", especially the disciplines with strong application of digital media technology, and pay more attention to students' practice. There are simulated projects and real projects, which can be selected according to students' personal interests. Students can complete projects based on the course content.

6.5 Discussion of the Mentor Workshop

Mentor workshop education mode is not only a bridge for students to enter the society, but also an incubator for production, learning and research. The workshop highlights the pertinence and practicality of education. In the case of a fixed tutor, students from different grades participate together, and students are able to work on practical projects in an orderly manner and collaborate with different team members.

6.6 Discussion on Vacation Practice Platform

The vacation practice platform is a comprehensive management platform for students to conduct social practice during winter and summer vacation. Each grade will match the above six teaching modes according to their own needs. Freshman students should pay attention to the study of professional knowledge. Sophomore students should pay attention to the development of innovative thinking and application ability. Junior and senior students should pay attention to the cultivation of comprehensive innovation ability and project practice ability [9]. As shown in Fig. 2.

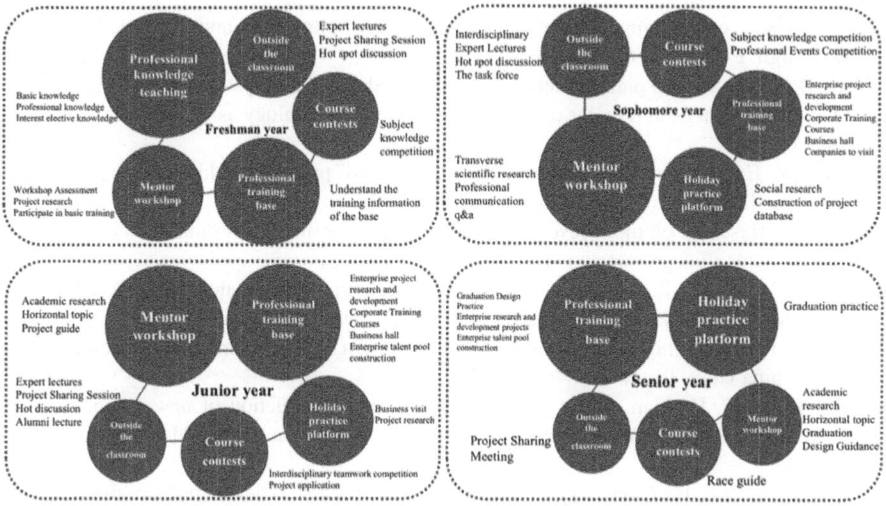

Fig. 2. Practice teaching reform design scheme of each grade

7 Conclusions

For the reform of digital media technology professional education, the implementation of the new engineering concept needs an innovative and comprehensive view of education. Interdisciplinary integration should be used to promote disciplinary innovation, and cross-disciplinary integration should be used to jointly promote the construction of practice platforms, with the adaptation to new technologies, new business models and the development of emerging industries as the main body and core. Keep close contact with the leading companies in the industry, pay attention to the needs of society and enterprises, and cultivate talents who can adapt to the new era of industry development. At the same time, according to the needs of students at different stages, the practical teaching program of each grade is designed to provide a reference for the subsequent reform of the professional practice of digital media technology.

References

1. Wang, S., Li, X., Wang, J.: Some consideration on the construction of traditional machinery undergraduate major under the background of new engineering. J. Jilin Radio TV Univ. (01), 1–2+55 (2020)
2. Dong, Z., Tian, J.: Development status, opportunities and educational strategies of digital creative industry. Art Des. Res. (01) (2020)
3. Zhang, L.: Reform and practice of art education for engineering students under the background of new engineering – taking digital media technology major as an example. Art Des. (Theory) **2**(12) (2020)
4. Yu, B.: Discussion on the "multi-platform" extracurricular practice teaching system of industrial design under the new engineering background. Design (01) (2020)
5. Zhou, K., Zhao, Z.: Exploration on the cultivation mode of engineering capability "interdisciplinary, production-teaching integration". Res. High. Eng. Educ. (03) (2019)

6. Gu, P.: New engineering and new paradigm: concept, framework and implementation path. Res. High. Eng. Educ. **6**, 1–13 (2017)
7. Yu, B.: Discussion on practical teaching mode based on tutorial system "second classroom" – taking industrial design major of Ningbo Institute of Technology as an example. Design **21**, 94–95 (2016)
8. Yang, Y.: Exploration and practice of "project-oriented" practice teaching of industrial design specialty. Design **12**, 63–64 (2016)
9. Min, L.: Research on multi-level progressive practice ability cultivation model of industrial design major students. Design **3**, 120–121 (2017)
10. Zhang, H., Xiang, Z., Yang, J.: Exploration of industrial design talent training mode based on multidisciplinary intersection. Design **8**, 17–26 (2017). (in Chinese)
11. Lu, G.: Five breakthrough and preliminary exploration in the construction of "new engineering." China Univ. Teach. **5**, 38–41 (2017)
12. Hu, B., Feng, H., Han, W., et al.: Accelerating the construction of new engineering and promoting the reform and innovation of engineering education. Fudan Educ. Forum **2**, 20–27 (2017)
13. Liang, L., Zhao, H.: Contact system construction of industrial design practice teaching from the perspective of service design. Design **6**(15), 17–31 (2018)

Author Index

The manufacturer's authorised representative in the EU is Springer
Nature Customer Service Centre GmbH, Europaplatz 3, 69115 Heidelberg,
Germany. If you have any concerns regarding our products, please
contact ProductSafety@springernature.com

Printed and bound by CPI Group (UK) Ltd, Croydon, CR0 4YY
30/09/2026
02225234-0020